Investment Strategies in Emerging New Trends in Finance

Edited by Reza Gharoie Ahangar and Asma Salman

Published in London, United Kingdom

IntechOpen

Supporting open minds since 2005

Investment Strategies in Emerging New Trends in Finance
http://dx.doi.org/10.5772/intechopen.78097
Edited by Reza Gharoie Ahangar and Asma Salman

Contributors
Nouha Khoufi, Salma Zone, Darina Saxunova, Corlise Liesl Le Roux, D'Maris Coffman, Bhaskaran Rajan, Navjot Kaur, Harpreet K Athwal, Afzalur Rahman, Velmurugan P.S, Valentyna Michaylovna Michaylovna Molokanova, Hoang Van Hai, Phan Kim Tuan, Le The Phiet, Tom Fisher, Joel Hodroff, Leonard Mushunje, Maxwell Mashasha, Edina Chandiwana

First published in London, United Kingdom, 2021 by IntechOpen
IntechOpen is the global imprint of INTECHOPEN LIMITED, registered in England and Wales, registration number: 11086078, 5 Princes Gate Court, London, SW7 2QJ, United Kingdom
Printed in Croatia

British Library Cataloguing-in-Publication Data
A catalogue record for this book is available from the British Library

Additional hard and PDF copies can be obtained from orders@intechopen.com

Investment Strategies in Emerging New Trends in Finance
Edited by Reza Gharoie Ahangar and Asma Salman
p. cm.
Print ISBN 978-1-83962-965-5
Online ISBN 978-1-83962-966-2
eBook (PDF) ISBN 978-1-83962-967-9

For EU product safety concerns:
IN TECH d.o.o., Prolaz Marije Krucifikse Kozulić 3, 51000 Rijeka, Croatia, info@intechopen.com or visit our website at intechopen.com.

Meet the editors

Reza Gharoie Ahangar is a Ph.D. student in Decision Science with a minor in Economics and a teaching fellow and research assistant in G. Brint Ryan College of Business, University of North Texas, USA. He holds a BSc in Business Management, an MBA in Finance, an MSc in finance, and an MSc in Business Analytics. He is a member of the American Finance Association (AFA), Decision Sciences Institute (DSI), Production and Operations Management Society (POMS), Institute for Operations Research and the Management Sciences (INFORMS), and Association of Scientists, Developers, and Faculties (ASDF). Mr. Ahangar is a teaching assistant at UNT for six years and has authored eight books and book chapters as well as several journal and conference publications in finance and business analytics, with more than forty technical publications. His research works are cited by the top 0.1% of most-read authors in academia. He serves as an editorial board member for several scientific journals. His current research interests include investment, forecasting, optimization, FinTech, and the application of artificial intelligence in financial areas.

Professor Asma Salman is a blockchain developer and Professor of Finance at the American University in the Emirates, UAE. An Honorary Global Advisor at the Global Academy of Finance and Management, USA, she completed her MBA in Finance and Accounting and earned a Ph.D. in Finance from an AACSB member, AMBA accredited, School of Management at Harbin Institute of Technology, China. Her research credentials include a one-year residency at the Brunel Business School, Brunel University, UK. Prof. Salman also served as the Dubai Cohort supervisor for DBA students under the Nottingham Business School, UK, for seven years and is currently a Ph.D. supervisor at the University of Northampton, UK, where she is a visiting fellow. She also served on the Board of Etihad Airlines during 2019–2020. One of her recent articles on "Bitcoin and Blockchain" gained wide visibility and she is an active speaker on Fintech, blockchain, and crypto events around the GCC. She holds various professional certifications including Chartered Fintech Professional (USA), Certified Financial Manager (USA), Women in Leadership and Management in Higher Education, (UK), and Taxation GCC VAT Compliance, (UK). She recently won an award for "Blockchain Trainer of the Year" from Berkeley Middle East. Other recognitions include the Women Leadership Impact Award by H.E First Lady of Armenia, Research Excellence Award, and the Global Inspirational Women Leadership Award by H.H Sheikh Juma Bin Maktoum Juma Al Maktoum.

Contents

Preface

This book focuses on some interesting topics in finance, including portfolio and investment strategies. It contains nine chapters from different finance and investment perspectives from authors across the globe. This book is organized into the following sections: "Investment and Portfolio Strategies," "Behavioral Finance and Investment Decisions," and "Emerging New Trends in Finance." The target audience comprises researchers, scholars, and specialists in the field of finance.

The first section, "Investment and Portfolio Strategies," includes three chapters. In Chapter 1, "Implementation of a Value-Oriented Strategy of the Organization through a Portfolio of Projects", Valentyna Molokanova describes the methodological aspects of implementing the organization's strategy through project portfolio management and analyses the existing concepts, models, and methods of organizational development portfolios management. In Chapter 2, "Estimating Short-Term Returns with Volatilities for High Frequency Stock Trades in Emerging Economies Using Gaussian Processes (GPs)" Leonard Mushunje, Maxwell Mashasha and Edina Chandiwana examine the volatility and stock prices and returns with some engineering and analytic tools to find the most optimal values for the stock price and return. In Chapter 3, "Firm-specific News and Anomalies", Hoang Van Hai, Phan Kim Tuan and Le The Phiet investigate the relationship between idiosyncratic volatility and future returns around firm-specific news announcements and examine whether systematic risk affects news and non-news idiosyncratic volatility profits.

The second section, "Behavioral Finance and Investment Decisions," includes two chapters. In Chapter 4, "Financial Literacy as a Tool for Stimulating the Investment Behaviour of Rural Women: An Empirical Assessment" Rajan Bhaskaran et al. examines the influence of financial awareness on the saving and investment behavior of rural females. In Chapter 5, "Accounting Information Quality and Investment Decisions" Nouha Khoufi examines the relationship between the quality of information and investment decisions, which helps to reduce information asymmetry and improve investment efficiency.

The third section, "Emerging New Trends in Finance," includes four chapters. In Chapter 6, "Digital Transformation of World Finance," Darina Saxunova and Corlise Liesl Le Roux investigate the transformation process of finance from a global view. In Chapter 7, "The Trouble with Minding Markets: Emotional Finance in Context", D'Maris Coffman examines the main theoretical claims of emotional finance and discusses the nature of financial assets and asset price bubbles, phantastic, and groupfeel subjects. In Chapter 8, "From Money-Centered to People- and Planet-Centered Ledger Economics: Leveraging the Hidden Wealth of Underutilized Productive Capacity" Thomas Fisher and Joel Hodroff proposes a framework to deal with wasted wealth, which consists of a new asset-management strategy that challenges the current money-centered approach to economics. Finally, In Chapter 9, "Tunisian Fintech: An Ecosystem under Construction - Can COVID 19 be the Fuel to Ignite the Construction of Tunisian Fintech?" Salma Zone examines the effect of the COVID-19 pandemic on the fintech industry and describes its future challenges.

We would like to express our cordial gratitude to all the authors for their contributions. The successful completion of this book has been the cooperation of many people, and we would like to thank Ms. Kristina Kardum Cvitan, Author Service Manager Ms. Ana Simcic, and Mr. Luka Cvjetkovic for their support during the publishing process.

Reza Gharoie Ahangar
G. Brint Ryan College of Business,
University of North Texas,
USA

Asma Salman
Professor of Finance,
College of Business Administration,
American University in the Emirates,
UAE

Section 1

Investment and Portfolio Strategies

Chapter 1

Implementation of a Value-Oriented Strategy of the Organization through a Portfolio of Projects

Valentyna Michaylovna Molokanova

Abstract

The article deals with the methodological aspects of implementing the organization's strategy through project portfolio management. The existing concepts, models, and methods of organizational development portfolios management are analyzed. The types of organizational cultures are considered in accordance with the evolutionary theory of values. The article shows that the success of the implementation of the organization's development strategy is impossible without taking into account its dominant values. The organization development model links the spiral nature of systems development and the organization's strategy in the form of a project portfolio. The model of the projects' portfolio formation based on the definition of organizational values at the stages of the life cycle of the system is shown. The application of the competitive analysis method for the projects' portfolio formation using the principles of value-oriented and reflexive management for making management decisions is presented.

Keywords: organization development strategy, project portfolio, value-oriented portfolio management, organizational values, portfolio components

1. Introduction

The current state of society shows that the future is becoming increasingly uncertain and unpredictable and management systems do not keep up with the changes that are taking place. As a result, acute problems become the subject of theoretical research after they have become quite acute [1]. In the process of human activity, there are always crises. The history of humankind perceived as an endless stream of crises. Systems management theory recommends developing anti-crisis measures in advance and training staff to act in conditions of endless change and improvement.

Today, most business leaders recognize the important role of strategic planning and professional portfolio management in organizational development [2]. In modern economics, the expediency of development, at the center of which is only material production, has long been criticized. This necessitates a change in the general paradigm of human development from the ideology of accumulation of material wealth and competition for resources to the ideology of reasonable sufficiency and mutual assistance. This paradigm is used in the theory of sustainable development management, the main provisions of which are already sufficiently lighted up in specialized publications [3–5]. It is substantiated that strategic goals require systematic, systematic technology of development and implementation of appropriate project portfolios for harmonized strategic goals achievements.

However, there is a common misconception about how well a portfolio of projects should match an organization's development strategies. Creating strong links between the strategy and many projects allows concentrating on the strategy implementation. However, the links between strategy and projects are the weakest points in the portfolio management methodology. The task of transforming the developed strategy into a projects' portfolio is poorly structured, it lacks unambiguous methodological unity, and needs to update in connection with the emergence of new theories and scientific schools.

The analysis of the literature shows that in most cases the portfolio is considered only as a set of assets [6–8]. Managers use portfolio analysis in a variety of ways, mostly just to decide which markets or industries to invest in. Nevertheless, in our study, we consider the project's portfolio management as a professional discipline that aims to maximize the business value of the organization through the selection, optimization, and supervision of investment projects that are consistent with the development organization strategy [9, 10].

In modern methodology, the main idea of the project portfolio management is to create new value by implementing a strategy in the form of programs and projects [11]. This value arises during the portfolio realization and becomes a source of additional assets for the organization [12]. Theoretical and methodological problems of project management optimization in the conditions of social evolution of values considered only sporadically, without application of the system approach, scientifically substantiated conclusions, offers, and recommendations. With this in mind, our study aims to create conceptual foundations, models, and methods that form the base of the value-oriented project portfolio management. The work is based on the hypothesis that the value orientation of organizations' development management provides a single content and communication basis for improving the processes of strategic portfolio management. Based on the evolutionary theory of values of K. Graves [13], it is proposed to consider project portfolio management from the standpoint of a fundamentally new paradigm - as a systematic activity to develop dominant values in the organization through the projects' portfolio. In the context of this methodology, we use the statement that the project is a commitment to creating value. The second element is the statement that the highest level of organization maturity, which leads to its continuous improvement, is the project portfolio management. The third element of the methodology is the continuous improvement of the project environment through the definition and change of value priorities of all stakeholders. Without the application of this methodology, it is impossible to ensure stable organization development.

2. Literature review

As defined earlier, portfolio management is the tactical level of the organization's development strategy implementation. Portfolio management covers the widest range of strategic issues of system development and provides significant benefits for organizations [14]. It improves decision-making on which projects the resources should spend on in line with the organization's strategic goals. The concept of dynamic project portfolio management provides an understanding of how firms use resources to achieve their goals [15].

Projects are the main means of providing new business opportunities and effective change management in enterprises. Thus, the formation of a portfolio of projects is necessary to comply with the market changes, and processes of the identification, prioritization, and implementation of relevant projects depend on them [16].

There are several definitions of project portfolio management (PPM), which emphasize different aspects of PPM. For example, the US Project Management Institute emphasizes coordination between projects to achieve strategic goals: "A portfolio is a set of projects or programs and other work that are grouped together to help effectively achieve strategic business goals [17]. The UK Department of Public Trade takes a forward-looking approach, stating, "PPM is a process at the corporate strategic level to coordinate the successful implementation of the firm's entire set of programs and projects" [18]. Some publications have described PPM as an area of new product development [19].

PPM has aspects related to financial portfolio management, such as risk balancing and rewards [20, 21] and describes real options used in financial portfolio management to help prioritize project portfolios based on an overall risk strategy. The concept of PPM in world standards and models, interpreted from different points of view, significantly affects for the procedure of project portfolio formation. Thus, in some American companies, the approach is used [22], according to which all projects of the organization are divided into four portfolios: large technology projects, small technology projects, internal organizational projects, and administrative projects' portfolio. In some companies, projects are divided into three portfolios: alternative projects, independent projects, and combined projects' portfolios [18].

In the context of PPM, the complexity increases due to the great variety of project types [23], the difficulty of identifying and evaluating many benefits [24] for specific investments. Portfolio formation methods focused on obtaining the maximum return on the investment portfolio are based on known investment indicators (ROI, NPV, DPP, RI). For such a portfolio, the task of maximizing the total profit of all projects is solved, taking into account budget constraints, resource provision, and time constraints. The list of candidate projects may include numerical indicators of their value obtained through preliminary project analysis. Recently researches emphasize the need to adapt the strategy and portfolio management to the uncertainty of dynamic environmental conditions [25]. Recent research mainly develops strategies for predicting asset returns in environments with significant uncertainty and volatility [26–29].

In terms of value approach, the indicators that need to be improved do not necessarily have to connect with financial returns; they may be any parameters that are a measure of the value of the portfolio. Strategic project portfolio management is a continuous process of creating and evaluating a set (portfolio) of strategic initiatives designed to achieve sustainable results and benefits in increasing the market value of the organization. In such project portfolios, we have to solve a multicriteria decision-making task and deal with a set of alternatives, a set of criteria, and a set of criteria evaluation scales.

3. Research methodology

The scientific and technical problem of creating basic methodological principles and models of value-oriented project portfolio management was solved based on the evolutionary theory of values and modern project management methodology. In the process of research were used: methods of project, programs and portfolios management (to analyze the creation of organizational values through project implementation); systems theory and systems analysis (to formalize the processes of portfolio management of organizational development); means of mathematical modeling and dynamic programming (for modeling value-oriented management of organizational development).

4. Value-oriented principles of organization development portfolio management

In project management, the importance of "soft components" has been steadily growing in recent years, which is associated with the defining role of the individual in project management. This human side of project management has become much more important in recent years, not only in practice but also in scientific research on project management [30]. The dominant factors for the analysis of human behavior in project management continue to be the project manager personality, project teams, and a specific project environment.

During the last century, the management theory transformed from the management by instructions (MBI) to management by objects (MBO), which is still popular. From the end of the last century in the organizational management, there were signs of methods of management on the basis of values (management by values or MBV) [31]. The main goal of this management is to take into account the personal human parameters of managerial thinking at a theoretical and practical level. The concept of "value" is one of the fundamental concepts of modern science. Value is a form of social being, a special social relationship, thanks to which the needs and interests of a person are transferred to the world of things, giving them certain social properties that sometimes are not directly related to their utilitarian purpose. Based on this, the definition of the concept of "value" in the project context formulated as a personal perception of the project product due to its unique properties to create certain benefits in the various contexts of life.

K. Graves, the founder of the values evolution theory [13], considered that the stage of development of the organization values could be characterized well in terms of the manifest rules, norms, and principles of internal relations. According to the theory of K. Graves, the development of an organization follows a double spiral. The external spiral is the living conditions and problems that the organization faces in a certain historical time. The inner spiral is the individual characteristics of the organization, cognitive processes, that is, the collective intelligence and mental abilities with which the organization "filters" the outside world. External conditions constantly interact with the internal structures of the organization. The strategy arising from this interaction determines strengthening the current level of organization's values or the transition to another level of organizational values. Later, R. Dawkins in his book "The Selfish Gene" [32] hypothesized that the value meme is a unit of information located in the human brain and is a certain mutated in cultural evolution virus.

Organizational values are the mental platform, the spiritual core of the organization, based on which the norms and behavioral patterns in the organization are built [11]. It is the values shared and declared by the founders or the most authoritative members of the organization that often become the key link on which the cohesion of employees depends, the unity of views and actions is formed, and the achievement of the organization's goals is ensured.

Strategic projects' portfolio management is a continuous process of establishing, optimizing, and strategic initiatives assessing, which are important for achieving strong competitive challenges. Strategic goals and project portfolio link and influence each other. The main task of PPM is along with the constant strategy development management to get the maximum values from the investment.

As defined earlier, the issues of methodology of value-oriented portfolio development have not been the subject of special systematic research so far. Some works of foreign and domestic scientists cover only certain general aspects related to the problematic issues of this subject area.

Since the main objects of transformation in projects are artificial and natural systems, the project management methodology is based on systems' theory. A systems approach is an effective tool for rationalizing and improving project processes. It provides the logical structure and sequence within which data is collected and analyzed. Besides that, we identify causal relationships, action priorities, and alternative projects. A systematic approach need not only develop a holistic project structure but also through systemic issues consider the project as a final product or service.

The standard design methods that take place in projects with material objects are called the hard system approach (HSA), and the soft system approach (SSA) is the methods that used when we are dealing with something intangible, for example, projects connected with the relations of the human community.

The main difference between "soft" systems from "hard" ones is the fact that for "soft" systems a person is the most important fuzzy element [33]. However, it is not always correct to consider the presence of a person in the system as the main criterion separating hard and soft approaches. Rather, the hard and soft systems approaches should be distinguished by the nature of the approach to problem solving. If all the factors of the problem are rigidly formalized, determinated, then in this case the situation is presented as "hard". The soft systems approach associated with non-material categories concerns such concepts as motivation, dynamic leadership, the hierarchy of values, dedication to work. Such poorly studied factors associated with human behavior, as a rule, are not taken into account in the complex formulation of management tasks. However, these factors are often the only reason for project management failure, requiring the integration of the efforts of all stakeholders. All these forces project managers to study more deeply and use the acquisition of other natural sciences, such as the theory of evolution, the theory of knowledge, cognitive and humanistic psychology, and social informatics. The main differences between the hard and soft systems approaches are presented in **Table 1**.

The main objects of transformation in project management are artificial and natural systems, and the basis of project-oriented management are several system

Hard system approach	**Soft system approach**
The problem has a solution	Too many problems need to be solved
The problem has a number of achievable goals	Goal achievement is difficult to measure
The problem answers the question "How?"	The focus of the problem is not only on the question "How?", but on the question "What?"
The problem has a deterministic complexity	The problem has an unforeseen, non-deterministic complexity
It is possible to determine the parameters of failure	It is very difficult to deal with the problem
The solution of the problem does not depend on the values of system	The decision depends on the values of system and professional mentality of the staff
Logically consistent connections	Intuitive metaphorical connections

Table 1.
The difference between hard and soft system approach.

concepts [34, 35]. The most important trend in project management development is manifested in the structuring of project management at three levels: project portfolio, programs, and individual projects. If a company chooses the wrong project (program, portfolio), it cannot succeed in its development, even if it successfully achieves the goal of the project. The success of a wrong or ill-conceived project can lead to the destruction of corporate values. Project selection is an investment of valuable corporate resources. Therefore, the company must choose a project that will create significant corporate value.

In mature organizations, project management at the highest level is used in the form of portfolio management of projects in line with the development strategy. Compared to managing a single program, the project portfolio has a broader context. The structure of the required organizational platform for system project management is as follows (**Figure 1**).

Modern project management, based on the increasing importance of "soft" project components, allows you to create new ways of thinking and generating ideas that create added value to projects. In this case, the strategy is considered as a generalized model of designing activities to achieve the desired future, consisting of basic conceptual provisions and a set of design tools aimed at the evolution of the company's values.

In the second half of the last century, the eminent psychologist K. Graves, having processed a huge amount of experimental and statistical data, created a spiral model of the evolution of the human value system. The Spiral vortex best depicts the development of human systems as they evolve through levels of increasing complexity. Each upward turn of the spiral marks the awakening of a more elaborated version of what already exists [13]. The image of the development spiral arose as a dialectical negation and synthesis of two metaphysical processes of development; the image of translational motion in a straight line and the image of motion in a closed circle. The special value of Graves' theory in its cholic approach. Each subsequent level of development of society is considered as the next stage of changes, and the higher levels of development of society do not deny but include all previous stages. An important feature of the evolutionary spiral model is that each odd level focuses mainly on individual values, and each even level focuses on collective values.

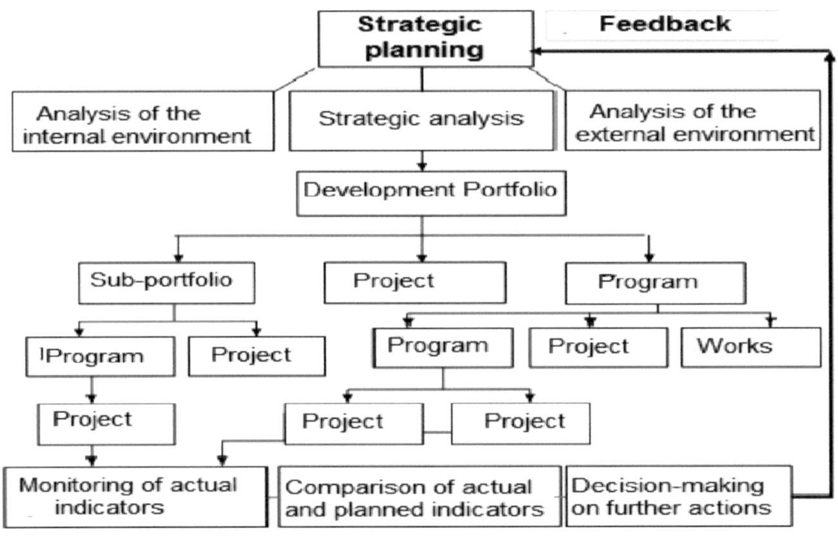

Figure 1.
Organizational platform for the implementation of development strategy.

An integrated model of values allows us to build a value profile of the organization. Without understanding the profile of the organization values it is impossible to effectively manage project-oriented development or any changes in general. According to K. Graves' theory, after the phase of full prosperity of the organization, it is not necessary to experience aging and gradual death, if you prepare in advance for its revival or transition to another level of organizational values (introducing new value memes). The semicircle of rotation of the organization in a spiral according to K. Graves [13] corresponds to the full life cycle of the company according to I. Adizes [35]. Although such a transition is accompanied by a period of a temporary decline in organizational efficiency and increasing uncertainty (**Figure 2**).

The development of the organization in a spiral is from a lower level of complexity to a greater one; from the mode of activity required to solve one set of problems, to the mode of activity essential for solving complex problems of the next level of living conditions. Those who adapt to new conditions survive, no matter what it requires, although sometimes it requires a complete replacement of the built intellectual model. At the same time, very often a number of significant variables in living conditions lie beyond the capabilities of the set of value memes of current leaders. Until new value memes are initiated or activated by change leaders, only stagnation and, more likely, degradation can be expected.

Each step of the spiral movement solves one set of problems and generates a new one for the future, that is, the evolutionary movement of the organization in a spiral, like any constant improvement, has no limits. This portfolio lifecycle modeling has two purposes: the model determines the sequence of management actions to add value and serves as a basis for the formation of detailed projects' plans. In the first case, we are dealing with a conceptual model of organizational values, and in the second - the model becomes a planning tool.

4.1 Conceptual model of organization development through a portfolio of projects

Portfolio management, as the highest level of mature project management in organizations, must comply with the laws of evolutionary development of systems. However, before forming a value-oriented development portfolio, it is necessary to

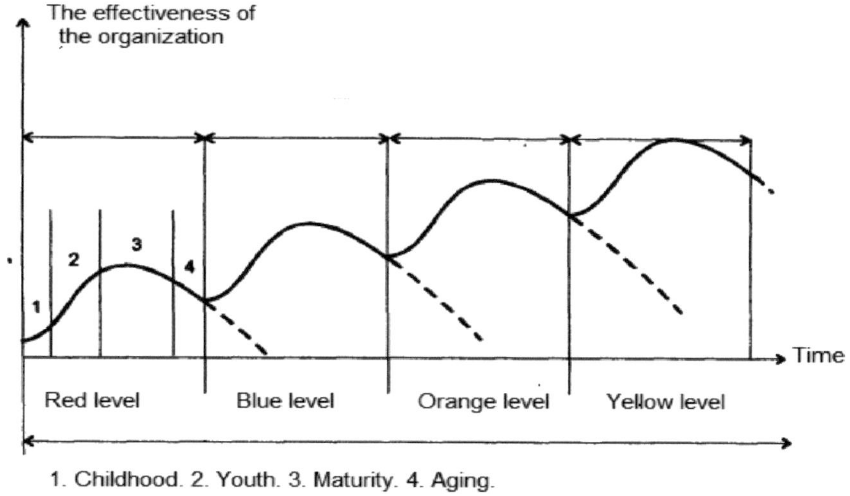

Figure 2.
Transition of an organization by value levels.

form a strategic vision of the future development of the organization, solving the problem of identifying internal organizational values and their possible change.

Defining evolutionary levels of values becomes a key concept in shaping development strategy through projects. Each level of spiral dynamics of values is a description of a unique world. The description of the company's value system helps to solve problems and successfully implement projects. Properly defining the company's dominant value system helps not only to answer the question of whom, how, and what should do in the company, but also it helps to determine the strategy of long-term changes. In this case, the spiral dynamics of the evolution of values does not refute the old theories, but organically integrates them into the overall dynamic models [36–38].

Defining strategic directions of organization development serves as a foundation for further creation of a portfolio of initiatives. The results and benefits gained from the implementation of these initiatives contribute to the implementation of the strategy and allow evaluating the effectiveness of the strategy and initiatives in creating value for the organization. This relationship could be illustrated in the form of a cycle consisting of four constantly repeated stages:

1. Transformation of strategy into separate projects.

2. Project portfolio planning.

3. Portfolio management.

4. Re-evaluation of strategy and portfolio.

The gradual increase in the capabilities of the system as project management develops is not the first time depicted in the form of a spiral untwisting from the center. According to this simple model, the development of an organization through project management is described as the gradual coverage of an ever-increasing plane that expands as projects move from stage to stage and from iteration to iteration. This model emphasizes that spiral development leads to a gradual expansion of the scope of the subject area of the organization. Conceptual scheme of modeling the development of the system based on a value-oriented approach, which includes four stages, are presented in **Figure 3**.

The value approach to the formation of a portfolio of organizational development is such that progress in each area characterized by a single integrated indicator. Each indicator may include several key performance indicators (KPIs), which assess the state of organizational values. Thus, the current state of organizational values could be described as a matrix of indicators in various aspects:

$$V_f = \left\{V_1, V_2, V_3, \ldots V_j\right\} \tag{1}$$

In the PMI knowledge system, portfolio management aggregate into two groups of processes [17]:

- Aligning Process Group — this group determines how components will be categorized, evaluated and selected for inclusion, and managed in the portfolio;

- Monitoring and Controlling Process Group — this group reviews performance indicators periodically for alignment with strategic objectives.

The formation of the portfolio of development of the organization begins with an assessment of the current state of the organizational and technical system.

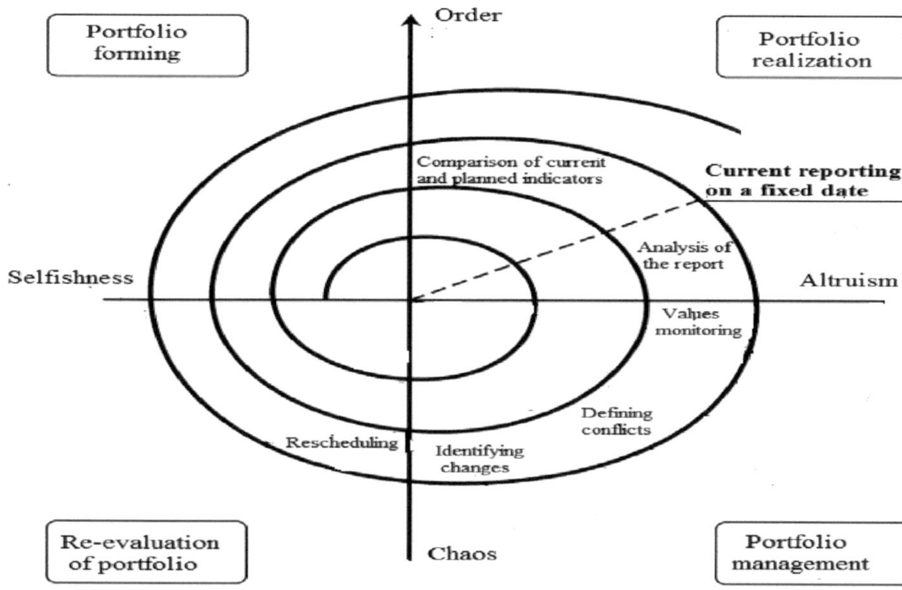

Figure 3.
Spiral development of the system based on a value-oriented portfolio.

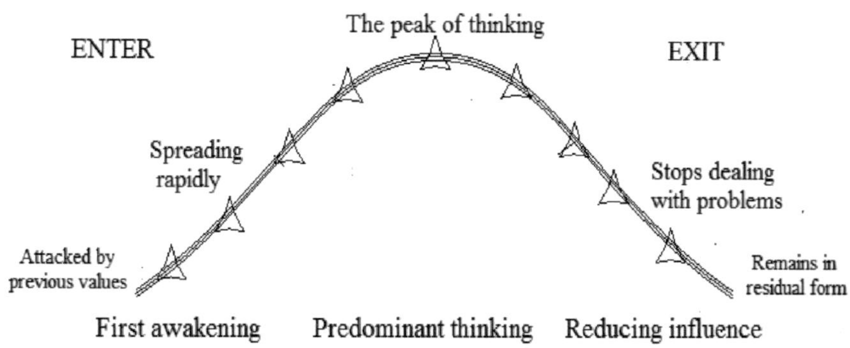

Figure 4.
The transition of the organization to another level of values [39].

Value-oriented portfolio affects all elements of the management system, i.e. it is aimed at organizational transformations, which, changing the existing value system, contribute to the maximum use of the managerial potential of the organization to move to a new level. The value-oriented portfolio should transfer the organization to a new higher level of development, without denying the values of the lower level. In **Figure 4** presents the sequence of such transitions in the direction of increasing the maturity of the organization [39].

This model shows that the organization in the course of development needs for constant organizational change, defined by the strategy of growth of dominant values. A holistic view of the organization's development strategy at certain stages of the life cycle requires a detailed consideration of the values based on which the portfolio is formed. The viability of an organization is determined by its ability to change values through project portfolios depending on changes in the external environment.

For a more detailed consideration of the dependence of the development strategy from the stages of the organization's life cycle and the state of internal organizational values, we assume that because of the implemented projects some organizations (**Figure 5**) moves to a bifurcation point (point A).

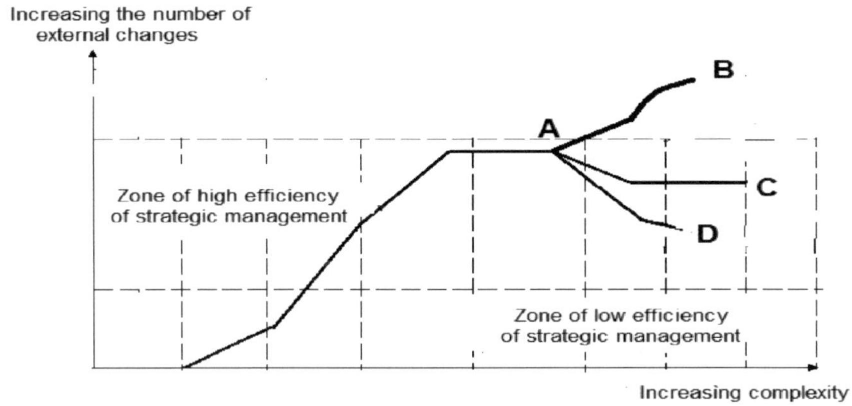

Figure 5.
Changing of the system value-oriented strategic movement.

After the phase of full prosperity (point A), either the organization must move to another level of organizational values (point B), or it is doomed to a gradual death. Consider three possible options for the development strategy of an organization in its blossom stage.

1. Wrongly chosen strategic position after the heyday leads the company to point D, which means a return to lower values and can cause an unexpected "death" of the company. It can be due to various reasons, such as a change in the rules of the game in the market, to which the company did not respond in time, or the withdrawal of one of the owners of the company.

2. One of the most common situations is when a company runs by a person blinded with the desire of "quick money", who does not know how to predict the future and does not feel the need for constant development. Such a straight road leads to a slow and painful agony at point C.

3. It is less common when the organization takes the right strategic position with entrepreneurial intuition. This stimulates the entry into a new cycle of development based on a new dominant value (point B), revenue growth due to new qualities of goods and services. The new quality should understand as a new focus on other quality values. Such evolutionary development can last forever, each time returning to the beginning of the cycle. Never less, the shape of the spiral requires constant review, taking into account the rapid changes in the environment.

The main principles of effective management are the reliability of sustainable development of the organization, the growth of its value over time. Strategies for achieving this goal can be different. It is clear that the "ideal" strategic position of the company is constantly changing over time, so the task of finding the best strategy is facing any organization. That is, at each of the selected stages of the life cycle of the organization there is an opportunity to choose a strategy for further development: to continue to increase the values of the current level; or prepare for the transition to the next level of values or freeze organizational projects, profiting from the existing level of values. The following set of strategic decisions should be presented in the form of:

$$G_k^p = \{G_C^p, G_N^p, G_D^p\}, \quad (2)$$

where G_k^P is a strategic decision at a certain value level of existence of the organization, *P* takes a meaning from 1 to 7 and corresponds to seven known levels of values, and *K* takes meaning 1–3. So we get:

$$\begin{aligned} &k = 1: G_1^p = G_C^p - \text{to continue increasing the current level values;} \\ &k = 2: G_2^p = G_N^p - \text{transition to the next level of values;} \\ &k = 3: G_3^p = G_D^p - \text{to return to lower level values.} \end{aligned} \tag{3}$$

The strategic decision is made by the management of the organization based on the understanding of the dominant organizational values at the current time. This requires tools to measure such values and their representation in numbers. An evolutionarily evolving system has the opportunity to move to the next hierarchical level of values, to begin to form information links of a new level of values.

Based on a generalized design algorithm, a model of the desired state of increasing organizational values increasing on a certain level is proposed. The model of organizational values based on identifying inconsistencies between the current state and the desired state of organizational values. Some aspects have been identified for assessing current and desired organizational values. Better strategic management of a company's projects based on a system of balanced scores proposed by Harvard School of Economics professors Robert Kaplan and David Norton [40, 41]. They studied the performance measurement systems of large companies that sought to improve their management systems by including non-financial indicators. The results of the study led to the emergence of relatively new technology - a system of balanced scores [40, 41]. The essence of this system is formulated in two main provisions:

- financial indicators alone are not enough to fully and comprehensively (balanced) describe the state of the organization, they need to be supplemented by other indicators;
- this system of indicators can be used not just as a comprehensive indicator of the state of the organization, but as a management system that provides a link between strategic goals and operational activities of the organization's management.

The system of balanced indicators translates the company's mission and strategy into a system of clearly set goals and objectives, as well as indicators that determine the degree of their achievement in four projections:

- finance (as assessed by investors);
- customers (as assessed by customers);
- internal business processes (to realize competitive advantages);
- training and growth (opportunities for the development of the company).

The main structural idea of this method is to balance the system of indicators in the form of four groups. The first group "finance" includes traditional financial indicators. No matter how we prove the importance of the market orientation of the organization and the perfection of internal processes, the owner will always be primarily interested in indicators of financial return on investment. Therefore, a balanced system must begin and end with financial indicators.

The second group indicators "business processes" characterizes the internal processes of the organization: innovation process; product development; organization culture; supply of basic resources; production; marketing; after sales service, etc.

The third group indicators "customers" describes the external environment of the organization, its relationship with customers. The focuses of attention: the ability of the organization to customer satisfaction; the ability of the organization to retain the client; ability to attract a new client; customer profitability; market volume; market share in the target segment.

The fourth group indicators "learning and growth" allows to describe the organization's ability to learn and grow, which focuses on the following factors: people with their abilities, skills and motivation; information systems that allow to deliver critical information in real time; organizational procedures that ensure interaction between the participants in the process and determine the decision-making system.

There is a causal link between the metrics and the goals of all four projections. For example, an increase in the absolute return on investment can be achieved by increasing the number of clients, which in turn is associated with a reduction of the errors in project planning (project implementation in terms of cost and time), as well as the level of staff competence. Thus, in the proposed model, value indicators are formed within the four projection, which characterizes the financial processes, management structures, team intelligence, and design technologies (**Table 2**).

Determining the discrepancies between the indicators of the organization on four types of balanced indicators between the current state and the desired can be represented in matrix form:

$$R = \begin{matrix} P_1 \\ P_2 \\ \cdots \\ P_n \end{matrix} \begin{bmatrix} \Delta(P_1,A_1) & \Delta(P_1,B_1) & \Delta(P_1,C_1) & \Delta(P_1,D_1) \\ \Delta(P_2,A_2) & \Delta(P_2,B_2) & \Delta(P_2,C_2) & \Delta(P_2,D_2) \\ \cdots & \cdots & \cdots & \cdots \\ \Delta(P_n,A_n) & \Delta(P_n,B_n) & \Delta(P_n,C_n) & \Delta(P_n,D_n) \end{bmatrix} \quad (4)$$

Level	Financial control	Management structures	Team intelligence	Design technologies
Beige.	Survival processes	Free groups	Automatic thinking	Repair of old infrastructure
Violet	Traditional are provided with a circular guarantee	Clans	Animistic thinking	Creation of new myths, ideological projects
Red	Operation	Hard hierarchies	Thinking is egocentric	Crisis management
Blue	Authoritarian bureaucracy	Pyramidal bureaucratic	Absolutist thinking	Construction of new systems
Orange	Strategic	Matrix, such as delegating	Multiple thinking	Creative projects
Green	Consensus, leveling	Horizontal, equalizing	Relativistic thinking	Ecological, socially oriented projects
Yellow	Integrating system	Interactive, network	Systemic thinking	Information technologies projects
Turquoise	Ecological, cholic	Global	Holistic thinking	Synergetic programs

Table 2.
The structure of values according to the levels of spiral dynamics.

Based on the definition of discrepancies, we form a portfolio of development to increase organizational values. The set of measures to eliminate discrepancies is presented in the form of a set of projects that are combined into a portfolio. An appropriate model was developed for the transition of the enterprise from the current state to the planned one by forming a development portfolio (**Figure 6**).

Structural decomposition of the portfolio into projects and programs means the ability to model the organization with varying degrees of detail, from the enterprise as a whole to a separate structural unit. Today, many companies face conflicts based on different development priorities within the company. Conflicts arise not because there are different views on development priorities, but because the company does not have a single agreed system of priorities. "Value-oriented management" is the search for and adoption of such priorities that will ensure the company's long-term evolutionary development. The main task of value-oriented management is to organize the joint coordinated work of all conflicting units because after agreeing on value priorities, the company becomes a community of like-minded people, which ensures the successful achievement of its goals.

Thus, understanding the essence and reasons for the spiral nature of systems development allows you to look at the development of the organization through the management of project portfolios from a new angle. Diagnosis of the dominant evolutionary values of the company's management system determines the strategy of formation and implementation of a value-oriented portfolio of projects, due to which the organization moves to a new level of evolutionary development. The current management of the evolutionary development of the organization can be implement through the portfolio management with using its methods, techniques, and tools. The proposed information technology model of enterprise development (see **Figure 6**) defines the basic tools of project portfolio management. All these steps can be formalized by placing information in a repository or retrieving it from the repository upon request.

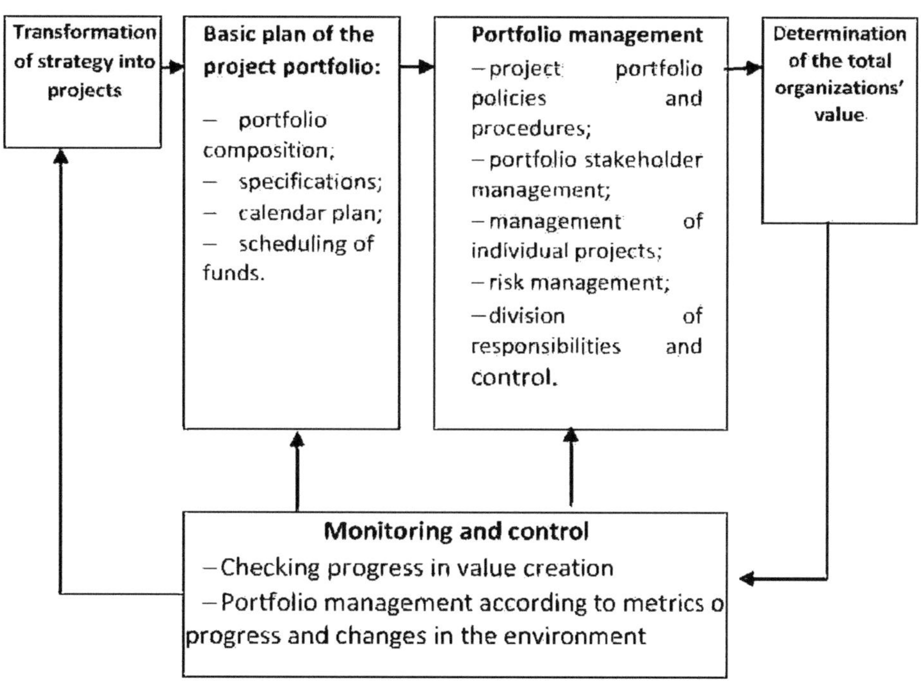

Figure 6.
Model of organization development portfolio formation.

The basic principles of portfolio formation, among other things, should determine: the desired composition of projects and programs within the portfolio; the level of risk to which the company is prepared in connection with the implementation of the portfolio, standards and restrictions, as well as key performance indicators for their further control. The dominant level of environmental values must also be taken into account when building the strategic focus of the organization, only so it is possible to implement the unique properties of the organization to create its competitive advantage.

The task of determining the profile of organization's values does not have an unambiguous solution, but it is very important for the development strategy of the firm. Project analysis offers methods and tools [9] that determine the interaction of the project organization with the project environment (economic, political, legal, social, etc.).

4.2 Formation of a value-oriented portfolio of organization development

In a narrow sense, the term "project portfolio formation" means determining which of the set of possible projects to start, which will be next, etc., provided that there are projects that can be started simultaneously and claim available resources. The overall process of project selection and resource allocation can be seen as the process of sequentially filling the order portfolio. The decision maker needs to know what funds can be spent on each of several possible projects in each of the time periods. At the end of each time period, the composition of the portfolio changes according to the projects that are currently in operation. Many of the existing projects consist of projects that are currently underway and projects that are in reserve.

In the general formulation of the problem of forming a value-oriented portfolio of development of the organization we have n projects, each of which is characterized by the corresponding costs and value. Restriction B is set on the amount of portfolio financing. It is necessary to form a portfolio of projects so that the total value of the portfolio was the maximum, provided that the amount of costs does not exceed B.

In accordance with the development strategy of the organization, the maximum number of options for strategic initiatives in the form of projects is developed. Before starting to form a portfolio of projects, they are preliminarily reviewed and discarded knowingly inefficient components, which reduces the number of alternatives in each area of activity. Let us denote $x_i = 1$, if the i-th project is included in the portfolio, $x_i = 0$ otherwise, then the mathematical formulation of the problem has the following form:

$$f(x) = \sum_{i=1}^{n} V_i x_i \to \max, \qquad (5)$$

$$\varphi(x) = \sum_{i=n} c_i x_i \le B,$$

$$x_i \in \{0;1\}, i = \overline{1,n},$$

where c_i - costs of the i-th project; V_i is the value of the i-th project.

However, this model of portfolio formation does not take into account the interdependence of the values of individual components of the portfolio. Meanwhile, the very consideration of interdependencies reflects the possibility of creating either a synergistic effect of the components of the portfolio or their mutual destruction (the effect of cannibalism). The synergetic effect of the value-oriented portfolio means the case when the value from the implementation of the entire portfolio exceeds the sum of the values from the implementation of its individual components.

To take into account the interdependencies of portfolio components in the proposed model, a matrix of project dependencies is used to determine the additional values obtained from the implementation of dependent portfolio projects. The matrix of project dependencies is a square matrix of dimension $n_p \cdot n_p$, where n_p, is the number of projects. Experts determine the values of the coefficients of dependencies of projects. Each element of the matrix d_{ij} can take values from 0 to 1 depending on the degree of connection of projects. The value of the coefficient d_{ij} shows the level of dependence of the project i on the project j. If the coefficient becomes 0, then the implementation of project i does not depend on the successful implementation of project j. A value of 1, in contrast, means that projects i and j are dependent, i.e. the success of one project directly depends on the implementation of another project, and as a result, both projects must be included in the portfolio. This matrix can be represented as follows:

$$\begin{bmatrix} d_{11} & d_{12} & \cdots & d_{1n_p} \\ d_{21} & d_{22} & \cdots & d_{2n_p} \\ \cdots & \cdots & \cdots & \cdots \\ d_{n_p1} & d_{n_p2} & & d_{n_pn_p} \end{bmatrix} \tag{6}$$

Once the interdependence matrix is formed, it is necessary to determine how the values obtained in the process of project activities are distributed among the dependent projects. To do this, a new parameter of the model V_i is introduced, which shows the share of the expected value in the case of the *i*-th project, if other dependent projects will not be launched. The remaining part of the value from the implementation of the *i*-th project and related projects in the amount $1-V_i$ is distributed among the dependent projects in proportion to the value of the relationship factors d_{ij}. The share of value allocated to dependent projects is reflected in the model by the following coefficients:

$$k_{ij} = (1 - V_i)\frac{d_{ij}}{\sum_{a=1}^{n_p} d_{ia}}. \tag{7}$$

The value D_{ij} from project *i*, obtained in the calendar year *t* is calculated based on a normalized matrix of dependencies (Eq. (4)). To assess the effect, it is necessary to enter a matrix of Boolean variables y_{it}, where $y_{it} = 1$, if project *i* is planned to start in year *t*, if not $y_{it} = 0$. The value obtained from the implementation of only dependent projects without taking into account the probability of their success can be determined by the following formula:

$$D_{it} = \sum_{j=1}^{n_p} k_{ij} Y_{it}. \tag{8}$$

The model assumes that a project starts only once and is funded throughout its life cycle. To simplify the model, it is assumed that the cost of the project does not depend on the year in which the project was launched (discounting is not taken into account). The costs for each component of the portfolio C_{it} are described in the form of a corresponding matrix. The model also includes projected revenue from each project by year, which depends on the year in which the project was started. The value of each element in the income matrix R_{it} is the income from project *i* in calendar year *t*. To account for the probability of success of each project on the basis of expert assessments, the probability P_i is assigned, and then the projects are ranked depending on the probability of success.

The model takes into account two types of restrictions: the budget and the number of projects in the portfolio. The budget B_t means the maximum amount of financial resources allocated for the implementation of portfolio projects in each calendar year *t*. The total cost of portfolio projects in each year may not exceed the budget. Therefore, we can write the following budget constraint:

$$\sum_{i=1}^{n_p} C_{it} Y_{it} - B_t \leq 0, t = 1,2,\ldots,n, \tag{9}$$

where n – the duration of the settlement period of the portfolio.

The limit on the number of projects implemented in year *t* is recorded as:

$$\sum_{i=1}^{n_p} Y_{it} - Q_t \leq 0, t = 1,2,\ldots,n. \tag{10}$$

The selection of projects for funding in each calendar year is based on maximizing the total value of portfolio *V*, subject to the restrictions. The function does not take into account the discounting factor to simplify the model. Under these conditions, the objective function has the following form:

$$\max \sum_{t=0}^{n_t} \sum_{i=1}^{n_p} Y_{it} R_{it} P_i \left(V_i - D_{it}\right) - \sum_{t=0}^{n_t} \sum_{i=1}^{n_p} Y_{it} C_{it} \leq 0. \tag{11}$$

Thus, the objective function of the model is to maximize the total value of the portfolio subject to budget constraints and the number of projects implemented simultaneously. The optimization model is calculated using Matlab software. With the practical use of the model, there may be no acceptable solutions, in which case it is possible to set a stricter limit on the number of projects in the portfolio.

In the general case, when forming a portfolio it is necessary to select projects with a large set of parameters, i.e. to solve a multicriteria decision-making problem and deal with many alternatives, many criteria, and multiple scales of evaluation criteria. To simplify this problem, a sequential convolution of the values of the characteristics of alternatives is used, for example, based on the method of analysis of hierarchies proposed by T. Saati at the end of the last century [42].

The task of selecting the components of the optimal portfolio is a difficult task and to solve it better by methods of mathematical programming. At the entrance of this task, we need information on possible projects (with a certain value) and weight about the criteria of values. Only those projects that bring the necessary value and, most importantly, correspond to the strategy at a certain value level of the organization's existence should be included in the portfolio.

As a result of solving the problem (for example, the simplex method), we obtain a set of projects from which should a portfolio consist of. However, this model can only be applied if the projects are independent. Taking into account the interdependence of projects in the portfolio is a very important point that reflects the possibility of creating a synergistic effect on the implementation of the project portfolio. Therefore, in the beginning, it is possible to estimate the total value of the portfolio without taking into account the interdependence of its components, and then calculate the total effect from the implementation of all components of the portfolio as a whole (synergistic effect).

4.3 Monitoring and control of the implementation of the development portfolio

Control of the implementation of the development portfolio based on deviations of actual indicators from the planned ones and determining the expediency of adjusting the strategy. Since the portfolio is a dynamic system, it means that the quantitative characteristics of its elements and the intensity of the relationship between them change over time, i.e. each current state of the portfolio structure corresponds to the actual current values of the properties of system elements.

Monitoring of the implementation of the strategy is carried out in order to provide all stakeholders with data that confirm or deny the existence of progress in achieving the goals and objectives of the strategy. In other words, it is the process of regularly collecting and recording data on key elements of the strategy implementation during the period of its implementation in order to determine intermediate and final results, timely identify problems and deviations from the planned results and make necessary adjustments to minimize negative consequences. Minimizing this inconsistency is the task of ongoing project portfolio management. Depending on the magnitude of this inconsistency in the system, problematic situations are possible, which are, respectively, states of advanced development, stability and stagnation of the organizational system.

An important task of monitoring is to document its procedures and results. This is primarily the responsibility of those directly involved in implementing the strategy or its individual elements, conducting monitoring procedures, and being responsible for data collection and processing. The project team members and the regional working group should carry out the synthesis of all obtained monitoring results.

The last step of management is the process of evaluating the achievements associated with the identification of public utility resulting from the implementation of projects and programs. Monitoring and evaluation of results should be made public in order not only to assess progress but also to make adjustments and monitor the sustainability of the results obtained. Unfortunately, not all project managers have practical tools for monitoring the implementation of projects and programs, understanding the political sustainability of the results, methods, and skills of preserving the experience of lessons learned.

Monitoring and control of portfolio performance and evaluation of the feasibility of adjusting the development strategy.

Because the enterprise is a dynamic system, this means that the quantitative characteristics of the elements that make up the system and the intensity of the relationship change over time:

$$S^d(t) = \left(E^d(t), R^d(t)\right), \tag{12}$$

where S – a certain structure, which is a set of elements E with ordered relations R.

The properties of the system also change over time, each current state of the enterprise structure corresponds to the actual current values of the system properties.

$$P^F(t) = F[S(t)]. \tag{13}$$

Comparison of $P^F(t)$ with target $P^d(t)$ allows determining the amount of inconsistency:

$$\Delta P(T) = P^d(t) - P^F(t). \tag{14}$$

Minimizing this inconsistency and taking into account rapid environmental changes is the task of ongoing project portfolio management.

Based on the law of positive dynamics, the external environment is a purposeful metasystem that has a vector of development aimed at achieving positive goals. Only processes that implement positive goals reduce the entropy of the system. The realization of the portfolio can be considered, first, as an approximation to the ideal state, the "portrait" of which at a certain stage of its development was "painted" by one or another social system. As you know, the system cannot be successful in its development if it successfully implements the "wrong" projects. Thus, all components of the development portfolio should correspond to the main vector of development of the organizational system. Mastering the project management methodology by Ukrainian managers would allow the country's leadership to implement its strategic priorities and commitments.

4.4 Method of the decisions preparation for the value-oriented portfolio management of the organizations

In the course of the research, the theoretical and methodological bases of management of development of the organizations by realization of the value-oriented portfolio of the projects formed based on the evolutionary theory of civilizational values were opened. For this purpose, the processes of project portfolio management in terms of their value significance were considered. The obtained results make it possible to describe the method, which should give a holistic view of the process of collecting, analyzing and preparing information on strategic decision-making in the management of value-oriented portfolio of development of organizations.

The formalization of the method is the basis for algorithmization and programming, without which the computerization of knowledge and research processes cannot do. Formalization of the method eliminates ambiguity, inaccuracy and uncertainty. When formalizing the method instead of statements about formalization we use a systematic representation in the form of clear structural elements. Based on the essence of the above models, we describe each of the structural elements.

The scope of the method of preparing information for strategic decision-making in the portfolios of organizational development is the practical activities of managing the development of the organization as a holistic open system in a changing environment. If the organization takes the right strategic position, it becomes possible to enter a new cycle of development based on a new dominant value. Such evolutionary development can take a very long time, each time returning to the beginning of the cycle. Wrongly chosen strategic position at the stage of the company's prosperity can lead it to painful agony and bankruptcy. This happens when an organization, due to the limited thinking of managers, "gets stuck" at a certain level of values, while external circumstances push it to move to a new level.

The essence of the value-oriented method of preparing information for strategic decisions in project portfolio management is to obtain information based on the ratio of the values of the components of the portfolio in the intermediate configuration. Indicators of the values of the components of the portfolio are obtained using integrated indicators, which are formed based on the concept of a system of balanced scores, and expert assessments of stakeholders, taking into account the opinion of the decision maker. As for the objective basis of the method, it should reveal the essence of the description of the object of the method, which allows you to track the relationship between objects and their properties [43].

In the method of preparing information for acceptance strategic decisions in development portfolios, the objective basis of the method is a single-order essence of indicators that characterize the state of the components of the portfolio, taking into account the different options for its further development.

Elements of the method of preparation of information for making strategic decisions in the portfolios of development of organizations based on the evolutionary theory of values are summarized in **Table 3**.

The proposed method allows taking into account both internal and external aspects of the value of the components of the development portfolio at different times, which allows choosing a strategy for further development of the enterprise as a system. The method became the basis of the methodology of decision preparation for the value-oriented portfolio management of organizations. The proposed method was piloted to identify the features of its implementation, which was reflected in the terms of reference for software development with subsequent testing in real enterprises.

Structural element	The essence of the structural element of the method
Name	Method of preparation of decisions for formation of the value-oriented portfolio of development of the organization
Scope	It is used to form and implement a portfolio of development of the organization to justify the choice of one of the possible options for further development.
Goal	Obtaining recommendations for the customer on the choice of strategy for further development of the organization through project portfolios.
Essence	Recommendations for choosing one of the three possible strategies for further development of the organization. At each stage of the life cycle of the organization there is an opportunity to choose a strategy for further development: to continue to increase the values of the current level; prepare for the transition to the next level of values or freeze organizational development projects. The decision is made based on comparing the level of internal organizational values and the level of values of the external environment. If an organization gets stuck at a certain level of values, while external circumstances push it to a transition to a new level, it is likely to face a painful bankruptcy.
Basic conditions	Ranking of indicators that characterize the level of values of an individual projects and the strategic value of the projects portfolio at the current date
Objective basis	The number of experts must be at least eight, with the obligatory involvement of at least two representatives for each projection of the balanced scorecard.

Table 3.
Method for the value-oriented portfolio formation.

5. Conclusions

The generalization of the obtained results, scientific positions, the achieved goal and the solved tasks of the research allow drawing conclusions that are meaningfully correlated with the proved consequences of the basic hypothesis:

1. Theoretical provisions of management of development of the organizations by the realization of the value-oriented portfolio of the projects formed based on the evolutionary theory of values, which allowed formalizing a method of preparation of decisions for the formation of the value-oriented portfolio, to open essence of its structural elements, and basic rules are presented.

2. Methodological bases of value-oriented development management in the form of system principles, basic terms, stages of modeling and methods of estimation of dominating values of the organization which differ from the traditional approach by interpretation of reality according to a set of value memes of project managers are developed.

3. The method of competitive analysis of portfolio components for forming the composition of the value-oriented portfolio by generalizing the principles of value-oriented, and competitive approaches has been improved.

4. A conceptual model of the decision support system has been developed, which allows solving the problems of current management of the value-oriented portfolio of enterprise development, which differs in the presence of the preliminary stage of building value-oriented strategy and elaboration of its implementation through projects portfolio.

In the future, the author plans to continue studying the processes of value-oriented portfolio management in a behavioral economy, as well as to explore the nature and impact of the mental platform of organizations on portfolio components.

Author details

Valentyna Michaylovna Molokanova
Dnipropetrovsk' Regional Institute for Public Administration, National Academy for Public Administration under the President of Ukraine, Dnipro, Ukraine

*Address all correspondence to: molokany@gmail.com

References

[1] Burnes Bernard, Rune By. Leadership and Change: The Case for Greater Ethical Clarity. Journal of Business Ethics. 2012;108(2):239-252

[2] The Standard for Portfolio management. Project Management Institute, Inc. Four Campus Boulevard Newtown Square, Pennsylvania USA; 2008. 203 p.

[3] Global Sustainable Development Goals 2030. [Internet]. Access mode: http://www.un.org.ua/images/documents/3615/entili_web(2).pdf.

[4] Forum on Sustainable Development of Ukraine. [Internet]. Access mode: http://www.sustainable-cities.net.ua.

[5] Promotion of sustainable development in Ukraine. [Internet]. International project under the initiative of the UNDP and the USA for International Development. Access mode: http://www.undpsust.kiev.ua/.

[6] Daniel Kent, Sheridan Titman, Characteristics or Covariances. Journal of Portfolio Management. Summer 1998; 24:24-33.

[7] Markowitz HM. Foundations of Portfolio Theory. Journal of Finance. 1991; 46:469-477.

[8] Ferson WE, Campbell RH, Sources of Predictability in Portfolio Returns. Financial Analysts Journal. May/June 1991; 47:49-56.

[9] PMBOK guide. A guide to the project management body of knowledge (PMBOK® guide). Sixth edition. Newtown Square, PA: Project Management Institute; 2017. 168 p.

[10] Daniel Elizabeth, Ward John, Franken Arnoud. A dynamic capabilities perspective of IS project portfolio management. Journal of Strategic Information Systems. 2014;23(2):95-111.

[11] Molokanova VM, Changes in portfolios management of organization projects in conditions of behavioural econome Applied Aspects of Information Technology. 2019;2(4):345-358.

[12] Zhang Y, Dolan S, Zhou Y. Management by values: A theoretical proposal for strategic human resource management in China. Chinese Management Studies. 2014;3(4):272-294. doi.org/10.1108/17506140911007468.

[13] Clare W. Graves. Compared with other theories. [Internet]. Access mode: http://www.clarewgraves.com/theory_content/compared/CGcomp1.htm.

[14] Killen C, Jugdev K, Drouin N, Petit Yv. Advancing project and portfolio management research: Applying strategic management theories. International Journal of Project Management, Elsevier. 2012;30(5):525-538. doi: 10.1016/j.ijproman.

[15] Jeffery M, Leliveld I. Best practices in IT portfolio management. MIT Sloan Management Review. 2004;45(3):41-49.

[16] Value Methodology Standard and Body of Knowledge. SAVE International. [Internet]. Access mode: https://www.value-eng.org/page/ValueStandards.

[17] The Standard for Portfolio management. Project Management Institute, Inc. Four Campus Boulevard Newtown Square, USA, 2006. 203 p.

[18] Best management practice portfolio. UK Office of Government Commerce. [Internet]. Access mode: https://www.gov.uk/government/publications/best-management-practice

[19] Killen CP, Hunt RA. Dynamic capabilities through project portfolio management in service and manufacturing industries. International Journal of Managing Projects in Business. 2010;3(1):157-169.

[20] Maizlish B., Handler R. IT Portfolio Management: Unlocking the Business Value of Technology. Wiley: Chichester; 2005. 367 p.

[21] Weill P, Aral S, Generating premium returns on your IT investments. Sloan Management Review. 2006;47(2):39-48.

[22] Bardhan I, Bagchi S, Sougstad R. Prioritizing a portfolio of information technology investment projects. Journal of Management Information Systems. 2004;21(2):33-60.

[23] Kendal I. Modern methods of project portfolio management and project management office. ROI maximization. M.: PMSOFT; 2004. 576 p.

[24] Cepeda G, Vera D. Dynamic capabilities and operational capabilities: A knowledge management perspective. Journal of Business Research 2007;60(5):426-437.

[25] Wang CL, Ahmed PK. Dynamic capabilities: a review and research agenda. International Journal of Management Reviews. 2007;9(1):31-51.

[26] Merali Y, Papadopoulos T, Nadkarni T. Information systems strategy: past. present, future. Journal of Strategic Information Systems.2012;21 (2):125-153.

[27] Kong, A., D.E. Rapach, J.K. Strauss, and G. Zhou. Predicting Market Components Out of Sample: Asset Allocation Implications. Journal of Portfolio Management.2011;37(4): 29-41.

[28] Neely, C.J., D.E. Rapach, J. Tu, and G. Zhou. Forecasting the Equity Risk Premium: The Role of Technical Indicators. Management Science. 2014;60(7): 1772-1791.

[29] McCahery, J., Z. Sautner and L. Starks. Behind the Scenes: The Corporate Governance Preferences of Institutional Investors', Journal of Finance. 2017;71(6): 2905-2932.

[30] Kahneman D, Tversky A. Prospect theory: An analysis of decision under risk. Econometrica. 1979;47(2):263-291.

[31] Simon LD, Bonnie AR. Management by values (MBV): a new philosophy for a new economic order. Handbook of Business Strategy.2006;7(1):235-238.

[32] Dawkins R. The selfish gene. Oxford: Oxford University Press; 1978. 218 p.

[33] Shigenobu Ohara. A Guidebook of Project & Program Management for Enterprise Innovation. Project Management Association of Japan (PMAJ); 2005. 235 p.

[34] Neely A, Mills J, Platts K, Richards H, Gregory M, Bourne et al. Performance measurement system design; developing and testing a process-based approach. International Journal of Operations & Production Management. 2000;20(10):63-80.

[35] Adizes I. Managing Corporate Lifecycles. Complete Edition. Adizes Institute Public; 2011. 384 p.

[36] McDaniel RR, Driebe DJ. Uncertainty and Surprise: An Introduction. Uncertainty and Surprise in Complex Systems. Springer. New York; 2010 311 p

[37] Guastello SJ, Guastello DD. Dynamics of Attitudes and Genetic Processes. Nonlinear Dynamics, Psychology, and Life Sciences. 2008;12:75-86.

[38] Miller JH, Page SE. Complex Adaptive Systems. An Introduction to Computational Models of Social Life. Princeton: Princeton University Press;2007.

[39] Don Beck, Chris Cowan. Spiral Dynamics: Mastering Values, Leadership, and Change. Blackwell Publishing;2005. 343 p.

[40] Kaplan RS, Norton DP. Putting the Balanced Scorecard to Work. Harvard Business Review. 1993;71(5): 134-147.

[41] Kaplan RS, Norton DP. The Balanced Scorecard: Measures that drive performance. Harvard Business Review. 2005;83(7/8):172-180.

[42] Saati T. Decision making. Method of analysis of hierarchies: trans. from English. M.: Radio and communication. 1989. 316 p.

[43] Rach VA, Ignatova OV. Methodology of the systemic approach to scientific advances: a master book. Luhansk: SNU. 2010. 210 p.

Chapter 2

Estimating Short-Term Returns with Volatilities for High Frequency Stock Trades in Emerging Economies Using Gaussian Processes (GPs)

Leonard Mushunje, Maxwell Mashasha and Edina Chandiwana

Abstract

Fundamental theorem behind financial markets is that stock prices are intrinsically complex and stochastic in nature. One of the complexities is the volatilities associated with stock prices. Price volatility is often detrimental to the return economics and thus investors should factor it in when making investment decisions, choices, and temporal or permanent moves. It is therefore crucial to make necessary and regular stock price volatility forecasts for the safety and economics of investors' returns. These forecasts should be accurate and not misleading. Different traditional models and methods such as ARCH, GARCH have been intuitively implemented to make such forecasts, however they fail to effectively capture the short-term volatility forecasts. In this paper we investigate and implement a combination of numeric and probabilistic models towards short-term volatility and return forecasting for high frequency trades. The essence is that: one-day-ahead volatility forecasts were made with Gaussian Processes (GPs) applied to the outputs of a numerical market prediction (NMP) model. Firstly, the stock price data from NMP was corrected by a GP. Since it not easy to set price limits in a market due to its free nature, and randomness of the prices, a censored GP was used to model the relationship between the corrected stock prices and returns. To validate the proposed approach, forecasting errors were evaluated using the implied and estimated data.

Keywords: short-term volatility, stock prices, stock returns, Gaussian process, GARCH, Numerical market prediction

1. Introduction

Stock prices are towards the determination of investors' portfolio status and their consideration is important not only in stock markets. In South Africa, Stocks listed at Johannesburg Stock Exchange (JSE) are actually going through volatilities whose coefficients are high, and this is most common in almost all emerging economies. Volatility is defined as a tendency for prices to change unexpectedly, Harris [1].

The frequency of the short time scaled volatility hits often poses several investment and operational challenges. Thus volatility prediction is an essential process towards securing the economies of the investment portfolios of investors. Short-term volatility forecasts with a prediction horizon from one hour to several days are critical to optimize stock returns and any associated costs. Broadly speaking, there are two approaches to short-term price volatility forecasting: statistical models and physical models. The former uses only historical stock price data to build statistical models, such as autoregressive integrated moving average (ARIMA), autoregressive conditional heteroscedasticity (ARCH), generalized autoregressive conditional heteroscedasticity (GARCH), artificial neural networks, Kalman filters, support vector machines. The cross-field application of these models appears in wind power generation forecast, (see [2–6]). While Statistical models are robust mainly for very short-term forecasts (between 1 and 3 hours ahead), physical models are good in some ways. They can provide better estimates and predictions for longer horizons (days, weeks, months), because they include (3-Dimension) spatial and temporal factors in a full fluid-dynamics model. However, this type of model has limitations, such as the limited observation set for model calibration. To overcome these limitations, some authors have combined statistical and physical models, Salcedo-Sanz et al. [6] and Al-Yahyai et al. [7] where data from a physical model is used as inputs to a statistical model.

This study proposes a forecast model combined with NMP data in which one-day-ahead price volatility forecasting is realized based on historically recorded close prices, volumes, and other market information. We shall combine our NMP data with the Gaussian Processes (GP). Such integrated methods will be used to tailor make corresponding return predictions. Related to our study, are the works of Ladokhin [8], who examines the accuracy of several of the most popular methods used in volatility forecasting. A comparative approach is employed where historical volatility models such as Exponential Weighted Moving Average, ARMA model and GARCH family of models are compared with Artificial Neural Networks based models. Taylor [9] proposed a simple but less accurate method of estimating volatility where daily squared returns are taken. The jumps associated with intra-day prices are not captured yet these jumps significantly affect volatility.

Other related works were done on the prediction of the stock/index returns by: White [10], Sharda [11], Kimoto [12], Brown [13], Gencay [14] where the Artificial neural networks were used. In addition, Sullivan (n.d) [15] employs a variation of a type of Recurrent Neural Network called Long-Short Term Memory (LSTM) in order to predict stock price volatility in the US equity market. Among their results, they found that greater deal of tuning is required on the deeper network, and in particular, the increased use of dropout layers could help reduce the variance problem associated with the employed model so as to accurately estimate the price volatilities. Recent work on stock market prediction is by Sang and Pierro [16] who focuses on the application of LSTM to predict financial time series in the stock market, using both traditional time series analysis and using technical analysis metrics. This is directly related to the successful application of the traditional (LSTM) to address the problem of volatility prediction in the stock market, Xiong et al. [17] and Sardelicha and Manandhar (n.d) [18]. Bhowmik and Wang [19] on the other hand provides a literature review using a systematic database to examine and cross-reference snowballing where previous studies featuring a generalized autoregressive conditional heteroskedastic (GARCH) family-based model stock market return and volatility are reviewed. They also conduct a content analysis of return and volatility literature reviews over a period of 12 years (2008–2019) and in 50 different papers to see the trends and concentration of volatility linked studies. Their results show that significant studies have been done on volatility. However, a focus on short term trades still lacks. With respect to volatility and deviation modeling, researchers have proposed different distribution models in order to better describe the thick tail of the daily rate of return. For instance, Engle [20] first proposed an autoregressive conditional heteroscedasticity model (ARCH model) to characterize some possible correlations of the conditional variance of the prediction error. In 1986, Bollerslev extended the ARCH model to form a generalized autoregressive conditional heteroskedastic model (GARCH model). Later, the GARCH model rapidly expanded to other forms such as TARCH, EGARCH, ETARCH to form the so-called the GARCH family. As indicated across the literature, researchers proved that GARCH is the most suitable model to use when one has to analyze the volatility of the returns of stocks with big volumes of observations, (for more see [20–25]).

From the reviewed literature, short-term volatility forecasting has been slimly done and little attention has been paid to jumps in association to these short- timed price swerves. For the volatility studies done, statistical models have been employed as stated earlier in this paper. In this paper, stock prices and some related factors such as returns and volumes' datasets including (NMP) results are analyzed and used to develop volatility forecasting models over a horizon of up to one day, with a (GP) method. The main contributions and thrust of this can be summarized into 4 categories as: 1. The predicted price volatility from an NMP model is corrected using a GP. This process helps to improve performance compared with earlier methods for combining statistical and physical models. 2. To build the relationship between corrected stock prices and stock volumes we employed the censored Gaussian Process (CGP). The method accounts for the probabilistic character of the values that are not known precisely because of censoring. 3. High-stock prices data display different features based on the initial values of the models. As such, we shall be treating one of its subset separately. 4. Past stock price data from the JSE databases is used as an additional input to the forecasting model over the time horizon of 1–3 hours-ahead. This time interval is actually the efficient and supportive to our model. The idea paves a great way for high-frequency trades that are proving to dominate the markets and investment world.

2. Methodology

2.1 Data

The datasets used in this study were extracted from Johannesburg stock exchange (JSE) databases with a time scale from June 2017 to May 2018. The idea is that we shall use a whole year dataset as a training set, and the remainder as an independent test set, from where we will make our suitable inferential conclusions. The missing values were less than 30% and to cater for them, we used the K-nearest neighbor (KNN) approach in R environment; otherwise the obtained data was tied.

2.2 Numerical market prediction model and volatility forecasting

Numerical market prediction uses statistical physics and statistical historical models related to financial markets' mechanics. They are used to predict prices based on certain initial-value and boundary conditions. This study uses the stock price data (SPD) (from JSE) and the NMP model. SPD (stock price data) is extracted from the frequently updated JSE electronic stock price databases. The databases are prepared and well-kept for the interests of investors. In general, short-term price volatility forecasting needs predictions from a NMP model with high spatial resolution. The stock price data from JSE is suitable directly for this application, and hence no needs for extra actions like backward and forward interpolation. The prediction data is produced once each day, and is usually available at 4:00 PM CAT, where closing valuations are done for most investment assets. The data including stock prices, volumes and returns is provided at an interval of 30 minutes for the following 24 hours. It is no secret that investors and market regulators require accurate stock price and return forecasts: In this study we stress that the forecasting error of 1–3 hours ahead should be less than 10% of the actual recorded figures. Therefore, all the forecast errors contained in this study are calculated using hourly data.

3. The Gaussian process (GP)

The method of Gaussian processes is not new, however less seem to be considerably known on its application to financial data. Moreover, it has been successfully applied to many machine learning tasks. Rasmussen [26] duped a well detailed systematic explanation of Gaussian process regression and Automatic Relevance Determination (ARD). Further, the extension of the Gaussian Processes (GP) to censored data is found in Groot [27].

3.1 Gaussian process model

Let us consider a Gaussian process $f(x)$ for a classic regression problem. Now, assuming that we have training set D with n observations such that $D = \{(x_i, y_i) | i = 1, \dots, n\}$, where x denotes an input vector and y denotes a scalar output, the task is to build a function that satisfies the following multiple linear equation.

$$\boldsymbol{y_i} = \boldsymbol{f}(\boldsymbol{x_i}) + \boldsymbol{\epsilon_i} \tag{1}$$

$\boldsymbol{\epsilon_i}$ is the additive noise parameter which is non-observable and is assumed to follow a Gaussian distribution such that $\boldsymbol{\epsilon_i} \sim N(0, \sigma_n^2)$. Note that y is a linear combination of Gaussian variables and hence using the invariant transformation property of linear functions, is itself Gaussian. Therefore, we have $p(y|X, k) = N(0, K + \sigma_n^2 I)$, where $K_{ij} = k(x_i, x_j)$, and the joint distribution for a new input x_* can be written in matrix form as:

$$\begin{bmatrix} y \\ f_* \end{bmatrix} \sim \left(0, \begin{bmatrix} K(X,X) + \sigma_n^2 & k(X, x_*) \\ k(x_*, X) & k(x_*, x_*) \end{bmatrix}\right), \tag{2}$$

where, $k(X, x_*) = k(x_*, X)^T = [k(x_1, x_*), \dots, k(x_n, x_*)]$, which we will shortly express as k_*. Consequently, following the properties of joint Gaussian distributions, we predict the distribution of our target variable using the following function:

$$\overline{f_*} = k_*^T (K + \sigma_n^2 I)^{-1} y \tag{3}$$

$$V[f_*] = k(x_*, x_*) - k_*^T (K + \sigma_n^2 I)^{-1} k_* \tag{4}$$

As a result of the stock price control strategies available in the market, there is always a defined upper limit $\boldsymbol{S_{upper}}$ and lower limit of 0 for the stock prices at JSE. Therefore, in statistics, the true values (unrestricted price output) are 'censored' in that they are not observed but are replaced by the threshold value. In our modeling, we assume that Gaussian process (GP) has some latent values $y^* = f(x)$. We then used the censored GP model by Groot [27] to incorporate our modeling assumption. Expectation propagation is used to approximate the censored distribution of the latent variables. This is accompanied by an exploratory analysis whose results suggest that 4.6% percent is within 5% of the upper limit. Thus, it is in the good range where the noise distribution overlaps significantly with the censored range. This normally guarantees the robustness of our results.

4. Modeling process

Our modeling process follows the same approach used in wind power prediction demonstrated in Chen et al. (n.d). Our proposed forecasting framework used in this paper employs GP models through the incorporation of three additional features and these features are fundamental to our modeling process. The three features are: 1. Automatic Relevance Determination (ARD) which is used to select model data points for inputs; 2. Predicted stock prices from the NMP model are corrected before any volatility forecasting and lastly, 3. detailed adjustments were applied to improve our forecasting accuracy using some adjustments in detail, such as using historical data and a separate model building for high stock prices. The NMP data usually includes several market variables such as trading volumes, stock returns, interest rates and inflation. It is clear that stock returns mainly depend on the actual stock prices, however, we do not know for sure if any other market variables play an important role too, and even if we know, we may fail to know the extent to which the variable can affect the returns. To cater for this case, an ARD is used to investigate the selection of input variables. There are two main ways that can be used to obtain stock returns from NMP data: 1. by learning directly the model between NMP data and stock returns data using a censored GP and correcting the error in NMP stock price prediction and then building a second model for the relationship between stock prices and derived stock returns. 2. Can be obtained qualitatively based on the ideas behind a large body of empirical analysis, which states that there are some systematic and stochastic biases present in the original NMP forecasts. For formality sake, we denote the first way of modeling stock returns as GP-direct, and the second as GP-CPrice (meaning based on corrected price):

For illustration, we give a simple schematic diagram of the modeling process as shown in **Figure 1** below.

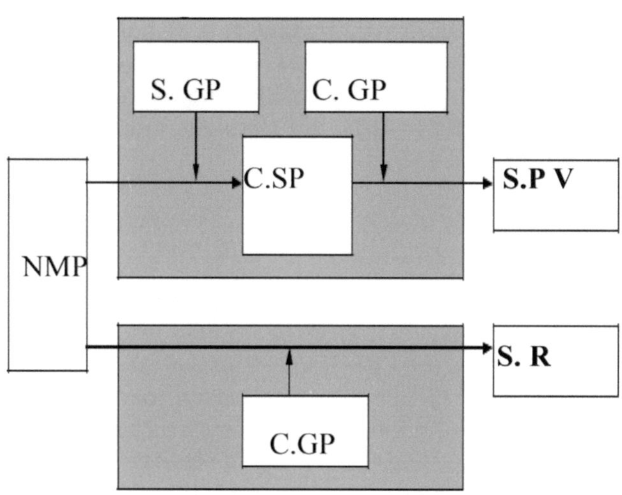

Figure 1.
Model building structure.

The terms in the diagram above are defined as follows:

NMP-Numerical market prediction.
S.GP-Standard Gaussian Process.
C.GP-Censored Gaussian Process.
C.SP-Censored Stock price.
S.PV-Stock price volatility.
S.R-Stock returns.

Further, we then apply our proposed correction model process, taking into account certain constraints to improve the accuracy of modeling. First of all, the process provides forecasts of price volatility and then returns. The main aim is to explore the effect of price volatility on stock returns. As mentioned earlier, the main call of this paper is to develop an efficient price volatility model that can be used to make relevant and frequent volatility estimates. The knowledge of such forecasts and explorations are useful then when modeling stock returns which is the reason behind all investment trades within stock markets.

5. Forecasting accuracy evaluation

Evaluating forecasting accuracy and efficiency can be done using several criteria. This study employed two methods to evaluate our proposed approach and for model evaluation and model comparison: The Root Mean Square Error (RMSE) and the Mean Absolute Error (MAE). We defined the error measures as follows:

$$e_t = y_t - \hat{y}_t \tag{5}$$

$$RMSE = \left(\frac{1}{n}\sum_{i=1}^{n} e_i^2\right)^{\frac{1}{2}} = \sqrt{\frac{1}{n}\sum_{i=1}^{n} e_i^2} \tag{6}$$

$$MAE = \frac{1}{n}\sum_{i=1}^{n} |e_i| \tag{7}$$

Here y_t denotes the actual observation value at time t, $\hat{y}_t$ represents the forecast value for the same period, n is the number of forecasts, and the error is denoted by e_i. The forecasting error threshold for the above specified methods 10%. The accuracy should be less or equal to 10%. Interestingly, our MAE and RMSE are all below 10% as shown in the subsequent tables.

5.1 Experimental validation

Two datasets based on JSE records and estimates are used in this paper to evaluate our approach. We first compared the implied price volatility with the forecasted price volatility. We used the Root Mean Square Error (RMSE) to compute the forecasting error to validate our modeling approach. Secondly, we used the Mean Absolute Error (MAE) method to validate our stock return forecasts where we compared the actual returns and the estimated returns. The two sets of pair wise data are independent from each other as they are extracted differently. Conclusions made are based on that, small values of both MAE and RMSE indicate a high degree of accuracy.

6. Root mean square error (RMSE) results

As shown in **Table 1**, the implied volatility coefficients are not significantly different the estimated coefficients. As implied volatility measures the realized volatility associated with price changes (short and long term), our estimated volatilities proved to be more reliable. This is well indicated by small RMSE values. Another interesting outcome is that, during holidays and weekends, volatility is high due to less market stability and reduced liquidity levels (**Table 2**).

	Implied Volatility (%)	Estimated Volatility (%)	Errors
Time (month)	(1)	(2)	(3)
1	0.280	0.279	0.001
2	0.23	0.223	0.007
3	0.296	0.283	0.013
4	0.178	0.170	0.008
5	0.312	0.291	0.021
6	0.337	0.32	0.017
7	0.117	0.112	0.005
8	0.49	0.48	0.01
9	0.413	0.419	(0.006)
10	0.60	0.60	0.000
11	0.556	0.532	0.024
12	0.80	0.798	0.003

****RMSE = 0.012168.*

Table 1.
Implied volatility versus estimated volatility.

	Actual returns (%)	Forecasted returns (%)	Errors
Time (month)	(1)	(2)	(3)
1	0.360	0.379	(0.019)**
2	0.655	0.635	0.02
3	0.698	0.6901	0.0079
4	0.738	0.738	0.000**
5	0.712	0.691	0.021
6	0.831	0.832	(0.001)*
7	0.8273	0.8121	0.0152
8	0.749	0.748	0.001
9	0.713	0.409	0.304**
10	0.635	0.62	0.015
11	0.756	0.732	0.024
12	0.57	0.568	0.002

*MAE = 0.03584 = 3.58%. The footnote ** is representing the extreme values obtained from the analysis. This can either be too low or too high and such numbers are of interest in our analysis.*

Table 2.
Actual stock returns versus forecasted stock returns.

Mean absolute error (MAE) results: As depicted in the above presented table. Our model proved to be more accurate as indicated by small MAE values. The forecasts errors are not significant, indicating small deviations of our estimated returns from the true (observed returns).

6.1 Model evaluation

As a preliminary step, the ARD was applied to determine which NMP variables should be included as inputs to the correction model. For clarity, we tabulated the measured conditional stock price values as our target variable in the presence of other selected variables-trading volumes, insider news, inflation, exchange rates and stock returns (**Table 3**).

The intensity and effect of the variables on our prediction accuracy for both stock returns and volatility is at all different. However, we noted that stock prices and trading volumes do impact our prediction much than the rest of factors and at the same time, volatility is mostly influenced by trading volumes and insider news in the market. Therefore, we use trading volumes and stock prices (historic) to predict our stock returns and associated short-term volatility as inputs in the GP correction process. This should be kept in mind that in some market environments and set ups, all of the above variables can be used though their intensity factors vary from market to market.

7. Simulation results

This section presents the results of our stock return-prediction framework and price volatility against some benchmarks. We employed the persistence model and a multi-layer perceptron (MLP) neural network model. We used the approach used by Chen et al. (n.d) and Amjady *et al.* [28], where they apply the MLP method to forecast wind power generation. The idea behind the persistence method is that it simply uses the current value as the forecast, which means that at time, t, the prediction, $\hat{y}_{t+1} = \hat{y}_{t+2} = \cdots \hat{y}_{t+30} = y_t$.

Since stock data-prices are Markovian, we excluded the historical data in this model at the pre-processing stage), The Markov property states that the future values of, a stock or its price is well explained by the current/present values than its past. As such, we use the current stock price and volume data in this model, and calculate both the stock returns and price volatilities by stock price-yield curve and volatility smile functions respectively, which can be obtained by training historical

	Modeling period	**Modeling period**
Variable	(1)	(2)
Stock prices	0.380	0.313
Trading volumes	0.33	0.364
Trade Frequency	0.206	0.21
Interest rates	0.10	0.08
Inflation	0.08	0.121
Insider news	0.27	0.29
Variable effect in percentages: Higher percentage higher effect.		

Table 3.
ARD results for stock prices at JSE.

Model	RMSE	MAE	NMAPE
	(%)	(%)	(%)
CReturns	14.59	12.79	10.45%
GP-Direct	12.40	12.09	9.53%
GP-CReturns	8.36	7.29	5.73%

Table 4.
Stock returns forecast error.

Model	RMSE	MAE	NMAPE
	(%)	(%)	(%)
MLP-CPrice	15.59	12.79	9.26%
GP-Direct	13.10	11.49	7.53%
GP-CPrice	9.36	8.69	4.73%

Table 5.
Price volatility forecasts error.

dataset. MLP networks are seen in application to short-term wind power forecasting than to stock markets data, for example Amjady *et al.* [28]. This study is making use of the networks, that is, an MLP based model which first corrects stock prices and then predicts stock returns is chosen for comparison. Using the empirical results (model comparison on a validation set), the first MLP model, which corrects stock prices, used NMP stock prices, trading volumes and exchange rates as input variables, and measured returns as the output variable, with a 11-neuron hidden layer. The second part of the MLP-Stock price model used corrected stock prices as input, and has 8-neuron hidden layer, then outputs the final prediction of stock returns. From our empirical results, we can conclude that one well-trained forecast model can be applied to other financial assets data of the same type at JSE. The results of applying the proposed model to the test datasets are shown in **Tables 4** and **5**.

From **Tables 4** and **5**, we note that the proposed GP-Stock Price model has better performance than the other models, and especially presents an outstanding performance in 1–3 hours forecast horizon. In terms of MAE, the improvement of accuracy is 17.98% is required. If comparing to MLP-Stock Price model, the improvement would be 11.61%. The normalized mean absolute percentage error (NMAPE) is the best measure of the forecasting error in our study. This is supported by its ability to provide non-deviating estimates. For easy reference the NMAPE is calculated as:

$$\frac{1}{n}\sum_{i=1}^{n}\left|\frac{e_i}{M}\right| \times 100,$$

where $n$the number of sample items, M is the market type, in this case we have the stock market (Johannesburg stock exchange.

8. Conclusions

Stock markets are by no means easy to predict. Both stock prices and returns are very stochastic. This poses some difficulties in forecasting their behavior. Volatility is a key aspect that needs always to be paid attention in the investment world. In this paper, we investigated short-term volatilities associated with stock prices using another approach. We employed the combination of numeric and probabilistic models to forecast one-day interval ahead returns and prices. We used the Gaussian Process (GP) and a Numerical market prediction (NMP) model. To improve the model prediction accuracy, we used a step-wise approach where predicted stock prices are firstly corrected by GP before it is used to forecast stock returns. A censored GP is applied to build the price-return model, mainly to cater for unobserved or missing price records; ARD is used to choose effective NMP variables as inputs to each model; for very short-term forecasts, historical data is added into modeling process; and a high stock prices subset is treated separately by building a single forecast model as we considered it as a special case. The simulation results show that, compared to an MLP-Stock Price model, the proposed model has around 11% improvement of forecasting accuracy, hence the effectiveness and performance of the GP-Stock Price model is proved. Precisely, we proved that the GP performs well in volatility forecasting based on the robustness test done using the forecasting error measures like the RMSE and MAE. Therefore, this paper suggests future works to be carried out on high-frequency trades using the proposed model to make informative forecasts on short-term volatilities.

Author details

Leonard Mushunje[1,2*], Maxwell Mashasha[1] and Edina Chandiwana[1]

1 Department of Applied Mathematics and Statistics, Midlands State University, Zimbabwe

2 Commercial Bank of Zimbabwe

*Address all correspondence to: leonsmushunje@gmail.com

References

[1] Hong, Chang, and Chiu. Hour-ahead wind power and speed forecasting using simultaneous perturbation stochastic approximation (spsa) algorithm and neural network with fuzzy inputs. Energy, 35(9):3870–3876, 2010.

[2] Hussain, Murthy, Singh, (2019) Stock market volatility: A review of the empirical literature. IUJ J. Manag., 7, 96–105.

[3] Liu, Erdem, and Shi, (2011). Comprehensive evaluation of arma arch (−m) approaches for modeling the mean and volatility of wind speed. Applied Energy, 88(3):724–732.

[4] Li and Shi, (2010). On comparing three artificial neural networks for wind speed forecasting. Applied Energy, 87 (7):2313–2320.

[5] Louka, Galanis, Siebert, Kariniotakis, Katsafados, Pytharoulis, and Kallos. Improvements in wind speed forecasts for wind power prediction purposes using kalman filtering. Journal of Wind Engineering and Industrial Aerodynamics, 96(12):2348–2362, 2008.

[6] Sancho Salcedo-Sanz, ngel, Bellido, Emilio,Garca, Figueras, Prieto, and Paredes, (2009). Hybridizing the fifth generation mesoscale model with artificial neural networks for short-term wind speed prediction. Renewable Energy, 34(6):1451–1457.

[7] Al-Yahyai, Charabi, and Gastli (2010). Review of the use of numerical weather prediction (nwp) models for wind energy assessment. Renewable and Sustainable Energy Reviews, 14(9): 3192–3198.

[8] Leung, M. T., Chen, A., & Daouko, H. (2000). Forecasting exchange rates using general regression neural networks. Computers and Operations Research, 27(11–12), 1093–1110.

[9] Taylor, S. (1986). Modelling Financial Time Series. Chichester: John Wiley & Sons Ltd.

[10] White, H. (1988). Economic Prediction Using Neural Networks: The Case of IBM Daily Stock. Proceedings of the IEEE International Conference on Neural Networks, 451–458.

[11] Sharda, S. A. (1990). Neural Networks as Forecasting Experts: An Empirical test. Proceedings of the International Joint Conference on Neural Networks, 491–494.

[12] Ladokhin, (2009). Forecasting Volatility in the Stock Market. BMI Paper

[13] Brown, S. G. (1998). The Dow theory: William Peter Hamilton's track Record Reconsidered. Journal of Finance, 1311–1333.

[14] Groot, (2012). Gaussian process regression with censored data using expectation propagation. In Sixth European Workshop on Probabilistic Graphical Models.

[15] Sullivan. Stock Price Volatility Prediction with Long Short-Term Memory Neural Networks. Department of Computer Science Stanford University Stanford, CA (unpublished paper)

[16] Sang, C., & Di Pierro, M. (2018). Improving trading technical analysis with tensor flow long short-term memory (lstm) neural network. The Journal of Finance and Data Science.

[17] Xiong Ruoxuan, Eric P. Nichols, Yuan Shen, Deep Learning Stock Volatility with Google Domestic Trends, 2015.

[18] Sardelicha and Manandhar, “Multimodal deep learning for

short-term stock volatility prediction,"
https://arxiv.org/abs/1812.10479.

[19] Bhowmik and Wang, (2020). Stock Market Volatility and Return Analysis: A Systematic Literature Review. Entropy 2020, 22, 522; doi:10.3390/e22050522, www.mdpi.com/journal/entropy

[20] Gencay, R. (1998). The Predictability of Security Returns with Simple Technical Trading Rules. Journal of Empirical Finance, 347–359.

[21] Bollerslev, T (1986). Generalized Autoregressive Conditional Heteroskedasticity. Journal of Econometrics, 31, 307–327.

[22] Engle, R.F. Autoregressive conditional heteroskedasticity with estimates of the variance of U.K. Inflation. Economics 1982, 50, 987–1008.

[23] Kimoto, T. A. (1990). Stock Market Prediction System with Modular NeuralNetworks. Proceedings of the International Joint Conference on.

[24] Leung, M.T.; Daouk, H.; Chen, A.S. Forecasting stock indices: A comparison of classification and level estimation models. Int. J. Forecast. 2000, 16, 173–190

[25] Scott, L.O. Financial market volatility: A survey. Staff Pap. Int. Monet. Fund **1991**, 38, 582–625.

[26] Rasmussen, Williams, (2006). Gaussian processes for machine learning. Cambridge: MIT Press.

[27] Harris, L. Trading and Exchanges: Market Microstructure for Practitioners; Oxford University Press: Hong Kong, China, 2003.

[28] Amjady, Keynia, and Zareipour, (2011). Short-term wind power forecasting using ridge let neural network. Electric Power Systems Research, 81(12):2099–2107.

Chapter 3

Firm-specific News and Anomalies

Hoang Van Hai, Phan Kim Tuan and Le The Phiet

Abstract

This study investigates the relation between idiosyncratic volatility and future returns around the firm-specific news announcements in the Korean stock market from July 1995 to June 2018. The excess returns of decile portfolios that are formed by sorting the stocks based on news and non-news idiosyncratic volatility measures. The Fama and French three-factor model is also examined to see whether systematic risk affects news and non-news idiosyncratic volatility profits. The pricing of our news and non-news idiosyncratic volatility are confirmed in the cross-sectional regression using the Fama and MacBeth method. Market beta, size, book to market, momentum, liquidity, and maximum return are controlled to determine robustness. Our empirical evidence suggests that the pricing of the non-news idiosyncratic volatility is more strongly negative compared to the news idiosyncratic volatility, which is contrary to the limited arbitrage explanation for the negative price of the idiosyncratic volatility. We find that the non-news idiosyncratic volatility has a robust negative relation to returns in non-January months. Macro-finance factors drive the conditioned on the missing risk factor hypothesis, the pricing of idiosyncratic volatility. This study contributes to a better understanding of the role of the conditional idiosyncratic volatility in asset pricing. As the Korean stocks provide a fresh sample, our non-U.S. investigation delivers a useful out-of-sample test on the pervasiveness of the non-news volatility effect across the emerging markets.

Keywords: idiosyncratic volatility, news idiosyncratic volatility, firm-specific news, macro-finance factors, Korea

1. Introduction

Idiosyncratic volatility (IV) has been recently well documented in the field of empirical finance. However, empirical results on the nature of the idiosyncratic volatility and future return are mixed and show the significantly negative to the insignificant or significant positive relationship (see [1–6]). Of these studies on the relationship between IV and expected returns, Ang et al. [1, 7] have received a lot of attention. Thus, a large number of studies have been trying to solve the IV puzzle, such as missing risk factor [8, 9], lottery preference [10], limited arbitrage [11], Liquidity and microstructure issues [12]; Lag and expected IV [3], and influence of macroeconomic and financial variables [13].

IntechOpen

More recently, the short-sale constraints were reported to keep an important role in the IV puzzle explanation [11]. This is the most promising interpretation of the negative price relation and the "mispricing-correction" stemming from the idiosyncratic volatility limited arbitrage. However, the mispricing correction hypothesis cannot sufficiently resolve the deep idiosyncratic volatility puzzle as the firm-specific news moves prices and the news announcements should increase the likelihood of mispricing [14]. Moreover, high mispricing should focus on stocks with great idiosyncratic volatility because of the limited arbitrage effect [11]. Consequently, the idiosyncratic volatility relative to the firm-specific news should be strongly negatively priced compared to the idiosyncratic volatility without the effect of firm-specific news. However, regarding the empirical tests, results reported by DeLisle et al. [14] are reverse of the mispricing correction hypothesis for the negative price of idiosyncratic volatility, stating that the non-news volatility is priced more strongly than news volatility. In addition, the non-news volatility is strongly significantly negative, which seems to violate the established features of the mispricing correction hypothesis.

On the other hand, the realized idiosyncratic volatility is believed to exist due to a risk factor that is neglected in the Fama and French [15] three factors model [16]. Additionally, the stock volatility and the macroeconomy are mentioned to be strongly related. In particular, Chen et al. [17] and Ferson and Harvey [18] propose that the term structure spread, inflation, industrial production, and spread of bonds are significant risk factors for the US stock market. Added to this, Shi et al. [19] postulate that the perceived negative IV-expected return relation can be the artifact of the confounding effect of public news arrivals. More recently, the negative relation between expected idiosyncratic volatility and stock returns are proved to reverse to a positive relationship when accounting for the macro-finance effects [13]. However, the IV around the firm-specific news return, which is not considered by DeLisle et al. [14], still remains highly statistically significant in all sample periods.

Motivated by these above discussions, in this study, the relationship between the idiosyncratic volatility and future returns around the firm-specific news announcements is examined in the Korean stock market. Based on this examination, the sufficiency of the limited arbitrage explanation of the pricing of idiosyncratic volatility can be evaluated. In particular, the pricing of idiosyncratic volatility news and no-news regarding the mispricing correction hypothesis will be examined as mention above. Next, portfolio analysis will be performed to understand whether idiosyncratic volatility is driven by some systematic variations, such as the macro-finance variables.

The Korean stock market can be regarded as an ideal setting to study the idiosyncratic volatility. The demand for IV is largely driven by individual investors than institutional investors [20]. The Korean market is driven by individual investors [21] and most of the explanations in the US market cannot be applied well in some emerging stock markets, such as China and South Korea [22]. Added to this, the test out-of-sample will be performed in one of the emerging equity markets characterized by its high volatility [23].

To test the hypotheses empirically, the firm-specific news is defined as a public announcement or declaration of 22 types of events. Following DeLisle et al. [14], the IVnews is defined as the idiosyncratic volatility around the firm-specific news announcements and the IVnonews is the idiosyncratic volatility unrelated to the firm-specific news announcements. Since the firm-specific news may fluctuate stock prices, news announcements should increase the likelihood of mispricing. Thus, we expect to see the stronger effect of IVnews compared to IVnonews in the empirical test.

From the empirical results, by conducting portfolio-level analysis and Fama and MacBeth [24] regressions, the IVnonews is found to be more strongly negatively associated with future returns, rather than the IVnews. The results from univariate portfolio sorting analysis show that the monthly equal-weighted (value-weighted) Fama and French [15] three-factor alpha on the high-minus-low (H-L) IVnonews portfolio is -0.0182 (-0.0179) with a Newey-West t-statistics of -5.09 (-5.11), while IVnews is not priced. This observation is consistent with that of DeLisle et al. [14] in the US market and is robust after controlling for several well-known predictors, such as market beta, book-to-market ratio, momentum, liquidity, and maximum return. The relationship between IVnonews and future returns is statistically significantly and economically negative, indicating that the pricing of idiosyncratic volatility must be driven by some factor that is beyond the limited arbitrage.

For further empirical tests related to the IVnonews characteristics, first, given the January seasonality in the monthly idiosyncratic volatility found by Peterson and Smedema [25], we examine the seasonality in the pricing of IVnonews. As a result, the IVnonews has a significantly positive and negative relation to the return in January and non-January months, respectively. In addition, motivating by recently empirical findings, such as Chen and Petkova [8] and Aslanidis et al. [13], the explanation of the IVnonews anomaly is also investigated based on the missing risk factor hypothesis. In more detail, we examine whether the more recent asset-pricing model of Fama and French [26] and macro-finance risk factors can price the portfolios formed on IVnonews relative to the Fama and French [15] three-factor model. For the construction of the macro-finance variables, we follow the recent trend in the financial literature exploiting information obtained from a large amount of macro-finance variables in predicting the asset returns (e.g., [27, 28]). The macro-finance factors are then constructed from a large set of macroeconomic and financial variables by using the first principal component of the variables in the group.

Consistent with the missing risk factor hypothesis and previous empirical findings, the IVnonews still exists after controlling for the Fama and French [26] five factors model. However, interestingly, results in this study show that the IVnonews is not priced conditional on the macro factors. Especially, the IVnonews coefficient attenuation is toward zero from the inclusion of macro-finance risk factors and is enough to eliminate the statistical significance. These observations indicate that the pricing of non-news volatility is driven by macro-finance factors. In other words, the macroeconomy can capture the common component in the idiosyncratic volatility [29].

The empirical results in the current study provide an important understanding of the idiosyncratic volatility puzzle on the asset pricing models, especially relative to the firm-specific news. First, this study empirically demonstrates the pricing of news and non-news idiosyncratic volatility in the Korean stock market. This finding is in line with that reported by DeLisle et al. [14] in the US market. Second, the limited arbitrage is also proved to not fully explain the negative relationship between IV and return in the Korean stock market. Third, the IVnonews is interpreted by considering the relationship between the idiosyncratic volatility and the macroeconomy.

The remainder of this study is organized in four sections: Section 2 addresses the dataset, variable constructions, and methodology; Section 3 presents the empirical test and reports the results; and the conclusion is provided in Section 4.

2. Data, variable constructions, and methodology

2.1 Data and variable constructions

The sample data used in this study is drawn primarily from the DataGuie database (http://dataguide.co.kr), containing the daily, monthly, and yearly data of all stocks listed and delisted in the Korean Stock Exchange (KSE) from July 1995 to June 2018. The financial firms, firms with a negative book value of equity, and other non-common stocks are excluded.

Following DeLisle et al. [14], we compute the monthly idiosyncratic volatility estimates with the daily data by applying the factors of Fama and French [15] three factors model, which is the excess market return (MKT), size (SMB), and book-to-market equity (HML). Specifically, the model can be defined as below (1), (2), and (3).

$$R_j = \alpha + \sum_{k=1}^{K} \gamma_{kj}\beta_k + \epsilon \tag{1}$$

$$\hat{i}_d = R_d - R_{fd} - \sum_{k=1}^{K} \gamma_{dk}\hat{\beta}_k \tag{2}$$

$$IV_{t-1} = \sqrt{\frac{30}{D_{t-1}}} \times \sqrt{\sum_{d=1}^{D_{t-1}} \hat{i}_d^2} \tag{3}$$

In more detail, first, the stock's loading on the kth factor is estimated in each month using the previous 60 months return data (from month t-61 to month t-2) following Eq. (1). A minimum of 36 months of valid returns is required during the study period. R_j is the excess return relative to the risk-free rate of month j, α represents the intercept of the month, γ_{kj} is the month j return of the kth factor portfolio (k = 3, $\gamma_{MKTj}, \gamma_{SMBj}, \gamma_{HMLj}$), β_k is the stock's loading on the kth factor ($\beta_{MKT}, \beta_{SMB}, \beta_{HML}$), and ϵ is a regression error term.

Then, we use the factor loading estimates in Eqs. (1) and (2) to estimate the daily idiosyncratic returns during month t-1. R_d is the raw return of the firm i in the day d, R_{fd} is the risk-free on day d, γ_{dk} is the day d return of the kth factor portfolio (k = 3, $\gamma_{dMKT}, \gamma_{dSMB}, \gamma_{dHML}$), and $\hat{\beta}_k$ is an estimate of the stock's loading on the kth factor ($\hat{\beta}_{MKT}, \hat{\beta}_{SMB}, \hat{\beta}_{HML}$). $\hat{i}_d$ is the estimate of day d idiosyncratic return. Finally, the stock idiosyncratic risk (IV) in Eq. (3) is measured in month t-1. D_{t-1} is the number of trading days in month t-1. $\hat{i}_d^2$ is square of the $\hat{i}_d$, estimated from Eq. (2). The scaling factor is selected as 30 because the potential for stocks has a different number of trading days in a month (we require a minimum of 15 trading days in a month to have a viable volatility estimate [1, 14]).

For the news and non-news idiosyncratic volatility measures, the firm-specific news is incorporated into the pricing of idiosyncratic volatility and the volatility is decomposed into the news and non-news volatility following Eqs. (4) and (5).

$$IVnews_{t-1} = \sqrt{\frac{30}{N_{t-1}}} \times \sqrt{\sum_{d=1}^{D_{t-1}} \left(\eta_d \times \hat{i}_d^2\right)} \tag{4}$$

$$IVnonews_{t-1} = \sqrt{\frac{30}{D_{t-1} - N_{t-1}}} \times \sqrt{\sum_{d=1}^{D_{t-1}} \left((1 - \eta_d) \times \hat{i}_d^2\right)} \tag{5}$$

where N_{t-1} is the number of trading days during month $t-1$ in which the firm-specific news announcement occurs, η_d is an indicator variable that equal to 1 in case the firm-specific news announcement occurs in day d. Otherwise, the η_d is zero. We employ an eight-day window (N_t = 8) around the reported announcement date, except the case where the news announcement is made on the first or last day of a calendar month. For instance, for a given firm, when a firm-specific news announcement is made on day d, the days from d-3 to d + 4 over month t-1 are defined as event dates and η_d equals one.

For the other controlling variables, several standard controls variables are used, including market beta, size and book to market ratio following Fama and French [15], momentum returns (the cumulative return over months t-7 to t-2), the turnover following Han and Lesmond [12], and the maximum daily return during month t-1 following Bali et al. [10].

Table 1 shows the time-series average of the cross-sectional statistics of idiosyncratic volatility (IV), news idiosyncratic volatility (IVnews) and non-news idiosyncratic volatility (IVnonews). The mean, standard deviation, median, Q1, Q3, and number of the monthly stock observation of the volatility measures are computed in each month. Then, these five statistics are averaged across cross-sections.

As can be seen in **Table 1**, the news volatility, rather than the non-news volatility, is higher and more dispersed across stocks. The time-series means of the cross-sectional news volatility and the non-news volatility are 0.1415 and 0.1235, respectively. The standard deviations of the news volatility and the non-news volatility in the typical cross-section are 0.0937 and 0.0888, respectively.

A number of 22 types of firm-specific news are obtained from the DataGuie database. The firm-specific news is defined as a public announcement or declaration of 1) Capital introduction technology, 2) Cash dividends, 3) Chane of the sector, 4) Change business objective, 5) Change of CEO, 6) DR issuance, 7) Facility investment or resource, 8) Investor relation, 9) Lawsuit, 10) Paid in the capital, 11) Paid in incineration, 12) Reverse stock split, 13) Sale transfer, 14) Stock dividend, 15) Stock split, 16) Suspension of the business case, 17) Take overbid, 18) Tangible asset acquisition disposal, 19) Write-down of income, 20) Merge, 21) Gratuitous pay-off, and 22) Patent application.

Similar to Ludvigson and Ng [28], the macro-finance variables in the current study are primarily obtained from Datastream and DataGuie database. Then, a number of 118 macro-finance variables are classified into five groups, including employment and hours; interest rate and import–export; compensation and labor cost; sale; and price. Details concerning the macro-finance variables are described in Appendix A. For each macro-finance variable group, a macro-finance factor, which is the first principal component of the variables in the group, is constructed. On average, the macro-finance factors account for 78.13% and 87.45% of the total variation of the group, indicating that they provide strong information about the macro-finance variables.

Variable	Mean	Std Dev	Median	Q1	Q3
IV	0.1387	0.0847	0.1146	0.0795	0.1768
IVnews	0.1415	0.0937	0.1170	0.0810	0.1799
IVnonews	0.1235	0.0888	0.0997	0.0714	0.1491

This table shows the grand averages of several summary statistics of the main idiosyncratic volatility estimates, including the summary statistics of idiosyncratic volatility (IV), news idiosyncratic volatility (IVnews) and non-news idiosyncratic volatility (IVnonews). The summary statistics for each monthly cross-section are computed in the sample and then the equal-weighted average of these statistics is calculated. In this table, we only use the firm-months having a firm-specific news announcement in the previous month. Due to data requirements and availability, the sample period is from July 1995 to June 2018.

Table 1.
Summary statistics.

2.2 Methodology

Motivated by the results of DeLisle et al. [14], the portfolio-level analysis and Fama and MacBeth [24] cross-sectional regressions are conducted to directly investigate whether the relationship between idiosyncratic volatility and future returns around the firm-specific news announcements is priced in the Korean stock market.

First, the time-series portfolios are constructed to examine the relationship between the idiosyncratic volatility and future returns conditional on firm-specific news. At the beginning of each month, the IV, IVnews, and IVnonews are sorted independently into quintile portfolios. Then, the significance of the value-weighted (VW) and equal-weighted (EW) portfolio returns is calculated and tested. Finally, the zero-investment "high minus low" (H–L) portfolios along with their Newey-West adjusted *t*-statistics are constructed by buying a portfolio of stocks in the highest IV (IVnews, IVnonews) quintile and shorting the stocks in the lowest one. Furthermore, three-factor alphas of the H-L portfolio and their Newey-West adjusted *t*-statistics are reported as FF3 alpha. Therefore, the significance of the H-L portfolio return and FF3 alpha indicate the existence of IV, IVnews, and IVnonews effects.

The portfolio sorts, which are interpreted easily, do not impose a functional form on the relationship between IV (IVnews, IVnonews) and expected returns. Therefore, the pricing of our idiosyncratic volatility (IV, IVnews, IVnonews) is confirmed in the cross-sectional regression using the Fama and MacBeth [24] method. Particularly, the procedure for estimation of the cross-sectional impact of the IV, IVnews, IVnonews measures follows this regression:

$$R_{it} - R_{ft} = \alpha + \beta_{IVn} IVn_{it} + \beta_{Xt} X_{it} + \varepsilon_{it} \tag{6}$$

where R_{it} is the return of firm i in month t, R_{ft} is the month t risk-free rate and IVn_{it} is one of our three idiosyncratic volatility measures (n = 1,2,3). X_{it} denotes a vector of control variables specific to firm i in month t. In all cross-sectional regressions, X_{it} is regarded as X_{it} = [BETA, LOGME, LOGBM, MOM, REV, LIQ, MAX].

To address the seasonal effect of the negative risk–return relation, we examine the pricing power of IV in the separated sample: January and Non-January. However, we focus only on the IVnonews, considered as an IV anomaly. To estimate the January effect, only observations in January are used. On the contrary, the January observations are excluded for the estimation of the Non-January effect.

Next, a possibly missing factor is tested by considering the recently well-known factor model, such as Fama and French [26] five-factor model and Macro-finance factors. The returns of zero portfolios are regressed and measured relative to the IVnonews on the MKT, SMB, HML, RMW, and CMA or five groups of Macro-finance factors. These two specifications are estimated as below:

$$(H - L)_t = \alpha + \beta_{MKT} MKT_t + \beta_{SMB} SMB_t + \beta_{HML} HML_t + \beta_{RMW} RMW_t + \beta_{CMA} CMA_t + e_t \tag{7}$$

$$(H - L)_t = \alpha + \beta_{MKT} MKT_t + \beta_{SMB} SMB_t + \beta_{HML} HML_t + \beta_{RMW} RMW_t + \beta_{CMA} CMA_t + \beta_X X_{t-1} + e_t \tag{8}$$

where $(H\text{-}L)_t$ is the IVnonews return on the H-L portfolio in month t. The independent variables include MKT, SMB, HML, UMD, RMW, and CMA following

Fama and French [26]. X_{t-1} is the vector of Macro-finance factors at time t-1 as mentioned above.

3. Results

3.1 Pricing of the news and non-news idiosyncratic volatility

3.1.1 Univariate portfolio sort

The portfolio-level analysis is firstly conducted to investigate the relationship between the idiosyncratic volatility (as in [1]) or the news idiosyncratic volatility and the non-news idiosyncratic volatility (as in [14]) in the Korean stock market. Specifically, at the beginning of each month *t*-1, the stocks are sorted into quintiles based on their idiosyncratic volatility, news volatility, or non-news volatility. We then hold these quintile portfolios over month t and estimate the average portfolio returns and Fama and French [15] three-factor alphas in month t on equal-weighted (EW) and value-weighted (VW) basis. Then, a zero-cost portfolio, that is short for the lowest quintile portfolio and long for the highest quintile portfolio, is formed. Next, the time-series average of monthly returns and Fama and French [15] three-factor alphas are reported.

Table 2 shows the results of the value-weighted (VW) and equal-weighted (EW) returns on portfolios sorted based on the idiosyncratic volatility (IV in Panel A, IVnews in Panel B, and IVnonews in Panel C). The zero-investment portfolio

	L	2	3	4	H	H-L	FF3 Alpha
Panel A: Idiosyncratic Volatility – IV							
EW	0.0108**	0.0120**	0.0106*	0.0077	−0.0045	−0.0153***	−0.0162***
	(2.19)	(2.14)	(1.87)	(1.21)	(−0.63)	(−3.14)	(−4.73)
VW	0.0100**	0.0114**	0.0100*	0.0072	−0.0051	−0.0151***	−0.0159***
	(2.03)	(2.04)	(1.77)	(1.13)	(−0.72)	(−3.14)	(−4.75)
Panel B: News Idiosyncratic Volatility - IVNEWS							
EW	0.0119**	0.0148**	0.0032	0.0103	0.0101	−0.0018	0.0017
	(2.25)	(2.44)	(0.54)	(1.42)	(1.11)	(−1.04)	(1.09)
VW	0.0113**	0.0146**	0.0031	0.0102	0.0099	−0.0014	0.0024
	(2.16)	(2.39)	(0.52)	(1.43)	(0.11)	(−1.07)	(1.23)
Panel C: Non-News Idiosyncratic Volatility – IVNONEWS							
EW	0.0127**	0.0135**	0.0125**	0.0088	−0.0042	−0.0169***	−0.0182***
	(2.51)	(2.38)	(2.15)	(1.35)	(−0.56)	(−3.29)	(−5.09)
VW	0.0119**	0.0129**	0.0119**	0.0082	−0.0048	−0.0167***	−0.0179***
	(2.37)	(2.27)	(2.05)	(1.26)	(−0.66)	(−3.29)	(−5.11)

*This table shows the average returns and Fama–French (1993) three-factor alphas for the idiosyncratic volatility sorted portfolios. In Panel A, the portfolios are formed based on idiosyncratic volatility. In Panel B (Panel C), the portfolios are formed based on the news (non-news) idiosyncratic volatility following DeLisle et al. [14]. In each month, all stocks are sorted into quintiles based on their idiosyncratic volatility in the last month and the portfolios are held for month t. Finally, the average return and alphas in the equal weighting (EW) and value weighting (VW) portfolio scheme are reported. In the (H–L) column, the return is for a zero-investment portfolio, that is long the quintile of stocks with the highest idiosyncratic volatility and shorts the quintile of stocks with the lowest idiosyncratic volatility. The sample period is from July 1995 to June 2018. The Robust Newey–West t-statistics are given in parentheses. The statistical significance at the 1%, 5%, and 10% levels are marked by the ***, **, and * characters, respectively.*

Table 2.
Return on portfolios sorted on news and non-news idiosyncratic volatility.

returns, that are long the quintile of stocks with the highest idiosyncratic volatility and short the quintile of stocks with the lowest idiosyncratic volatility, are seen in the rightmost columns of **Table 2**. The Newey and West [30] adjusted *t*-statistic are reported in parentheses.

Panel A presents the EW and VW returns of portfolios sorted on IV. The returns are roughly decreasing in IV for both the VW and EW portfolios. The average returns (FF3 alpha) of the EW H–L portfolio and the VW H-L portfolio are −0.0153 (−0.0162) and − 0.0151 (−0.0159), respectively and significant at the 1% level, suggesting that the IV puzzle is confirmed in the Korean data sample. This result is consistent with that reported by Nartea et al. [21], Cheon and Lee [31]. Panel B of **Table 2** shows the sorted IVnews. The average portfolio returns are fluctuant in the idiosyncratic volatility for both the VW and EW portfolios. The returns (FF3 alpha) of the EW H–L portfolio and VW H-L portfolio are −0.0018 (0.0017) and − 0.0014 (0.0024), respectively and statistically insignificant with the t-statistic of −1.04 (1.09) and − 1.07 (1.23), respectively. In Panel C, the returns are fluctuation and decreasing in IVnonews for both the EW and VW portfolios. The EW H–L and VW H-L portfolio returns (FF3 alpha) are −0.0169 (−0.0182) and − 0.0167 (−0.0179), respectively and both of them are significant at the 1% level.

As seen in **Table 2**, the results of IV and IVnonews are similarly priced feature while those of the IVnews are not priced. These findings are not consistent with the limits of arbitrage explanation, meaning that the pricing of IVnews should be significant and stronger than the IVnonews. This result is also in line with that reported by DeLisle et al. [14].

3.1.2 Firm-level cross-sectional regressions

In the current study, the firm-specific news effect on the pricing of idiosyncratic volatility has been observed in the Korean stock market using a single portfolio sort method. However, the portfolio tests are limited by the number of control variables at one time [32]. Therefore, the Fama and MacBeth [24] cross-sectional regressions, which are necessary to control the large set of potential covariates, are performed as a robustness test. Based on this test, we can re-examine the pricing of news and no-news idiosyncratic volatility in the firm-level regression and control other relevant variables affecting the pricing of news and no-news idiosyncratic volatility in the cross-section of stock returns. The control variables are size, book-to-market ratio [15], momentum, turnover [33], and maximum return [10]. The results are present in **Table 3**.

As seen in Model 1, the coefficient on IV is negative (−0.1769) and significant at 1% level (*t*-statistics of −4.02). The average slope of IV remains negative and statistically significant in Model 1, indicating that none of the control variables can explain the IV anomaly individually. This finding is consistent with that in previous studies [10, 34]. In Model 2, the coefficient of IVnews is positive (0.0074) and insignificant (*t*-statistics of 1.23), however, that of the IVnonews is negative (−0.0826) and significant at 1% level (*t*-statistics of −2.69). Moreover, the pricing of IVnews and IVnonews in Model 3 is same as that in Model 2. The predicting power of the other control variables is the same as that in Model 1, Model 3, and previous studies about the Korean stock market [21, 31].

As shown in **Tables 1** and **2**, there is no evidence of the predictive power of stock returns by IVnews. Nevertheless, a strong negative predicted power of the IVnonews, which cannot be eliminated by the other control variables, is observed in the Korean stock market. This finding is in line with that of the portfolio analysis and those in the US market [14], suggesting that the IVnonews is strongly priced in the Korean stock market. This result also indicates that the mispricing correction hypothesis is not sufficient to resolve the deep idiosyncratic volatility puzzle.

MODEL	IV	IVnews	IVnonews	BETA	LOGME	LOGBM	MOM	REV	LIQ	MAX
1	−0.1769***			0.0008	−0.0055***	0.0060***	−0.0019	0.0048	−0.0307***	0.0048
	(−4.02)			(0.49)	(−3.86)	(3.72)	(−0.41)	(1.59)	(−4.23)	(1.59)
2		0.0074	−0.0826***							
		(1.23)	(−2.69)							
3		0.0114	−0.1630***	0.0010	−0.0057***	0.0060***	−0.0020	0.0043	−0.0316***	0.0043
		(1.43)	(−4.34)	(0.58)	(−3.99)	(3.68)	(−0.42)	(1.45)	(−4.33)	(1.45)

*In this table, we present the coefficient estimates and t-statistics from the Fama-MacBeth (1973) cross-sectional regressions of individual stock excess returns on the listed variables. Model 1 is regression models with the idiosyncratic volatility and the other control variables. Model 2 is regression models with the news idiosyncratic volatility and the non-news idiosyncratic volatility. Model 3 is regression models with both news and non-news idiosyncratic volatility and the other control variables, including size, the book to market, momentum, liquidity, and maximum return. The sample period is from July 19,955 to June 2018. The Robust Newey–West t-statistics are given in parentheses. The statistical significance at the 1%, 5%, and 10% levels are marked with the ***, **, and * characters, respectively.*

Table 3.
The pricing of news and non-news idiosyncratic volatility in cross-sectional regressions.

3.2 Additional test

3.2.1 Seasonality in pricing of non-news idiosyncratic volatility

The January seasonality is reported to affect the relations between idiosyncratic volatility and future returns [25]. Therefore, in this part, the effect of seasonality on the relationship between IVnonews and return is also investigated in the Korean stock market. To address the seasonality, the average returns and risk-adjusted alpha (FF3) are calculated in only January (Panel A of **Table 4**) and non-January (Panel B of **Table 4**). The results of the portfolio-level analysis are also reported in **Table 4**.

In panel A, the stocks are sorted based on the IVnonews for only the January data. The portfolio returns fluctuate and both of the VW and EW H–L portfolio returns, as well as the FF3 alpha, are positive and significant. Particularly, the return of the EW (VW) H–L portfolio is 0.0251 (0.0252) and significant at the 5% level (5% level), whereas that of the EW (VW) FF3 portfolio is 0.0124 (0.0122) with the *t*-statistics of 1.95 (1.92).

Panel B reports results for the non-January data, which is expected to observe the strongly negative IVnonews. The results show that the returns monotonically decrease in the IVnonews for the VW and EW portfolios. In particular, the EW (VW) H–L portfolio return and the EW (VW) FF3 alpha portfolio return are −0.0206 (−0.0205) and − 0.204 (−0.0200), respectively and significant at the 1% (1%) level. Furthermore, the average return in **Table 4** is stronger compared to that in **Table 2**. The negative predicting power of IVnonews is strong and robust to the value weighting and equal weighting outside of January month. In general, these results are consistent with those reported by Peterson and Smedema [25] for the idiosyncratic volatility analysis, and DeLisle et al. [14] for the non-news idiosyncratic volatility in the US market.

	L	2	3	4	H	H-L	FF3 alpha
Panel A: January – IVnonews							
EW	0.0375*	0.0612**	0.0581**	0.0711**	0.0626**	0.0251**	0.0124*
	(1.67)	(2.04)	(2.31)	(2.51)	(2.66)	(2.26)	(1.95)
VW	0.0368	0.0604**	0.0580**	0.0706**	0.0620**	0.0252**	0.0122*
	(1.62)	(2.01)	(2.25)	(2.50)	(2.64)	(2.26)	(1.92)
Panel B: Non-January - IVnonews							
EW	0.0105**	0.0092	0.0084	0.0032	−0.0101	−0.0206***	−0.0204***
	(1.89)	(1.46)	(1.30)	(0.45)	(−1.27)	(−3.61)	(−5.43)
VW	0.0097*	0.0087	0.0078	0.0026	−0.0108	−0.0205***	−0.0200***
	(1.73)	(1.36)	(1.19)	(0.36)	(−1.36)	(−3.61)	(−5.49)

*This table shows the average returns and Fama–French (1993) three-factor alphas for the non-news idiosyncratic volatility sorted portfolios. In Panel A (Panel B), we form portfolios based on the non-news idiosyncratic volatility in January (Non-January). In each month, all stocks are sorted into quintiles based on their idiosyncratic volatility in the last month and the portfolios are held for month t. Finally, we report the average return and alphas in the equal weighting (EW) and value weighting (VW) portfolio scheme are reported. In the (H–L) column, the return is for a zero-investment portfolio, which is long the quintile of stocks with the highest idiosyncratic volatility and short the quintile of stocks with the lowest idiosyncratic volatility. The sample period is from July 1995 to June 2018. The Robust Newey–West t-statistics (estimated with six lags) are given in parentheses. The statistical significance at the 1%, 5%, and 10% levels are marked with the ***, **, and * characters, respectively.*

Table 4.
Seasonality return of portfolios sorted on non-news idiosyncratic volatility.

3.2.2 The non-news idiosyncratic volatility and missing risk factors

In this section, the time-series alphas are estimated for the zero-investment portfolios of the non-news idiosyncratic volatility measured by DeLisle et al. [14] mothed. We present the time-series results from regressing the VW (EW) H–L IVnonews portfolio returns based on the five control variables (i.e., MKT, SMB, HML, RMW, and CMA as in [26]), and the Macro-finance variables [13], for further details consult **Tables 6** and 7 in the Appendix. The procedure for portfolio construction is the same as that reported in **Table 2**.

For the FF5 alpha results, the results shown in **Table 5** are almost the same as those in **Tables 2** and **4**. The strongly negative time-series alphas are found in all months and non-January months after controlling for Fama and French [26] five factors model. The pricing power of the IVnonews is negatively stronger in the non-January months compared to the other months. For instance, the EW (VW) FF5 alpha in all months is −0.0180 (−0.0176) and significant at the conventional level, while those in the months excluding January is −0.0203 (−0.0210) with t-statistics of −5.44 (−5.49).

Next, we are interested in controlling for the macro-finance variables following Aslanidis et al. [13] findings. Regarding the results of the Macro-finance panel, the time series alpha is toward zero when the Macro-finance variables are included. Additionally, the time series alpha is strong enough to eliminate the statistical significance, suggesting that the IVnonews in the Korean stock market can be explained by the Macro-finance variables. Added to this, these coefficients are lower than their corresponding values in the FF5 alpha as well as in **Tables 2** and **4**. These observations reflect that the pricing of IV is driven by the macro variables, which is also consistent with the findings reported by Goyal and Welch [27], Aslanidis et al. [13].

The findings in this study are also supported by several recent empirical findings, such as the IV puzzle explanation based on the missing risk factor [1, 8].

	FF5 Alpha		**Macro-finance**	
	EW portfolios	**VW portfolios**	**EW portfolios**	**VW portfolios**
All months	−0.0180***	−0.0176***	−0.0120	−0.0143
	(−5.09)	(−5.11)	(−0.97)	(−1.01)
January	0.0126*	0.0129*	0.0553	0.0573
	(1.95)	(1.95)	(0.99)	(1.01)
Non-January	−0.0203***	−0.0210***	−0.0151	−0.0169
	(−5.44)	(−5.49)	(−0.90)	(−0.97)

This table presents the estimated alphas from the return regressions of the IVnonews zero-investment portfolios. In each month, all stocks are sorted into quintiles based on the IVnonews in the last month and the portfolios are held for month t. Finally, the estimated alphas in the equal weighting (EW) and value weighting (VW) portfolio scheme are reported. The returns of each portfolio are regressed on two specifications of the risk factor model. This procedure follows the below Equation.

$(H—L)_t = \alpha + \beta_{MKT}MKT_t + \beta_{SMB}SMB_t + \beta_{HML}HML_t + \beta_{RMW}RMW_t + \beta_{CMA}CMA_t + e_t$ (1)

$(H—L)_t = \alpha + \beta_{MKT}MKT_t + \beta_{SMB}SMB_t + \beta_{HML}HML_t + \beta_{RMW}RMW_t + \beta_{CMA}CMA_t + \beta_X X_{t-1} + e_t$ (2)

*The first specification, the Fama and French [26] factors, is illustrated in Eq. (1). MKT is the excess market return of the KOSPI index in the Korean stock market. SMB (HML) is the return on a value weight portfolio that is long a portfolio of small (value) stocks and short a portfolio of large (growth) stocks. Following Fama and French [26], RMW (Robust Minus Weak) is the average return of the two robust operating profitability portfolios minus the average return of the two weak operating profitability portfolios; CMA (Conservative Minus Aggressive) is the average return of the two conservative investment portfolios minus the average return of the two aggressive investment portfolios. X_{t-1} is a set of five macro-finance variables defined in the methodology section. The sample period is from July 1995 to June 2018. The robust Newey–West t-statistics are given in parentheses. The statistical significance at the 1%, 5%, and 10% levels are marked with the ***, **, and *, characters, respectively.*

Table 5.
Return on the portfolios sorted on the non-news idiosyncratic volatility for the five-factor model and macro-finance variables.

Additionally, this study also indicates that the common component, existing in the idiosyncratic volatility [29], is related to the macro-finance variables.

4. Conclusions

This study investigates the effect of firm-specific news on the idiosyncratic volatility and future return relationship in the Korean stock market from July 1995 to June 2018. The results show that the non-news volatility relative to the firm-specific news, defined as in DeLisle et al. [14], is negatively priced and positively priced in the months excluding and including January, respectively. These findings are robust after controlling for several important factors, such as market beta, size, book-to-market ratio, momentum, liquidity, and maximum return.

In addition, the effect of firm-specific news on the idiosyncratic volatility and future return relationship suggests that the usage of limited arbitrage content cannot fully support the interpretation of idiosyncratic volatility in the Korean stock market. The strong evidence of the significantly negative IVnonews is found, however, no evidence is observed for the IVnews in the Korean stock market. Thus, this study contributes to a better understanding of the role of the conditional idiosyncratic volatility in asset pricing. As the Korean stocks provide a fresh sample, our non-U.S. investigation delivers a useful out-of-sample test on the pervasiveness of the non-news volatility effect across the emerging markets.

Moreover, this study also shows that non-news volatility is driven by the macro-finance variables. The macro-finance factors are constructed from a large pool of macroeconomic and financial variables. This finding is confirmed by using different kinds of methods, including portfolio analysis and Fama and Macbeth [24] cross-sectional regression tests. These tests represent methods that aim to validate and qualify the data as well as the establishment of empirical evidence appropriate for the evaluation of the objectives.

Appendix: macro-finance variables

STT	VARIABLE	CODE
Employment and Hours		
1	KO ACTIVE POPULATION(LABOUR FORCE),ALL PERSONS(AGES 15 & OVER)	KOMLFT06R
2	KO ACTIVE POPULATION(LABOUR FORCE),FEMALES(AGES 15 & OVER) VOLA	KOMLFF06O
3	KO ACTIVE POPULATION(LABOUR FORCE),MALES (AGES 15 AND OVER) VOLA	KOMLFM06O
4	KO BOP: INCOME - COMPENSATION OF EMPLOYEES CURA	KOBPIEMNB
5	KO CALL MONEY/INTERBANK RATE NADJ	KOOIR060R
6	KO CIVILIAN LABOUR FORCE: TOTAL(DISC.) SADJ	KOOPL032Q
7	KO EMPLOYED REGULAR EMPLOYEES VOLN	KOEMPRGRP
8	KO EMPLOYED SELF-EMPLOYED WORKERS VOLN	KOEMPSELP
9	KO EMPLOYED TEMPORARY EMPLOYEES VOLN	KOEMPTPRP
10	KO EMPLOYEES: TOTAL (HOUSEHOLD SURVEY)(DISC.) VOLA	KOOEM103O
11	KO EMPLOYEES: TOTAL VOLA	KOMLF007O

STT	VARIABLE	CODE
12	KO EMPLOYMENT - 15-19 YEARS OLD VOLN	KOEMPM15P
13	KO EMPLOYMENT - 20-29 YEARS OLD VOLN	KOEMPM20P
14	KO EMPLOYMENT - 30-39 YEARS OLD VOLN	KOEMPM30P
15	KO EMPLOYMENT - 40-49 YEARS OLD VOLN	KOEMPM40P
16	KO EMPLOYMENT - 50-59 YEARS OLD VOLN	KOEMPM50P
17	KO EMPLOYMENT - 60 YEARS OLD & OVER VOLN	KOEMPM60P
18	KO EMPLOYMENT - AGRICULTURE, FORESTRY, HUNTING & FISHING VOLN	KOEMPAGRF
19	KO EMPLOYMENT - FEMALE VOLN	KOEMPFEMP
20	KO EMPLOYMENT - MALE VOLN	KOEMPMALP
21	KO EMPLOYMENT - MANUFACTURING & MINING VOLN	KOEMPMANF
22	KO EMPLOYMENT - MANUFACTURING VOLN	KOEMPMANP
23	KO EMPLOYMENT VOLA	KOEMPTOTO
24	KO EMPLOYMENT, FEMALES (AGES 15 AND OVER) VOLA	KOMLFF12O
25	KO EMPLOYMENT, MALES (AGES 15 AND OVER) VOLA	KOMLFM12O
26	KO EMPLOYMENT, MFG, ALL PERSONS VOLA	KOMLF005O
27	KO HARMONIZED UNEMPLOYMENT RATE: ALL PERSONS(DISC.) SADJ	KOOUN014Q
28	KO HARMONIZED UNEMPLOYMENT: LEVEL, ALL PERSONS (ALL AGES) VOLA	KOMLFT15O
29	KO HOURS WORKED - ALL EMPLOYEES VOLN	KOHWRWEMP
30	KO LABOUR FORCE: ALL PERSONS(DISC.) VOLA	KOOPL032O
31	KO LABOUR MARKET - NUMBER OF WORKING DAYS VOLN	KOLMNOWDP
32	KO LAGGING INDEX: REGULAR EMPLOYEES NUMBER (%MOM)(DISC.) NADJ	KOCYLAE5R
33	KO UNEMPLOYMENT LEVEL: SURVEY-BASED (ALL PERSONS)(DISC.) VOLA	KOOUN010O
Interest rate and Import–Export		
34	BOND YIELDS FINANCIAL DEBENTURES(3YAA-)(%)	E11.02.003.012
35	BOND YIELDS GOVERNMENT BONDS(10Y)(%)	E11.02.003.021
36	BOND YIELDS GOVERNMENT BONDS(1Y)(%)	E11.02.003.013
37	BOND YIELDS GOVERNMENT BONDS(20Y)(%)	E11.02.003.031
38	BOND YIELDS GOVERNMENT BONDS(3Y)(%)	E11.02.003.008
39	BOND YIELDS GOVERNMENT BONDS(5Y)(%)	E11.02.003.014
40	BOND YIELDS KEP(3Y) BONDS(%)	E11.02.003.019
41	BOND YIELDS MONEY STAB. BONDS(%)	E11.02.003.009
42	BOND YIELDS MONEY STAB. BONDS(2Y)(%)	E11.02.003.016
43	BOND YIELDS MONEY STAB. BONDS(91 DAYS)(%)	E11.02.003.032
44	CALL RATES OVERNIGHT(%)	E11.02.003.003
45	COFIX RATE FOR NEW LOANS(%)	E11.02.003.034
46	COFIX RATE FOR OUTSTANDING LOANS(%)	E11.02.003.033
47	CORPORATE BONDS(3YBBB-)(%)	E11.02.003.020
48	KO BOP: GOODS(FOB) - EXPORTS CURA	KOEXPBOPB

STT	VARIABLE	CODE
49	KO EXPORT PRICE INDEX - BASIC METAL PRODUCTS NADJ	KOEXMBMTF
50	KO EXPORT PRICE INDEX - CHEMICAL PRODUCTS NADJ	KOEPIPCHF
51	KO EXPORT PRICE INDEX - COAL PRODUCTS & PETROLEUM PRODUCTS NADJ	KOEXCPPPF
52	KO EXPORT PRICE INDEX - ELECTRICAL EQUIPMENT NADJ	KOEXPEEEF
53	KO EXPORT PRICE INDEX - FABRICATED METAL PRODUCTS NADJ	KOEXMETPF
54	KO EXPORT PRICE INDEX NADJ	KOEXPPRCF
55	KO EXPORT PRICE INDEX-AGRICULTURAL, FORESTRY & MARINE PRODS. NADJ	KOEXAGRIF
56	KO EXPORTS FOB (CUSTOMS CLEARANCE BASIS) CURN	KOEXPGDSA
57	KO IMPORT PRICE INDEX NADJ	KOIMPPRCF
58	KO IMPORTS CIF (CUSTOMS CLEARANCE BASIS) CURN	KOIMPGDSA
59	KO INCOME TERMS OF TRADE INDEX NADJ	KOTOTPRCF
60	KO TRADE BALANCE (CUSTOMS CLEARANCE BASIS) CURN	KOVISGDSA
61	OVERNIGHT: INTERBANK DIRECT TRANSACTIONS(%)	E11.02.003.002
62	OVERNIGHT: INTERMEDIATED TRANSACTIONS(%)	E11.02.003.001
63	UNCOLLATERALIZED CALL RATES(ALL TRANSACTIONS)(%)	E11.02.003.004
64	YIELD ON CD(91 DAYS)(%)	E11.02.003.005
65	YIELD ON CP(91 DAYS)(%)	E11.02.003.017
66	YIELDS OF FINANCIAL DEBENTURES(%)	E11.02.003.010
67	YIELDS OF NATIONAL HOUSING BONDS TYPE1(5YR)(%)	E11.02.003.007
Compensations and Labour cost		
68	KO BOP: INCOME - COMPENSATION OF EMPLOYEES CURA	KOBPIEMNB
69	KO BOP: INCOME - COMPENSATION OF EMPLOYEES, CREDIT CURA	KOBPIEMCB
70	KO CURRENT A/C.: INCOME-DEBIT, COMPENSATION OF EMPLOYEE (DISC CURA	KOCUIDCEB
71	KO FOREIGN DIRECT INVESTMENT BY PURPOSE - LOW LABOR COST CURN	KOFDOPLLA
72	KO LCI: 12MONTH SMOOTHED CHANGES(DISC.) NADJ	KOCY1200R
73	KO MONTHLY EARN: MFG - PROXY(DISC.) SADJ	KOMLC007E
74	KO MONTHLY EARN: MFG(DISC.) SADJ	KOOLC009E
75	KO MONTHLY EARN: PRIVATE SECTOR(DISC.) SADJ	KOMLC034E
76	KO REAL EFFECTIVE FX RATE (REER) BASED ON UNIT LABOUR COSTS NADJ	KOI.RELF
Sale		
77	KO AVG MONTHLY DAYS WORKED- WHOLESALE & RETAIL TRADE (DISC.) VOLN	KODWRWROP
78	KO AVG.MONTHLY EARN.: FEMALE - WHSLE. & RETAIL TRADE(DISC.) CURN	KOERAFWRA
79	KO AVG.MONTHLY EARN.: MALE-WHSLE.& RETAIL,HOTELS & R (DISC.) CURN	KOERAMWHA
80	KO BOK BUSINESS SVY: DOM.SALES GROWTH-MANUFACTURING, ACTUAL NADJ	KOBSIDMPR

STT	VARIABLE	CODE
81	KO BOK BUSINESS SVY: EXPORTS GROWTH - MANUFACTURING, ACTUAL NADJ	KOBSIXMPR
82	KO BOK BUSINESS SVY: SALES GROWTH - ALL INDUSTRIES, ACTUAL NADJ	KOBSISAPR
83	KO BOK BUSINESS SVY: SALES GROWTH - MANUFACTURING, ACTUAL NADJ	KOBSISMPR
84	KO BOK BUSINESS SVY: SALES GROWTH-NON-MANUFACTURING, ACTUAL NADJ	KOBSISNPR
85	KO BOK BUSINESS SVY: SALES PRICE - MANUFACTURING, ACTUAL NADJ	KOBSIPMPR
86	KO BOK CONSUMER SVY: EXPECT.OF HSG.& SHOPPING CENTER,NEXT (D NADJ	KOCSEHSCR
87	KO BUS SALES VOLN	KOSLSBUSP
88	KO CAR SALES VOLN	KOSLSCARP
89	KO CENTRAL GOVT.FINANCE: CASH-LIABILITIES, TRANSACTI(DISC.) CURN	KOICC3LBA
90	KO COINCIDENT INDEX: RETAIL SALE INDEX (%MOM) NADJ	KOCYCORSR
91	KO DAYS WORKED PER MONTH - WHOLESALE & RETAIL TRADE (DISC.) VOLN	KODAYWHSP
92	KO EMPLOYMENT - WHOLESALE & RETAIL TRADE VOLN	KOEMPWREP
93	KO EMPLOYMENT-W'SALE., RETAIL TRADE, HOTELS & RESTAURANTS VOLN	KOEMPWRHP
94	KO EXPORTS - COMMODITIES & TRANSACTIONS NEC(DISC.) CURN	KOEXNECXA
95	KO FOREIGN DIRECT INVESTMENT BY IND-W'SALE. & RETAIL TRADE CURN	KOFDOWRTA
96	KO IMPORT OF COMMODITIES AND TRANSACTIONS, N.E.C(DISC.) CURN	KOOICOMMA
97	KO INDUSTRIAL INVENTORIES - MINING VOLA	KOIPMINFG
98	KO INDUSTRIAL SHIPMENTS - MINING VOLA	KOIPMINEG
99	KO LIGHT TRUCK SALES VOLN	KOSLSLTRP
Price		
100	KO CPI - EXCLUDING AGRICULTURAL PRODUCT & OIL NADJ	KOCPCOREF
101	KO CPI NADJ	KOCONPRCF
102	KO CPI: ALCOHOL BEVERAGES & TOBACCO NADJ	KOCPALTOF
103	KO CPI: CLOTHING & FOOTWEAR NADJ	KOCPCLFTF
104	KO CPI: COMMUNICATION NADJ	KOCPCOMMF
105	KO CPI: EDUCATION NADJ	KOCPEDCNF
106	KO CPI: FOOD & NON-ALCOHOL BEVERAGES NADJ	KOCPFDBVF
107	KO CPI: FURNISHINGS, HOUSEHOLD EQP.& ROUTINE HOUSEHOLD MAINTENANCE	KOCPFUHEF
108	KO CPI: HEALTH NADJ	KOCPHLTHF
109	KO CPI: HOUSING, WATER, ELECTRICITY, GAS & OTHER FUELS NADJ	KOCPHWEFF
110	KO CPI: MISCELLANEOUS GOODS & SERVICES NADJ	KOCPMSGSF
111	KO CPI: RECREATION & CULTURE NADJ	KOCPRECUF

STT	VARIABLE	CODE
112	KO CPI: RESTAURANTS & HOTELS NADJ	KOCPREHOF
113	KO CPI: TRANSPORT NADJ	KOCPTRNSF
114	KO DUBAI SPOT PRICE OF CRUDE OIL (US$/BBL) CURN	KODUBOILA
115	KO FOREIGN DIRECT INVESTMENT CURN	KOFDI...A
116	KO INFLATION RATE NADJ	KOCPANNL
117	KO KERI BSI: BUSINESS CONDITIONS, PROSPECTS NADJ	KOBUSCBCR
118	KO PPI NADJ	KOPROPRCF

Below we list the data used to construct the macro factors. The data are monthly and obtained from Datastream and DataGuie database from 1995 to 2018. The table presents a brief series description, series mnemonic (code).

Table 6.
Macro-finance variables.

	Average variation explained (%)	Average correlation coefficient
Employment and Hours	81.91	0.61
Interest rate and Import–Export	80.94	0.52
Compensations and Labour cost	78.13	0.49
Sale, Order, and Purchase	83.39	0.56
Price and Inflation	87.45	0.68

The table show the average proportion of variation in the underlying 118 indicators of macro-finance variables by using the method of principal component analysis. The second column is the average correlation coefficient of the factor with the other factors. The data are monthly and obtained from Datastream and DataGuie database from 1995 to 2018.

Table 7.
Descriptive statistics for macro-finance factors.

Additional classification

JEL classification: G12, G17, G12

Author details

Hoang Van Hai[1]*, Phan Kim Tuan[1] and Le The Phiet[2]

1 University of Economics, The University of Da Nang, Viet Nam

2 Tay Nguyen University, Viet Nam

*Address all correspondence to: hoangvanhaidhkt@gmail.com

References

[1] Ang A, Hodrick RJ, Xing Y, Zhang X. The cross-section of volatility and expected returns. The Journal of Finance. 2006;**61**(1):259-299

[2] Bali TG, Cakici N. Idiosyncratic volatility and the cross section of expected returns. Journal of Financial and Quantitative Analysis. 2008;**43**(1): 29-58

[3] Fu F. Idiosyncratic risk and the cross-section of expected stock returns. Journal of Financial Economics. 2009; **91**(1):24-37

[4] Malkiel B, Xu Y. Idiosyncratic Risk and Security Returns. Working Paper: Princeton University; 2002

[5] Merton RC. A simple model of capital market equilibrium with incomplete information. The Journal of Finance. 1987;**42**(3):483-510

[6] Spiegel M, Wang X. Cross-Sectional Variation in Stock Returns: Liquidity and Idiosyncratic Risk. Yale School of Management: Working Paper; 2005

[7] Ang A, Hodrick RJ, Xing Y, Zhang X. High idiosyncratic volatility and low returns: International and further U.S. evidence. Journal of Financial Economics. 2009;**91**(1):1-23

[8] Chen Z, Petkova R. Does idiosyncratic volatility proxy for risk exposure? Review of Financial Studies. 2012;**25**(9):2745-2787

[9] Huang W, Liu Q, Rhee SG, Zhang L. Return reversals, idiosyncratic risk, and expected returns. The Review of Financial Studies. 2010;**23**(1):147-168

[10] Bali TG, Cakici N, Whitelaw RF. Maxing out: Stocks as lotteries and the cross-section of expected returns. Journal of Financial Economics. 2011; **99**(2):427-446

[11] Stambaugh RF, Yu J, Yuan Y. Arbitrage asymmetry and the idiosyncratic volatility puzzle. The Journal of Finance. 2015;**70**(5): 1903-1948

[12] Han Y, Lesmond D. Liquidity biases and the pricing of cross-sectional idiosyncratic volatility. The Review of Financial Studies. 2011;**24**(5):1590-1629

[13] Aslanidis N, Christiansen C, Lambertides N, Christos SS. Idiosyncratic volatility puzzle: Influence of macro-finance factors. Review of Quantitative Finance and Accounting. 2019;**52**(2):381-401

[14] DeLisle RJ, Mauck N, Smedema AR. Idiosyncratic volatility and firm-specific news: Beyond limited arbitrage. Financial Management. 2016;**45**(4):923-951

[15] Fama EF, French KR. Common risk factors in the returns on stocks and bonds. Journal of Financial Economics. 1993;**33**(1):3-56

[16] Detzel, A., Duarte J., Kamara, A., Siegel S. and Sun C. (2019), "The Cross-Section of Volatility and Expected Returns: Then and Now", *Critical Finance Review* (Forthcoming)

[17] Chen NF, Roll R, Ross S. Economic forces and the stock markets. Journal of Business. 1986;**59**(3):383-403

[18] Ferson WE, Harvey CR. The variation of economic risk premium. Journal of Political Economy. 1991; **99**(2):385-415

[19] Shi Y, Liu W-M, Ho K-Y. Public news arrival and the idiosyncratic volatility puzzle. Journal of Empirical Finance. 2016;**37**(C):159-172

[20] Fong WM, Toh B. Investor sentiment and the max effect. Journal of Banking and Finance. 2014;**46**:190-201

[21] Nartea G, Wu J, Liu HT. Extreme returns in emerging stock markets: Evidence of a MAX effect in South Korea. Applied Financial Economics. 2014;**24**(6):425-435

[22] Gu M, Kang W, Xu B. Limits of arbitrage and idiosyncratic volatility: Evidence from China stock market. Journal of Banking & Finance. 2018;**86**(C):240-258

[23] Karolyi GA, Lee K-H, Van Dijk MA. Understanding commonality in liquidity around the world. Journal of Financial Economics. 2012;**105**(1):82-112

[24] Fama EF, MacBeth JD. Risk, return, and equilibrium: Empirical tests. Journal of Political Economy. 1973;**81**(3):607-636

[25] Peterson DR, Smedema AR. The return impact of realized and expected idiosyncratic volatility. Journal of Banking & Finance. 2011;**35**(10): 2547-2558

[26] Fama EF, French KR. A five-factor asset pricing model. Journal of Financial Economics. 2015;**116**(1):1-22

[27] Goyal A, Welch I. A comprehensive look at the empirical performance of equity premium prediction. Review Finance Studies. 2008;**21**(4):1455-1508

[28] Ludvigson SC, Ng S. The empirical risk-return relation: A factor analysis approach. Journal of Financial Economics. 2007;**83**(1):171-222

[29] Herskovic B, Kelly B, Lustig H, Nieuwerburgh SV. The common factor in idiosyncratic volatility: Quantitative asset pricing implications. Journal of Financial Economics. 2016;**119**(2): 249-283

[30] Newey W, West K. A simple, positive semi-definite, heteroskedasticity and autocorrelation consistent covariance matrix. Econometrica. 1987;**55**:703-708

[31] Cheon YH, Lee KH. Time variation of MAX-premium with market volatility: Evidence from Korean stock market. *Pacific-Basin Finance* Journal. 2018;**51**(C):32-46

[32] Fama EF, French KR. Dissecting anomalies. The Journal of Finance. 2008;**63**(4):1653-1678

[33] Chordia T, Roll R, Subrahmanyam A. Market liquidity and trading activity. The Journal of Finance. 2001;**56**(2):501-530

[34] Annaert J, De Ceuster M, Verstegen K. Are extreme returns priced in the stock market? European evidence. Journal of Banking & Finance. 2013; **37**(9):3401-3411

Section 2

Behavioral Finance and Investment Decisions

Chapter 4

Financial Literacy as a Tool for Stimulating the Investment Behaviour of Rural Women: An Empirical Assessment

Bhaskaran Rajan, Navjot Kaur, Harpreet K. Athwal, Afzalur Rahman and Velmurugan P.S.

Abstract

Clapping with two hands create the sounds. Similarly, investment and saving behaviour are considered as the most vital elements for economic growth of an individual. This paper is to evaluate the influence of financial awareness on saving and investment behaviour of rural females in India. Investment pattern serves as a link between savings and wants of the common people. Economic growth of any nation can be critically measured through capital accumulation and investment trends in financial markets. In the present study, the investment behaviour on effect of financial awareness of 335 rural women in Jalandhar district has been evaluated. The relationship of financial literacy and saving & investment behaviour is also evaluated in the context of five basic domains of financial behaviour, such as demographic variables, financial control, financial planning, financial product selection and financial literacy. Results of the study revealed that rural women are conscious about the availability of various investment avenues in the market, but their investment pattern is still followed by some factors like familiarity, safety and assured returns, etc. This study suggests policymakers to focus on financial awareness rather to focus only on financial literacy.

Keywords: financial awareness, financial literacy, investment pattern, saving behaviour, rural women

1. Introduction

Women consist of half of the world population and it is an open secret that an independent and educated woman leads an educated and self-reliant family, which is further translated into a liberal, independent and an educated society. As per census of 2011, in India, the female population was 586.4 million (48% of the total population). Out of these total female population, 405.1 million (69% of the total female population) were living in rural areas [1]. Without women contribution or support, it is not possible to develop the country as a whole because half of the nation's human resources is women. Therefore, women are playing a very important role in the socioeconomic development of the country.

The constitution of India honours both men and women with equal rights. But women are not treated as equals as men [2]. Certain barriers still exist between men and women. The literacy level of the rural women population is less than that of urban women population. During 2009–10, 46.7 % of rural women population was illiterate as reported by the National Sample Survey Office [3].

Generally, the rural women face problems with regard to medical facilities, health care, malnutrition, environment, etc. Besides, finance is an essential part of their life. Hence, different financial inclusion programmes were launched by the Government for the rural population at different periods. Financial literacy is an integral part of the financial inclusion programme. It was introduced to rural women for the purpose of understanding the financial concept thoroughly and guiding them to take a decision on financial aspects [4]. This programme cultivates saving habits among the rural women. Also, it helps them to understand the financial affairs and motivate them to invest the savings in a profitable avenue.

Now-a-days, the financial institutions are offering a variety of schemes/products to the public. A careful selection of the product is important; otherwise, it leads to loss of their hard earned money. A large number of literature reports [5] that in India, financial literacy is not well developed particularly in rural areas and they are still waiting for revolutionary push. The purpose of the study is to investigate whether the learned knowledge on financial literacy by the Indian rural women population helps to invest their hard earned saving money in the profitable ventures or not?

2. Literature survey

A study on financial awareness among the salaried class people was carried out by Bhushan [6]; Umamaheswari and Kumar [7]. The studies reveal that certain demographic factors like general education level, gender, income level, employment etc. affect financial literacy. The financial literacy level between the salaried class persons is also varied. Vasagadekar [8] has informed that a working woman who has less knowledge in finance, finds difficulty in managing a portfolio. Hence, they should evaluate the available avenues before making investment [9].

Subha and Priya [10]; Agarwalla et al. [11] have reported that there are certain factors which affect financial literacy level viz. general literacy, income level, age, employment and place of work. Hence the government should take some sort of remedial measures to enhance financial attentiveness.

A variety of investment and saving products are available in the financial market, but people are still least aware. Therefore, a proper awareness about the products, among the public either through TV or radio is required as reported by Trivedi and Trivedi [12]; Goel [13]; Jappelli and Padula [14]; Kudva [15]. Awareness about the various investment avenues brings positive change in the lifestyle and investment pattern of people [16]. Only a few investors are aware about the industrial securities and most of the investors believe that such securities are insecure one [17].

A systematic analysis of the behaviour of rural and urban investors in terms of education, health care services, financial activities and priorities was carried out by Kumar and Mukhopadhyay [18]. The analysis reveals that both groups made an investment according to their requirements and rural investors' especially rural women need certain help for making the financial decision.

The awareness level of investors in a metro city is found to be higher than the investors in rural area [19]. The reason is that the metro investors are more concerned with financial gateways; news channels and finance or market related programs. In Pakistan, a study on impact of financial literacy on investment decisions was conducted. This study reveals that financial literacy has a positive trend on agreeableness, extraversion, openness and negative trend on neuroticism [20].

The difference between the saver and investor was clearly mentioned by Thilakam [21]. The investment decision made by the investors is fully based upon risk bearing, yield amount and their future plan [22, 23]. If they are aware of the basic concepts of finance under present condition, it helps them to identify the best investment opportunities [24].

Bhattacharya [25] has stressed that the financial literacy is an important requirement for resource planning. The investment behaviour of investors in India varies from time to time. Thulasipriya [26] has informed that in earlier stages, the investors invested in physical asset than financial assets. Later stage, their preference changed from physical assets to financial assets. Sharma and Pandey [27], Palanivelu and Chandrakumar [28] have expressed that Corporate bonds; post-office schemes; debentures; and bank deposits are the most promising investment avenues for the investors and more number of investors prefer these avenues. The rural people in India prefer to invest their savings in bank, insurance and post office only not in Public Provident Fund, Mutual Funds and Industrial Securities for the purpose of safety and security [29].

3. Scope of study

Financial literacy is an energetic universal concern. Availability of large number of financial resources, different financial schemes and low level of financial awareness has led to financial literacy. Earlier studies have mainly concentrated on investment behaviour of women. Most of the studies concluded that investors are interested in investing their savings in banking, insurance and post office schemes. No in depth study has been carried out on impact of financial literacy on investment behaviour of rural women. Scope of this study is to develop a model for assessing the level of financial literacy and to apply the same among the rural women of Jalandhar district in the state of Punjab.

4. Objectives

The main objective of the present study is to assess the relationship between the financial literacy programme and the investment behaviour of rural women. The sub objectives of the present study are:

1. Identify the level of financial knowledge obtained by rural women through the financial literacy programme.

2. Analyse the awareness of rural women towards the available investment avenues.

3. Ascertain the push and pull factors for rural women with regard to savings and investment behaviour.

4. Develop financial literacy score.

5. Research methodology

5.1 Sample size

Jalandhar district of Punjab has been selected as a sample district for this study. This district has five tehsils namely Jalandhar 1, Jalandhar 2, Nakodar, Phillour, and Sahakot. The present study attempts to evaluate the impact of financial literacy programme on investment behaviour of rural women. Hence, 2.5% of the potential rural women savers have been selected from each tehsil randomly. The total sample size is 335 rural women respondents.

6. Analysis and interpretation

6.1 Socio-economic factors

In respect of a wide diversity in socio-economic factors, the sample was drawn out of five tehsils in terms of rural women population across Jalandhar district. Data was collected through questionnaire. Age, occupation, education level, number of dependents, monthly income of family and the type of family were demographic traits on which data was collected. In addition to demographic attributes, the target group was required to respond on questions related to financial behaviour, financial planning and financial literacy. Details about the demographic variables of the respondents are shown in **Table 1**.

6.2 Awareness of investment avenues

The largest numbers of investment avenues are available in financial markets to serve the desires of investors. Thousands of investment schemes are available in the market. The art of rational investment decision is maximum returns with minimum of risk. Investment pattern differs from one another in terms of invested amount, risk bearing capacity and expected returns. In recent times, awareness about financial products has become an issue of discussion in financial markets. Past studies have revealed that people prefer to invest in traditional safe investment avenues. Bank, insurance and post office investment schemes were the most preferred investment avenues. There is an information gap between financial markets and a financier and due to this a majority of investor does not use modern investment products. Data collected under this section confirms that there is imbalance in-between traditional and modern investment avenues. As we can figure out easily that awareness level of respondents is fairly high in banking avenues, post office schemes, insurance schemes and other traditional avenues like gold/silver and real estate opportunities. On the other hand as evidenced in **Table 2**, there is lack of awareness in Chit Fund Schemes, Bonds, Debentures, Public Provident Fund, National Savings Certificate, Government Securities and Forex Market and Commodity Market. It is also stated by Mohd and Verma [29].

In terms of familiarity with financial products, data collected from the respondents revealed that rural female are most familiar with savings account (99.7%), followed by fixed deposit (99.4%), post office schemes (98.5%), life insurance (98.2%), real estate (94%) and gold/silver (91.9%) trading options. Furthermore, it is reported that rural females are most familiar with bank, post office, insurance and other traditional avenues of investment. Although, data do notreveal high familiarity of rural females with Debentures (58.2%), Bonds (57.9%), Forex Market

Variable	Detail	Frequency	Percentage
Age (in years)	20 and less	0	0
	21–30	43	12.8
	31–40	126	37.6
	41 and over	166	49.6
Education level	No formal education	43	12.8
	Primary school	109	32.5
	Matriculation	78	23.3
	Diploma	52	15.5
	Graduate/post-graduate	53	15.8
Marital status	Unmarried	28	8.4
	Married	230	68.7
	Widowed	77	23
No. of dependents	Two	3	0.9
	Three	17	5.1
	Four	49	14.6
	Five and more	266	79.4
Monthly income	1001–3000	28	8.4
	3001–5000	56	16.7
	5001–10,000	232	69.3
	More than 10,000	19	5.7
Family type	Nuclear family	188	56.1
	Joint family	147	43.9

Source: Primary data.

Table 1.
Details of demographic variable.

(40.3%) and Commodity Market (28.7%) in moderate risk avenues. But marginal divergence is found among respondents about few investment avenues like Mutual Funds (77.6%), Equity Share Market (74%), Public Provident Fund (63.3%), National Savings Certificate (62.7%), Chit Fund (62.1%) and Government Securities (61.5%).

6.3 Investment pattern

Investment pattern refers to the outline of savings into various financial products with the objective of risk diversification or high expected profits. The very first step for voyage investment is savings. Investor can take the benefit of large chunk of financial products only if he/she is aware about the relevance of portfolio or diversified pattern of savings. The current investment pattern of selected rural women respondents are represented in **Figure 1**.

From **Figure 1**, it is revealed that most of the female respondents are investing in Savings Account (96.7%), followed by Bank Fixed Deposit (84.2%) and Life Insurance (81.5%). These three are found to be the most prominent investment avenues in pattern of rural females. Post Office Savings (56.4%), Mutual Funds (57.3%) and Gold/Silver (53.1%) are found less popular in the investment pattern of rural

Financial product	Familiar		Non-familiar	
	Frequency	In percentage	Frequency	In percentage
I. Safe investment avenues				
Savings account	334	99.7	1	0.3
Bank fixed deposit	333	99.4	2	0.6
Public Provident Fund (PPF)	212	63.3	123	36.7
National Saving Certificate (NSC)	210	62.7	125	37.3
Kisan Vikas Patra (KVP)	259	77.3	76	22.7
Post office savings	330	98.5	5	1.5
Government securities	206	61.5	129	38.5
II. Moderate risk investment avenues				
Mutual funds	260	77.6	75	22.4
Life insurance	329	98.2	6	1.8
Debentures	195	58.2	140	41.8
Bonds	194	57.9	141	42.1
III. High risk investment avenues				
Equity share market	248	74	87	26
Commodity market	96	28.7	239	71.3
Forex market	135	40.3	200	59.7
IV. Traditional investment avenues				
Real estate	315	94	20	6
Gold/ Silver	308	91.9	27	8.1
Chit fund	208	62.1	127	37.9

Source: Primary data.

Table 2.
Awareness about investment products.

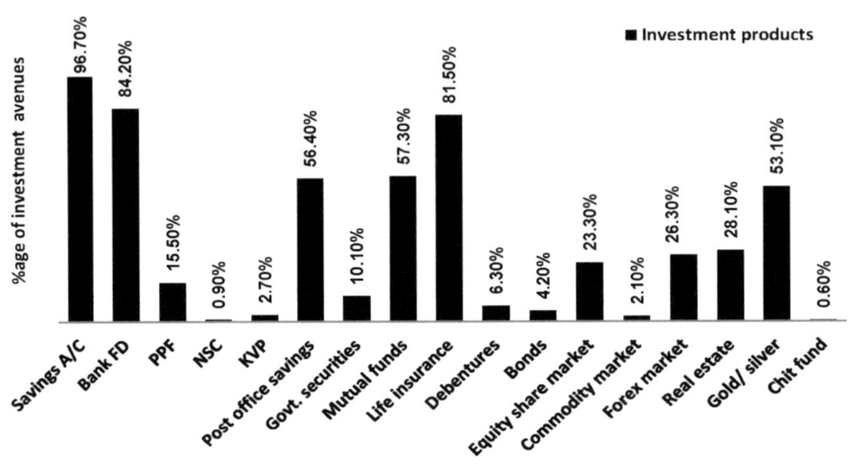

Figure 1.
Attitude of rural women towards various avenues. Source: Primary data.

females. On the other hand, KisanVikasPatra (2.7%), Government Securities (10.1%), Debentures (6.3%), Bonds (4.2%), Commodity Market (2.1%), National Saving Certificates (0.9%), Chit Fund (0.6%) are preferred by very few persons to diversify their portfolio.

6.4 Components of financial attitude

The reason for the selection of the financial instrument by the rural women is presented in **Figure 2**.

From **Figure 2**, it can be concluded that familiarity with any financial institution influences most of the times investment decisions of investors. 34% of total females have selected a financial institution because of familiarity, followed by the reason of assured returns. 23% of respondents has selected only those financial products which assure return on their investment quantum. 22% of respondents have preferred to select a number of financial products. Here, portfolio diversification is the main aim of investment. Interestingly, safe and low risk factors have the lowest preferred reason for financial selection. Only 21% of people has invested in safe and low risk investment avenues.

6.5 Statements describe the financial selection of rural females

Financial and investment behaviour of a person is a vital component in a given financial environment. Investment pattern is affected by the awareness about the financial markets and the ability to make rational decisions. Hence, the variable behaviour prior to the selection of investment policy was investigated for this research. Data related to behaviour and rationality prior to financial selection is presented in **Figure 3**.

Figure 3, illustrates the behaviour-wise allocation of responses. Among 335 households' surveyed 36.40% of respondents have preferred different financial or investment policies from one company only. It is clear that most of the respondents trust in the investment policies of only one company. 34.30% of responses belongs to those households who never compare different investment policies of one or more companies. They prefer to invest in pre-selected avenues. Consequently, 20.60% households compare various products from more than one company and 8.70% of sample population are found to be unaware of the availability of different financial avenues in the market.

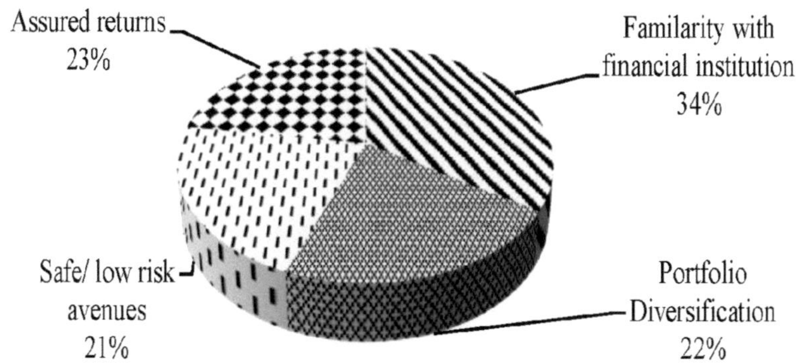

Figure 2.
Reason behind financial selection. Source: Primary data.

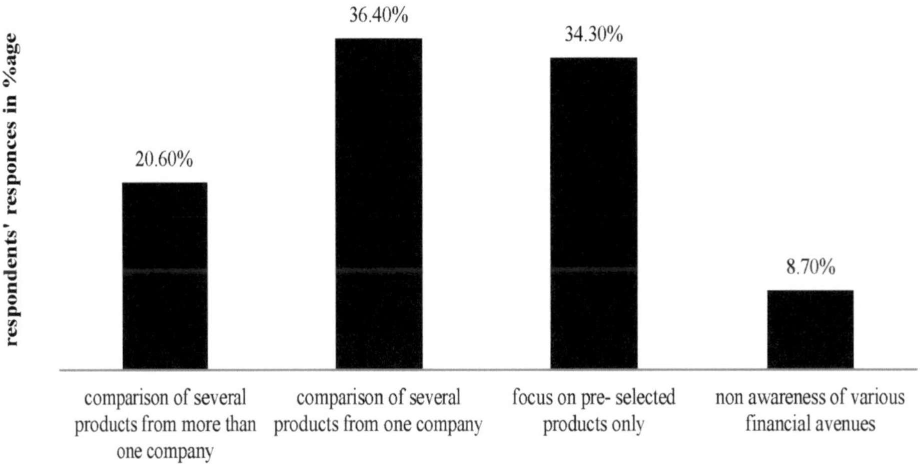

Figure 3.
Behaviour of rural women with reference to product choice. Source: Primary data.

6.6 Financial literacy scale

Financial literacy is the ability of a layman to understand the nature of finance and earning potential of his savings. In true sense, financial literacy allows a person to take a rational financial decision in specific areas like property or real estate matters, tax planning, banking and insurance and capital markets, etc. To achieve financial goals, basic knowledge about financial matters becomes the essential part of today's world; not only for the investors of stock market; but also for the persons having saving habits. It can be defined as the tricks used by the finance player to manage their earnings in terms of savings, budgeting, investing and insuring etc. Definition of financial literacy also declares that financially knowledgeable people are well aware about money management concepts and know in which manner financial institutions work. The financial literacy score is a platform to identify trends of financial awareness among individuals. To depict awareness trends in basic financial matters, financial literacy index of rural women was calculated. The financial literacy index is prepared on the basis of following basic financial literacy indicators:

- Simple interest rate
- Compound interest rate
- Affordability
- Financial security
- Portfolio diversification
- Loan ideology
- Financial awareness to life circumstances
- Product choice
- Credit card ideology
- Basic taxation ideology

In order to determine the financial literacy level, a set of question was asked and based upon the response, a rank was assigned. The rank "0" is assigned to the respondent who does not have knowledge about financial literacy. The ranks "1" and "2" are assigned for those having average and thorough knowledge on financial activities, respectively.

After assigning rank for the all the parameters, the total financial literacy score for the individual respondent is calculated as follows:

$$\text{Literacy Score} = \left(\frac{Actual\ value - Minimum\ value}{Maximum\ value - Minimum\ value}\right), \tag{1}$$

where 'actual value' is the sum of ranks the individual respondent scored, 'maximum value' is the theoretical maximum, here it is = 20, (that is 10 × 2) and 'minimum value' is the theoretical minimum, here '0' (i.e., 10 × 0).

In order to get the net score, Total of the literacy score all the respondents is divided by the total number of the respondents.

If the value is 0, it indicates that the financial literacy level is zero. Between 0.1 and 0.33 it specifies that level of financial literacy is at a minimum. Between 0.34 and 0.66 the level of financial literacy is of medium level. Between 0.67 and 0.99 the level of financial literacy is high and if the value is 1, it indicates that complete financial literacy level is achieved.

The calculated value of financial literacy is 0.69552. This revealed that the overall level of financial literacy is encouraging in rural parts of Jalandhar district. This indicates that efforts of government and non-government organisations are leading to a positive change. The results of financial literacy index are given in **Table 3** and **Figure 4**.

From the data collected from rural women of Jalandhar district, on the basis of combination of ten questions, it is revealed that the majority of respondents are falling in high level of financial literacy group followed by 38% of our total respondents who are coming under medium level of financial literacy.

Some differences concerned with investment pattern and financial selection include risk and portfolio choices. Choice of the portfolio, the level of risk bearing capacity is more concerned with the financial awareness of households. It is indicated that most of the rural females are aware of the ideology and framework of taxation (91%), Affordability and Financial security (73%). 72% of respondents confidently answer the calculation of simple interest rate. While portfolio diversification (64%), product choice (63%) and loan ideology (48%) are found lacking in this context. While in some typical financial matters financial knowledge of rural women is found lacking. Those financial concepts are Compound interest rate (24%), financial knowledge to life circumstances (22%) and Credit card ideology (10%). **Table 4** is dictates the financial literacy score for selected financial concepts.

6.7 Relationship between financial literacy and investment pattern

A financier, who is not financially literate, will not be able to select a suitable investment pattern. This behaviour is strongly evident in the rural society of India. Financial literacy is important not only for rural or uneducated one but even an urban educated can get him into financial suffering if he is not aware of financial concepts. The results highlight how important financial literacy is to make sound financial decisions. Financial control, Financial planning, Understanding of financial concepts and Selection of financial product are basic concepts to measure financial awareness of a person.

Respondent	Value for the respondent's response for different parameters										Actual score for individual respondent's (maximum value 20)	Financial Literacy score for individual respondent's
	Simple interest rate	Compound interest rate	Affordability	Financial security	Portfolio diversification	Loan ideology	Financial awareness to life circumstances	Product choice	Credit card ideology	Basic taxation ideology		
	(A)	(B)	(C)	(D)	(E)	(F)	(G)	(H)	(I)	(J)	(H)	$\left(\frac{\text{Actual value} - \text{Minimum value}}{\text{Maximum value} - \text{Minimum value}}\right)$
											Sum of (A to J)	
1	0	0	1	2	2	0	0	2	0	2	9	0.45
2	1	0	2	2	2	1	1	1	0	2	12	0.6
3	2	1	2	2	2	1	1	1	0	2	14	0.7
4	2	1	1	2	0	1	1	1	0	2	11	0.55
5	2	1	2	2	2	1	1	1	1	2	15	0.75
335	2	0	1	2	2	0	2	1	1	2	13	0.65
Total Financial Literacy Score for all the respondents												233.00
Total respondents												335
Average financial literacy Score for individual respondent												0.69552

****Data have been collected from 335 members for calculation of the individual respondent's score on financial literacy. But due to space constraint only responses of 5 members have been shown in **Table 3**.*

Table 3.
*Sample of financial literacy index calculations.***

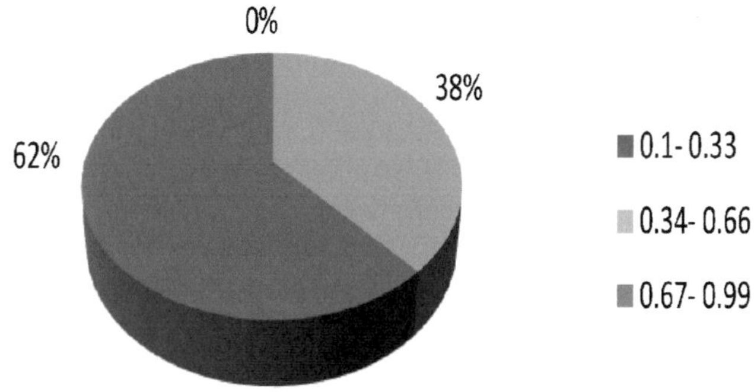

Figure 4.
Financial literacy index. Source: Primary data.

Financial concepts	Correct	Incorrect	Don't know
Simple interest rate	240 (72%)	69 (20%)	26 (8%)
Compound interest rate	79 (24%)	94 (28%)	162 (48%)
Affordability	252 (75%)	83 (25%)	NIL (0%)
Financial security	244 (73%)	47 (14%)	44 (13%)
Portfolio diversification	213 (64%)	61 (18%)	61 (18%)
Loan ideology	160 (48%)	128 (38%)	47 (14%)
Financial knowledge to life circumstances	166 (22%)	122 (16%)	47 (62%)
Product choice	211 (63%)	124 (37%)	NIL (0%)
Credit card ideology	60 (10%)	62 (11%)	213 (79%)
Taxation ideology	304 (91%)	18 (5%)	13 (4%)

Source: Primary data.

Table 4.
Financial literacy score.

For the purpose of finding out the relationship between financial literacy and pattern of investment, a correlation test is applied. Results obtained by correlation are given in **Table 5**.

From **Table 5**, it is observed that the value of correlation is 0.129. So it is evidenced that there is weak degree of positive correlation between financial literacy and investment pattern among rural females. The significance value revealed by

		Financial literacy	Investment pattern
Financial Literacy	Pearson correlation	1	0.129*
	Sig. (2-tailed)		0.018
	N	335	335
Investment pattern	Pearson correlation	.129*	1
	Sig. (2-tailed)	.018	
	N	335	335

Source: Primary data.

Table 5.
Relationship analysis through correlation.

correlation is 0.018 which is less than 0.05% level of significance. So it is strongly evidenced that correlation is statistically significant also.

7. Conclusion

Financial Literacy is a vital element to predict households' financial attitudes in developing nations. Indeed, in Indian heterogeneous household, levels of financial awareness vary greatly. From the empirical study it is revealed that most of the investors select financial institutions because of familiarity and their portfolio selection is largely based on comparison of number of financial products issued by the same familiar financial institution. So, guaranteed return, safety and diverse portfolio selection are contributing at large to describe the investment attitude of women.

The study reveals that there is a relationship between financial literacy and investment behaviour of the rural female. Through financial literacy programme, majority of the respondents (62% of total) have acquired more knowledge on financial concepts such as taxation, financial security, calculation of interest rate etc.

The awareness level of rural females in Investment Avenue is fairly high in banking avenues, post office schemes, insurance schemes and other traditional avenues like gold/silver and real estate opportunities. Their awareness level in investment avenue is very low in chit fund schemes, bonds, debentures, Public provident fund, National savings certificate, Government securities and Commodity market.

A website as a financial literacy guide was released by the Reserve Bank of India on 31st January 2013. This website was developed as a complete financial awareness guide and banks are advised to use this website as a fundamental curriculum to communicate basic financial knowledge. This financial literacy guide provides operational guidelines to organize financial awareness camps, as an initiative towards financial literacy.

Besides, various measures adopted by government and non-government institutions towards financial literacy, the results of the study reveal that still the investment pattern of rural women is followed by traditional avenues of investment. This, it is suggested to financial literacy program organizers to focusing on preferences and investment attitude of micro level segment investors. Hamza and Arif [20] have also suggested that policymakers and managers need to focus on profiling investors based on their status. It is strongly suggested to the program organizers to pass information on issue of budgeting, portfolio diversification, effective credit card management and loan ideology.

DOI: http://dx.doi.org/10.5772/intechopen.94532

Author details

Bhaskaran Rajan[1*], Navjot Kaur[2], Harpreet K. Athwal[3], Afzalur Rahman[4] and Velmurugan P.S.[1]

1 Department of Commerce, Central University of Tamil Nadu, Thiruvarur, India

2 College of Business and Law, University of Canterbury, New Zealand

3 KPMG LLP, USA

4 Department of Commerce, B.S. Abdur Rahman Crescent Institute of Science and Technology, Chennai, India

*Address all correspondence to: askaraudit@yahoo.com

References

[1] Chandramouli C. *Census of India 2011 – Rural urban distribution of population, Ministry of Home affairs, New Delhi dated 15th July 2011*. Retrieved from http://censusindia.gov.in/2011-prov-results/paper2/data_files/india/Rural_Urban_2011.pdf. Dated 6th June, 2015.

[2] Sharma A. Status of women: A socio-historical analysis in different ages of Indian society. Research Journal of Language, Literature and Humanities. 2014, January;**1**(1):10-14

[3] Report No. 515, *Employment & Unemployment Situation in India, 66th Round, July 2009 – June 2010*, National Sample Survey Office (NSSO), Govt. of India. (July 2009 – June 2010) November, 2011.

[4] Garg S, & Agarwal P. Financial inclusion in India – A review of initiatives and achievements. Journal of Business and Management. 2014;**16**(6): 52-61

[5] Mathivathani V, & Velumani M. A study on financial literacy among rural women in Tamilnadu. Indian Journal of Applied Research. 2014;**4**(1):556-557

[6] Bhushan P. Insights into awareness level and investment behaviour of salaried individuals towards financial products. International Journal of Engineering, Business and Enterprise Applications. 2013, March;**8**(1):53-57

[7] Umamaheswari S, & Kumar M.A. A study on investment pattern and awareness of salaried class investors in Coimbatore district. Indian Journal of Research. 2013, September; 2(9), 31-34.

[8] Vasagadekar P. A research paper on investment awareness among Indian working women with reference to Pune region. International Journal of Scientific & Engineering Research. 2014, June;**5**(6):1333-1350

[9] Bairagi U. & Rastogi C. An empirical study of saving pattern and investment preferences of individual households with reference to Pune city. ASM's International E-Journal of Ongoing Research in Management and IT. 2013; 1-11.

[10] Subha M, & Priya P. The emerging role of financial literacy financial planning. International Journal of Innovative Science, Engineering & Technology. 2014, July;**1**(5):400-408

[11] Agarwalla S. K, Barua S, Jacob J, & Verma J. Financial literacy among working young in Urban World Development. 2015, March; 67:101-109.

[12] Trivedi P, & Trivedi S. Financial literacy an essential prerequisite for financial inclusion. Global Journal for Research Analysis. 2014, March;**3**(3): 28-30

[13] Goel S. Performance of Mutual funds and Investors' Behavior (Published Ph.D. thesis), 2013, June. Jaypee Institute of Information Technology Noida, India.

[14] Jappelli T, & Padula M. Investment in financial literacy (Working Paper No. 272). 2011, January: Retrieved from Centre for studies in Economics and Finance, http://www.csef.it/WP/wp272.pdf

[15] Kudva V. Financial education and consumer protection. FICCI Banking & Finance Digest. 2011, September;**8**:1-9

[16] Virani V. Saving and investment pattern of school teachers – A study with reference to Rajkot city, Gujarat. National Monthly Refereed Journal of Research in Commerce & Management. 2014;**2**(4):13-27

[17] Bhardwaj B, Sharma N, & Sharma D. Income, saving and investment

pattern of employees of Bahra University, Solan. International Journal of Management & Business Studies. 2013, March;**3**(1):137-141

[18] Kumar L, & Mukhopadhyay J. Patterns of financial behavior among rural and urban clients: Some evidence from Tamil Nadu, India (Working Paper No. 9), 2013. Retrieved from Institute for Money, Technology & Financial Inclusion, http://www.imtfi.uci.edu/files/blog_working_papers/20139_kumarmukhopadhyay.pdf

[19] Brahmabhatt, Raghu Kumari P.S, & Shamira Malekar. A study of investor behavior on investment avenues in Mumbai Fenil. Asian Journal of Marketing & Management Research. 2012, September; 1(1), 49-71.

[20] Hamza N, & Arif I. Impact of Financial Literacy on Investment Decisions: The Mediating Effect of Big-Five Personality Traits Model. Market Forces College of Management Sciences. 2019, June;**14**(1):43-60. Retrieved from https://www.researchgate.net/publication/333965615_Impact_of_Financial_Literacy_on_Investment_Decisions_The_Mediating_Effect_of_Big-Five_Personality_Traits_Model accessed Oct 13 2020

[21] Thilakam C. Financial literacy among rural masses in India. Proceedings of an International Conference on Business and Management held in Phuket, Thiland, 6-7 September, 2012. (pp. 204-217).

[22] Altaf M. A changing financial investment behaviour of households (A case study of Baramulla town). International Journal of Scientific Research. 2013;**5**(1):1-5

[23] Karthikeyan B, & Ramprasath S. Individual investors' behaviour towards select investments: A study with reference to KattumannarKoilTaluk, Cuddalore district, Tamil Nadu, India. The International Journal of Business and Management. 2013, December;**1**(6):48-56

[24] Gallery N, Newton C, & Palm N. Framework for assessing financial literacy and superannuation investment choice decisions. Australasian Accounting Business and Finance. 2011;**5**(2):3-22

[25] Bhattacharya J. Investor awareness and protection. FICCI Banking & Finance Digest 8, 2011, September; 10-12.

[26] Thulasipriya B. Investment pattern of government employees - An empirical study. International Journal on Global Business Management & Research. 2014, August;**3**(1):35-41

[27] Sharma P C, & Pandey A. Indian mutual fund market: Retail investor's investment insight. International Journal of Research & Development in Technology and Management Science. 2014, March;**21**(1):1-16

[28] Palanivelu V.R, & Chandrakumar K. A study on preferred investment avenues among salaried peoples with reference to Namakkal Taluk, Tamil Nadu, India: Proceedings of an International Conference Business, Economics, and Accounting (IBEA) held in Bangkok, 20-23 March, 2013; (pp. 25-32).

[29] Mohd S, & Verma O.P. Saving and Investment Pattern of Rural Households of Himachal Pradesh. PRAGATI: Journal of Indian Economy. 2018;**5**(2):75-86

Chapter 5

Accounting Information Quality and Investment Decisions

Nouha Khoufi

Abstract

Accounting information quality has been said to play an important role in reducing information asymmetry. Thus, firms with high accounting information quality may enhance more investors' decisions. This paper aims to empirically examine the association between accounting information quality and investment decisions among firms in Tunisia. The sample of this study consists of 50 firms listed on the Tunis Stock Exchange covering 2012 to 2016. The findings imply that accounting information quality is significantly negatively related to investment inefficiency. The inclusion of control variables and the use of alternative models to measure accounting information quality provide consistent findings. This paper has several important contributions. First, this paper provides new empirical evidence in an emerging market. Although emerging markets make up the vast majority of economic activity around the world, they have received limited attention in academic research. Second, this paper can also help researchers to better understand and realize the governance role of accounting information, and push them to investigate the other role of accounting information deeply and broadly.

Keywords: accounting information quality, investment inefficiency, agency costs, financial constraint, asymmetry

1. Introduction

Many researchers have explored that the major objective of accounting information was to help its users make informed decisions. In addition, high-quality accounting information can also inform investors in a timely manner about the orientation of the firm's capital investments and help them to supervise managerial activities. Similarly, Bushman and Smith [1] find that high-quality information disclosures are beneficial to investors by monitoring management, encouraging them to make investment decisions efficiently and effectively and finally improving capital allocation efficiency and gaining more returns to investors. Houcine, [2] argue that investors are concerned with the quality of accounting information because it helps them to better understand the company's operating situation and other fundamentals. Therefore, high-quality accounting information affords external stakeholders a comprehensive understanding of firm fundamentals and allows them to take action to supervise management behavior.

An investment decision basically consists of the process of accepting or rejecting a particular investment project. Thus, it can be noted that, from a theoretical point of view, the decision is simple: projects for which the return is greater than the opportunity cost must be accepted, while others must be rejected. In real life, this process is not so easy, since the decision to accept or reject a project can be influenced by agents' interests in the decision-making process. Thus, accepting economically unviable projects or rejecting economically attractive projects can occur when the outcome of such deliberations offers benefits to decision makers, even when it causes losses to shareholders [3].

Firms use accounting information in investment decision-making to whether invest in physical project or invest in capital market. Firms need to invest in efficient investments with positive Net Present Value (NPV), and let go projects with negative NPV for better future growth and expansion. Accounting information is therefore important to facilitate informed decision [4].

This main objective of this study is to investigate the association of accounting information quality and investment decision using firm level observations in an emerging market such as Tunisia. The primary reason for choosing Tunisia is that we found an interesting research track in order to test the economic consequences of the quality of financial information in such an environment. Especially, in the face of this increasing doubt done over the quality of accounting results following the wave of financial scandals whereby Tunisia was not spared with BATAM case[1]. Also the Tunisian firms are characterized by a weak informational environment, namely a weak level of voluntary divulgation of information, little follow-up by financial analysts as well as quasi absence of media coverage by the economic and financial press, that turns the accountable information a component relatively more dominant among the set of information used by the different users of financial statements in their decision-making process [5].

The paper is organized into five sections including this introduction. Section 2 presents a brief theoretical framework discussing the determinants of the quality of accounting information, and the relationship between accounting information quality, investment decision, and financial constraint. Section 3 explains the empirical methodology, including the choice of variables and data issues. Estimation results are presented and discussed in Section 4 and we concluded in Section 5.

2. The association between the quality of accounting information and the investment decision

One of the main objectives of accounting information is to provide information that can facilitate the efficient allocation of capital. In other words, quality of financial information should be one of the most important inputs in decision-making regarding capital allocation that is investments [6]. The Financial Accounting Standards Board (FASB) states that one objective of financial reporting is to help present and potential investors in making rational decisions for investment. Firm is seen as investing efficiently if it invested in projects with positive Net Present Value (NPV). If the firm passed up on investment opportunities that would have positive NPV, then the firm was under-investing. On the other hand, when firm invests in investments with negative NPV, the firm was over-investing. Under or over-investment indicate that the firm is not investing efficiently. Hence, the level of firm's investment efficiency can be gauged from the absence of under or over-investment [1].

Based on 3600 firm-year observations of A-share listed companies on the Shanghai and Shenzhen exchanges from 2004 to 2006, Li [7] examines the

[1] It is a manipulation case of accounts that auditors, such as in the Enron case in the United States, did not report in time and that took on the emergence of a real financial scandal, affecting the credibility of the stock market as well as weakening seven local banks.

influence of accounting information quality on the under- and over-investment of listed companies. His results show that high-quality accounting information reduces the risks of moral hazard and adverse selection and inhibits both under-investment and overinvestment by ameliorating contracts and supervision, thereby improving capital allocation efficiency at the company level.

2.1 Quality of financial information, capital cost and information asymmetry

The accounting The accounting information represents an important source of information specific to the company that tends to reduce the level of information asymmetry between investors and the company and therefore contributing to a better functioning of financial markets [8].

Under lower external financing costs and investor's capital rationing, there is less possibility that managers pass up investments with positive NPV (lower under-investment). According to Jensen [9], lower adverse selection opportunity decreases the opportunity for managers to engage in value-destroying activities and self-maximizing decisions such as build an empire-building with ample capital (less over-investment).

Therefore, Easley and O'Hara [10] show that poor quality of accounting information leads to an undiversifiable information risk between informed and uninformed investors, thus increasing the cost of capital. On the other hand, the publication of better financial information in terms of quality and quantity would reduce this level of risk and therefore the cost of capital. Similarly, Yee [11] asserts that poor quality of the published information is considered to be a non-diversifiable risk factor leading to an increase in the risk premium, a component of the cost of capital. Also, Lambert [12] demonstrate how better quality of information accounting disclosure consents to reduce systematic risk by changing the perceptions of different stakeholders in the financial market regarding the distribution of future cash flows, and as a result, attenuating the cost of capital. For his part, Suijs [13] illustrates that better quality of financial information reduces the cost of capital by lowering the volatility of securities by improving risk sharing between generations of investors.

As well, in the light of literature developed above and empirical works, if a better quality of accounting information published, namely in terms of reliability, enables to reduce the levels of information asymmetry, and so the capital cost, it will be associated with a better decision of investment, facilitating the access to external funding sources for companies with a less cost, and consequently to reduce under-investment. Such an association was documented as well over the emerging developed markets, from which, we suggest testing the following hypothesis:

H1: A better quality of published accounting information is negatively associated with under-investment.

2.2 Quality of financial information, agency costs and control of managers

According to previous studies from the perspective of agency theory, the main reason for financial information is to alleviate the problem of information asymmetry by increasing shareholders, creditors, and others access to information about a company.

As the access to the accounting information increases, the privileged position held by managers in relation to private information decreases [9]. Based on this assertion, the accounting information is currently used as an input within contracts of inciting remuneration in order to motivate the managers to act in the interest of stakeholders and constitute an important source of information on which governance organs are based on controlling managerial activities [1, 2].

For instance, several past studies find that accounting information is used by shareholders to monitor managers [1, 12] and it is an important source for investors in monitoring firms' performances [4, 14]. Therefore, if higher financial information quality improved investors and shareholders ability to monitor managerial activities and detect their dysfunctional behavior such as over and under-investment, it could lead to managers investing more efficiently.

Based on the above theoretical arguments, we tend to check the hypothesis below:

H2: A better quality of published accounting information is negatively associated with over-investment.

3. Research methodology

3.1 Sample and data collection

In order to test our hypotheses in the Tunisian context, we select a sample of 50 companies listed on the Tunisian Stock Exchange (TSE). This number is limited because we have eliminated the financial companies due to their specific financial data. This study is based on observations from 2012 to 2016. The data are collected from the publications of the sample companies (annual reports, prospectuses...) available at the Financial Market Council, among some brokers or some companies' websites and on the publications of the TSE.

Table 1 provides distribution of the sample by industry based on the DataStream-industry classification. The sample is represented by 12 industries.

3.2 Investment decisions

First, we tested the association between the investment decisions and the quality of accounting information conditional on the assumption that the company is in a situation more prone to over or underinvestment. Similar with past studies [6, 15],

Industry	N	Percentage (%)
Construction and materials	7	14%
Electronic and electrical equipment	3	6%
Food producers	2	4%
Telecommunication	5	1%
Electronic and electrical equipment	6	12%
Oil equipment and services	3	6%
Health care equipment	2	4%
Industrial metals and mining	4	8%
Industrial transportation	5	1%
Software and computer services	6	12%
Support services	4	8%
Technology hardware	3	6%
Total	50	100%

Table 1.
Sample distribution by industries.

both overinvestment (positive deviations from expected investment) and underinvestment (negative deviations from expected investment) are considered inefficient investments. Specially, we use the model that predicts investment as a function of revenue growth. The model is described as follow:

$$\text{Invest}_{i,t+1} = \beta_{i,t+1+}\ \text{RevGrowth}_{i,t} + \varepsilon_{i,t+1} \tag{1}$$

Where:

$Invest_{i,t+1}$ = total investment expenditure for year t + 1, which relate to fixed capital investment and are measured by the difference between the gross values of fixed assets of t + 1 and t, deflated by the capital stock at the start of the period.

$RevGrowth_{i,t}$ = revenue growth and defined as percentage change in revenue from year $t-1$ to t.

εi, t: the residuals of the model, which represent the inefficiency of the investment.

Then, we will then use the residuals of model (1) as a specific proxy for the level of deviation of the company from its expected level of investment. The negative (positive) residuals from the regression model (1) indicate under investment (over investment). In our analyses, we use the absolute value of residuals as a proxy for investment efficiency.

Thus, based on the residual of the model, we could identify differences and make the necessary groupings, as shown in **Figure 1**.

3.3 Accounting information quality

There is no universally accepted measure of accounting information quality [6, 16]. But no number could be as attractive to users of financial statements as the accounting result [16]. According to Francis et al. [17], the quality of accounting results has several attributes, namely reliability, relevance, conservatism, punctuality, smoothing, predictability and persistence. At the level of this research, we will in particular be interested in two attributes of the accounting result, namely: the quality of accruals and accounting conservatism. Our choice focused on these two attributes since it has been widely demonstrated by the various previous works [6, 15, 18, 19] that it is mainly these two attributes of the accounting result which improve the investment behavior of companies. Practically, a better quality of accruals increases the accuracy and reliability of accounting results, lowering the cost of capital and thus reducing underinvestment. On the other hand, a more conservative accounting result, allocates to governance bodies to exercise better

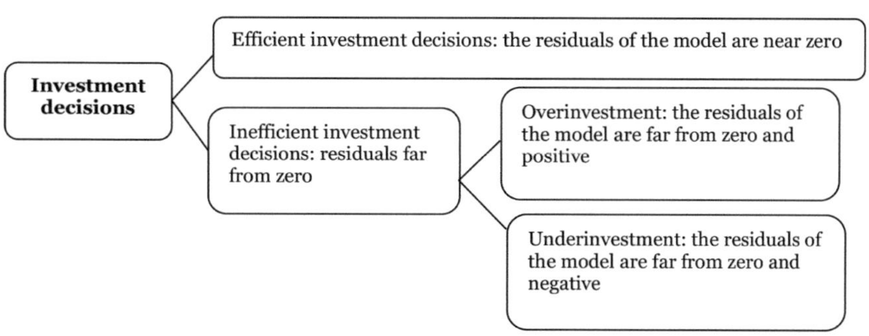

Figure 1.
Grouping of firms according to efficiency in investment decisions.

control over managerial decisions, and therefore to reduce ex-ante their incentive and ability to undertake unprofitable investments.

3.3.1 Measure of the quality of accruals

Managers can use their discretion to manipulate results via accruals and to alter the actual performance of the business. This is why the results, which quickly turn into cash flow, represent the most desirable quality of profits. Francis et al. [17], consider that this rapid transformation of results into cash flow, is at best captured by the model of Dechow and Dichev [20]. The DD model (2002) suggests that the quality of accruals is assessed by the degree of association between the change in total current accruals with cash flows from past, present and future periods. However, we will use the modified DD model (2002) as proposed by McNichols [21] to determine discretionary accruals. This model states that beyond cash flows, the change in net sales and the proportion of tangible fixed assets are variables important in forecasting with respect to currents accruals:

$$CUACC_{i,t} = ß_0 + ß_1 CFO_{i,t-1} + ß_2 CFO_{i,t} + ß_3 CFO_{i,t+1} + ß_4 ASi,t + ß_5 Asset_{i,t} + \varepsilon_{i,t}.$$

Where:

$CUACC_{i,t}$: the amount of current accruals of firm i for year t, calculated as follows: $\Delta CAit - \Delta CLit - \Delta LIQit + \Delta DEBit$.

Where:

Δ **CAit**: change in current assets between t - 1 and t;

Δ **CLit**: change in current liabilities;

Δ **LIQit**: change in liquidity t - 1 and t;

Δ **DEBit**: change in current debts between t - 1 and t;

$CFO_{i,t-1}$, $CFO_{i,t}$ *and* $CFO_{i,t+1}$: cash flow from operations for the years t-1, t and t + 1,

$AS_{i,t}$: change in annual sales between t-1 and t;

$Asset_{i,t}$: the proportion of tangible fixed assets in year t.

In this model, the absolute value of the residuals is used as a proxy the quality of accruals (QACC). We will multiply this value by (−1), so that a higher value corresponds to a better quality of the accruals, and therefore, of the accounting results. The quality of accounting information is therefore assumed to be inversely proportional to the company's propensity to manage the accounting result.

3.3.2 Measure of accounting conservatism

At the level of the current research, we are going be interested in an attribute of accounting result, namely accounting conservatism. In fact, a more conservative accounting result, allocates to governance organs to exert a better control on the managerial decisions, and thus to reduce ex-ante their incentives and their qualifications in order to undertake non-profitable investments. Yet, we will specifically be interested in conditional conservatism. According to Gively, and Haynes [22], there are two types of conservatism: conditional and unconditional. Unconditional conservatism results in under-evaluation of the accounting value of net assets since the start of the economic activity of the company, because of the selection beforehand, of accounting conservatism methods. While under-evaluation of assets led by the conditional conservatism is attributable to the delay of accountability between latent losses and gains. As we prepare to show that through asymmetric recognition of gains and losses, this form of conservatism endorses a role of control on the activities of managers, namely those that are reattached to the investment decision. We will use the accumulation of non-current accruals, in view of apprehending the degree of conservatism for every company-year.

The current measure was initially developed by Givoly and Haynes [22] and then repeated by several authors [19, 23]. These latter argue that the underlying intuition behind resorting to this measure lies in the fact that it captures caution and vigilance such as the trends of accountants to require more auditing so as to recognize the good news in terms of financial statements and manage to anticipate bad news. In fact, non-current accruals comprise accounting posts subject to the application of the precaution principle, such as: provisions, change effects at the level of accounting estimation methods, losses on asset disposals, impairment of assets, etc.

Though these rubrics must be mandated by the Generally Accepted Accounting Principles, both the schedule and size of these loads/expenses, are left to the discretion of the managers, which makes them largely subject to their discretion and therefore constitutes a measure of accounting conservatism [24].

Non-current accruals *NCUACC* are measured by the difference between total accruals (net outcome– operating cash flow) as well as current accruals.

We will estimate the size of *NCUACC* over a period of 3 years, ranging from t-2 to t. To better facilitate the interpretation, we will multiply this value by (−1). Thus, positive values are synonymous with conservative accounting practices.

3.4 The control variables

Consistent with past studies such as Verdi [3], Biddle et al. [15] and Chen et al. [6] following control variables are applied for this study:

$MTBi_{,t}$ = we retain the Market ratio to book as the first measure of growth opportunities. It was measured by Denis [25] via the rapport between the market value and the accounting value of proper capitals (*Market to book ratio*).

$XCE_{i,t}$ = done by Biddle et al. [15] we will include the sales growth as an additional measure of growth opportunities. It was measured by the variation of the company turnover between the year t and t-1.

$SIZE_{i,t}$ = logarithm of the total accounting asset. The firm size equally represents an explicative factor of investment expenditure, since it can have an impact on the access to external capitals.

$DEBT_{i,t}$ = ratio total debt divided by the total asset. With reference to Myers [26] the financial shift can lead to under-investment caused by the over-indebtedness problem.

3.5 Model specification

To test our hypothesis on whether accounting information quality in year t affects investment decisions in year t + 1, we estimate a model that connects inefficiency of investment with the various measures of the quality of accounting information and a set of control variables. We will estimate a logistic regression in order to take counts the binary nature of our dependent variable, which predicts the likelihood that a firm will belong to one of the two groups.

This specification considers simultaneously, but separately, the probability of on and under-investment. The model to be tested is as follows:

$$\text{InvestIneff}_{i,t+1} = \beta_0 + \beta_1 \text{ ACCOUNQUA}_{i,t} + \sum \beta_j \text{ CONTR}_{i,t} + \varepsilon_{i,t+1} \quad (2)$$

Where,

InvestIneff$_{i,t+1}$: Inefficiency of investment represents over or under-investment which is a binary variable that takes the value of 1(0) if the residuals of the model (1) are positive (negative), 0(1) otherwise.

ACCOUNQUA$_{i,t}$: the measurement of the quality of financial information, as described below.

CONTR$_{i,t}$: different control variables, as defined previously.

4. Analysis of results

4.1 Descriptive analysis

Table 2 shows that Tunisian companies have a poor quality of their accounting results compared to other countries. Indeed, the average of their accruals is around (−0.0322), this level is lower than that detected by Francis et al. [18] in the American context (−0.0442). At the same time, it appears from **Table 1** that Tunisian companies exhibit an average level NCUACC of (0.008), revealing that they practice low conservative accounting compared to the average value (0.01) detected by Xu et al. [19] on the Chinese market.

4.2 Multivariate analysis

Before moving to multivariate analysis, it is first important to evaluate the multicollinearity by using Variance Inflation Factor (VIF), and the results show that VIF values are also relatively small and there is no multicollinerity issue among variables (**Table 3**).

Table 4 presents the multivariate results in panels testing the relationship between the quality of the accounting result and the probability of under and overinvestment. The Logit model applied to panel data can be estimated using a fixed or random effect. If the estimation of fixed effects is adopted, the constant is treated as an unobservable characteristic specific to firm i in correlation with the other variables in the model.

Since the dependent variable is binary and the specific effect must be eliminated, only companies that have changed status from one period to another are taken into account in the estimate, which implies the exclusion of observations which have not changed over time [22].

On the other hand, if the estimate adopted follows a random effect, the constant is considered as a non-observable random variable and not correlated with the other variables, which allows it to be integrated into the model [27]. So for these reasons,

Variable	Average	Gap Type	Minimum	Maximum
QACC	−0.032	0.352	−0,511	2.987
CONSV	0.008	0.073	−0.244	−1.205
MTB	1.886	2.217	−0.431	14.566
XCE	0.4178	0.755	−3.236	1.490
SIZE	16.566	0.998	16.258	22.314
DEBT	0.722	4.534	0.033	0.927

Table 2.
Descriptive statistics of variables.

	Tolerance	VIF
QACC	0.993	1.020
CONSV	0.991	1.009
MTB	0.981	1.007
XCE	0.972	1.022
SIZE	0.934	1.042
DEBT	0.993	1.004

Table 3.
Tolerance values and VIF without bias.

we opted to adopt the random effect model so as not to exclude observations that do not vary over time. Before interpreting our results, it is important to note that the prediction quality of our models is very strong (90%) and this, for the different specifications selected. The models also have very good overall significance, insofar as the likelihood ratio test (LR test) is significant at the 1% level.

It is possible to note in **Table 4** that the quality of the accruals increases the probability of underinvestment, while it has no significant impact on the probability of overinvestment. Our results can, however, be explained by the contextual specificities of the Tunisian market as well as the behavior of the Tunisian investor. Thus, we can first argue that the low quality of financial information displayed on average by Tunisian companies may explain our results.

In fact, according to the descriptive statistics, Tunisian firms display on average a lower quality of their accruals in comparison to American or Chinese firms. A priori, this level of quality does not seem sufficient enough in the eyes of the Tunisian investor, to constitute a means making it possible to attenuate the levels of asymmetry of information with regard to the firm, to reduce its cost of capital. Then, we can invoke the behavioral dimension of the Tunisian investor in the explanation of our results. Indeed, the latter may not have enough confidence in the accuracy of the financial information conveyed through the accounting results, so that it cannot reduce the levels of information asymmetry towards the firm. On the contrary, for the Tunisian investor, publicly disclosed financial information would increase the levels of information asymmetry, since the latter does not consider such information as a reliable source of information and would have more confidence in information collected on its own and through private channels. In fact, Loukil and Yousfi, (2012) [28] recently noted that the Tunisian investor has no confidence in the public information disclosed by companies and would have more confidence in private information. The authors specifically found that only private information reduces the levels of information asymmetry on the Tunisian stock market. As for accounting conservatism, it remains to have no effect on the probability of over and under investment. Such a result is contradictory to that found by Xu et al., (2012) [19] on the Chinese market, but can be explained by the low conservative accounting practiced by Tunisian companies in comparison to Chinese companies.

Furthermore, the results tell us that neither the quality of the accruals nor the accounting conservatism have a significant effect on overinvestment decisions. We can explain our results by the fact that the low level of accruals displayed on average by Tunisian firms, does not allocate to financial information to take on a governance role, to reduce the agency costs associated with the control of managers and to improve the selection process investment projects. In other words, the role of governance granted to accounting conservatism is conditioned by a set of control mechanisms, which are lacking in the Tunisian context.

	UNDINVEST		OVERINVET	
	QACC	CONSV	QACC	CONSV
ACCOUNQUL	0.341 (2.26)**	0.351 (0.33)	−0.915 (−0.29)	−1.419 (−0.41)
MTB	−0.656 (2.35)***	−0.735 (−2.34)***	0.735 (2.51)***	0.709 (2.53)**
XCE	−0.67 (−1.82)***	−0.654 (−1.75)*	0.789 (1.72)*	0.603 (1.57)*
SIZE	−5.489 (4.16)***	5.769 (4.31)***	−5.06 (−4.21)***	5.863 (−3.73)***
DEBT	0.332 (0.22)	0.321 (−0.12)	−0.009 (−0.03)	−0.614 (−0.41)
Constant	−91.123 (−2.86)***	−91.560 (−3.28)***	94.861 (4.00)***	93.312 (3.43)***
Log likelihood	−55.881	−53.635	−57.019	−54.361
LR test	25.73***	23.43***	23.37***	21.03***
Quality of Prediction	91.42%	90.24%	89.68%	91.45%
Specific Effect	Random	Random	Random	Random

**Coefficient significatif à 10%.*
***Coefficient significatif à 5%.*
****Coefficient significatif à 1%.*

Table 4.
Results of the estimation of the relationship between the quality of accounting results and the probability of under-investment and over-investment.

With regard to control variables, the results show that the MTB, Cash-Flow and liquid assets ratios increase (decrease) the probability of overinvestment (underinvestment). While the size of the firm decreases (increases) this probability. As for the debt ratio, this variable persists in having no significant effect on the probability of over and under investment. These different results are similar to those found by Biddle et al. [19].

5. Conclusion

This study focuses on the importance of the quality of accounting information quality on the investors' decisions making. Indeed, prior studies state that better financial information, contributes to making better investment decisions, as it reduces the level of information asymmetry. This finding can be explained by the fact that high-quality financial information facilitates the process of monitoring managers because, by reducing existing asymmetries, it inhibits opportunistic behavior, ensuring the rights of both shareholders and creditors. We are extending this current of research to the context of emerging market, particularly Tunisia, because of the importance of its challenges for businesses. In order to test our hypotheses, we have used two attributes of the quality of accounting results, namely: conditional conservatism and the quality of accruals.

The results of this study indicate that the quality of the accruals increases the likelihood of underinvestment. We attribute such a result to the lack of confidence that the Tunisian investor places in the accounting information vehicled through the accounting results. On the other hand, the results reveal that the quality of accruals has no effect in reducing the probability of overinvestment. The low level of accruals displayed on average by Tunisian firms could explain such a result.

Furthermore, we reveal that accounting conservatism has no significant effect and therefore cannot constitute a lever for action in improving the investment decisions of Tunisian companies. We can explain these results by the fact that the Tunisian firms practice a weak conservative accounting so that this level is not sufficient to allow this attribute of the result to assume an informational role allowing to attenuate the problems of asymmetry of information present between the firm and its capital providers.

Our findings suggest that countries, especially emerging markets, can benefit from improved financial information quality. Hence, these countries should take initiative to improve their market infrastructures such as adopting better accounting standards and encourage greater disclosure as well as enhancing the role of enforcement agencies. In addition to this, these findings could be of interest to the international organizations such as "World Bank" and "International Monetary Fund", whose missions are to aid countries with developing and transitional economy, and improve living conditions of their citizens. It is likely that more efficient investments will lead to better allocation of capital and resources and this may lead to higher social welfare. One limitation of this paper is that the relationship between accounting information quality and capital investment choice may differ with the different development stage of the industry. Maybe this issue is an important topic for future research.

Acknowledgements

This study was supported by the University of Sfax and the GFC research laboratory (Governance, Finance and Accounting), for which we gratefully acknowledge.

Conflict of interest

The author declares no conflict of interest.

Notes

1. There are two types of conservatism: Conditional and unconditional. Unconditional results in under-evaluation of the accounting value of net assets since the start of the economic activity of the company, because of the selection beforehand, of accounting conservatism methods (Givoly et al.; 2007). While under-evaluation of assets led by the conditional conservatism is attributable regarding the delay of accountability between latent losses and gains.

2. *QACC* = measure of the quality of accruals, as estimated according to the model of Dechow and Dichev (2002); *CONSV* = measure of conservatism by means of non-current Accruals; *MTB* = market to book ratio (market value of equity compared to accounting value); *XCE* = Rate of sales growth of year t, measured by the variation of the firm's turnover between the year t and t-1;

SIZE = logarithm of the total accounting assets of the firm; *DEBT* = total debts reported to the accounting value of the total asset.

3. The **Table 3** presents the results of estimates of panel logistic regression with random effects. The dependent variable is based on the unexplained level of investment. *UNDINSVT* = Firms classified among those which underinvest; *OVERINVST.*

Author details

Nouha Khoufi
University of Sfax(s), Tunisia

*Address all correspondence to: nouhakhoufi@yahoo.fr

References

[1] Bushman R, Smith, A. Financial accounting information and corporate governance. Journal of Accounting and Economics, 2003, 31: 237-333

[2] Houcine A. The effect of financial reporting quality on corporate investment efficiency: Evidence from the Tunisian stock market, Research in International Business and Finance, 2017, 42: 321-337.

[3] Verdi R. S. Financial reporting quality and investment efficiency, SSRN, eLibrary, 2006. DOI: http://papers.ssrn.com/sol3/papers.cfm?abstract_id=930922

[4] Zhai J,Wang, Y. Accounting information quality, governance efficiency and capital investment choice. China Journal of Accounting Research, 2016, 9 (4): 251-266

[5] Mirshekary S, Saudagaran SM. Perceptions and characteristics of financial statement users in developing countries: Evidence from Iran. Journal of International Accounting, Auditing and taxation, 2005, 15: 33-54

[6] Chen F, Hope O, Li Q et al. Financial reporting quality and investment efficiency of private firms in emerging markets. The Accounting Review, 2011, 86 (4): 1255-1288

[7] Li Q, Wang T. Financial reporting quality and corporate investment efficiency: Chinese experience. Nankai Business Review International, 2010, 1(2)*:* 197-213

[8] Healy P, Palepu K. Information Asymmetry, Corporate Disclosure, and the Capital Markets: a Review of the Empirical Disclosure Literature. Journal of Accounting and Economics, 2001, 31 (1-3): 405-440

[9] Jensen M. Agency Costs of Free Cash Flow, Corporate Finance, and Takeovers. American Economic Review, 1986, 76(2):323-329

[10] Easley D, O'hara M. Information and the Cost of Capital. *The Journal of Finance*, 2004, 59 (4):1553-1583

[11] Yee KK. Earning quality and the equity risk premium: A benchmark model. Contemporary Accounting Research, 2006, 23: 833-877

[12] Lambert R. Contracting theory and accounting. Journal of Accounting and Economics, 2001, 32 (1-3): 3-87

[13] Suijs J. On the value relevance of asymmetric financial reporting policies. Journal of Accounting Research, 2008, 46(5): 1297-1321

[14] Holmstrom B, Tirole J. Market liquidity and performance monitoring. Journal of Political Economy, 1993, 101: 678-709

[15] Biddle G, Hilary G, Verdi R. et al. How Does Financial Reporting Quality Improve Investment Efficiency? Journal of Accounting and Economics, 2009, 48: 112-131

[16] Dechow P, Ge W, Schrand C. et al. Understanding earnings quality: A review of the proxies, their determinants and their consequences. Journal of Accounting and Economics, 2010, *50*: 344-401

[17] Francis J, LaFond R, Olsson P.M, Schipper K. The market pricing of accruals quality. Journal of Accounting and Economics, 2005, 39 (2): 295-327

[18] Francis J, LaFond R, Olsson P.M et al. Cost of equity and earnings attributes. The Accounting Review, 2004, 79 (4): 67-1010

[19] Xu X, Wang X, Han N. Accounting Conservatism, Ultimate Ownership and

Investment Efficiency, China Finance. Review International, 2012, 2 (1): 53-77

[20] Dichev I, Dechow P. The quality of accruals and earnings: the role of accrual estimation errors. The Accounting Review, 2002, 77: 35-59

[21] McNichols M. Discussion of the Quality of Accruals and Earnings: the Role of Accrual Estimation Errors. *The Accounting Review,* 2002, 77:61-69

[22] Givoly D, Haynes C. The Changing Time-Series Properties of Earnings, Cash Flows and Accruals: Has Financial Accounting Become More Conservative? Journal of Accounting and Economics, 2000, 29 (3): 287-320

[23] Ahmed A, Duellman S. Evidence on the Role of Accounting Conservatism in Monitoring Managers' Investment Decisions. Accounting and Finance, 2011, 51(3): 609-633

[24] Kwon S, Yin J, Han J. et al. The Effect of Differential Accounting Conservatism on the Overvaluation of High-Tech relative to Low-Tech firms. Review of Quantitative Finance and Accounting, 2006, 27 (2): 143-173

[25] Denis D.J. Investment opportunities and the market reaction to equity offerings. Journal of Financial and Quantitative Analysis, 1994, 29(June): 159-77

[26] Myers S. and Majluf N. Corporate financing and investment decisions when firms have information that investors do not have. Journal of Financial Economics, 1984. *13*, 187-221.

[27] Cameron A, Trivedi P. K, and Zimmer D. M. Modelling the Differences in Counted Outcomes Using Bivariate Copula Models With Application to Mismeasured Counts. Econometrics Journal, 2004, 7: 566-584

[28] Loukil N, Yousfi O. Firm's information environment and stock liquidity: Evidence from Tunisian context. Journal of Accounting in Emerging Economies, 2012, 2 (1): 30-49

Section 3

Emerging New Trends in Finance

Chapter 6

Digital Transformation of World Finance

Darina Saxunova and Corlise Liesl Le Roux

Abstract

The boundary between the physical and a virtual world is not clearly visible nowadays, the 4.0 industry utilizes artificial intelligence, distributed ledger technology, quantum computing, advanced visualization and other advanced technologies. The surge of capital flows in financial technology is visible wherever we look. Classical businesses face a challenge to connect and create partners with the companies that are technology savvy because this may impact their future success. The strategy for digital business must be thought over very thoroughly since it represents the success threshold in contemporary digital environment. The classic banking system faces the threat or opportunity of an open banking system and banks are forced to be prepared to offer next generation services benefiting from third party channels. The short history on the banking industry including digital banking along, with fintech as a financial institution showing its power to compete sophistically, will shift the studied digital transformation phenomenon into a dilemma whether we indeed face a cashless society challenge, whether the governments should start to accelerate their decisions on Central Bank Digitalized Currency – CBDC or how far several countries already are to become a cashless society. At last, potential security, trust and fraud issues will close this chapter.

Keywords: digital transformation, digital strategy, modern banking, fintech, CBDC-Central Bank Digital Currency and Cashless Society

1. Introduction

Emerging digital technologies, such as artificial intelligence (AI), AI enabling machine learning, blockchain, internet-of things (IoT), robotics and automation have enormous effects on contemporary businesses that are evident everywhere presently. Expectations of digital-era customers have been growing, forcing enterprises to innovate and introduce new business models relying on digital technological progress. Consequences of zero activity may lead to losing millennial customers because of becoming obsolete in the digital competitive market. To stay competitive, traditional businesses requires to stop avoiding digital the transformation process, on the contrary they must seize opportunities, resulting in beginning a transition towards adoption of a model meeting digital economy expectations.

Emerging digital channels such as web, search, messaging, applications, digital media and others are a big challenge for the traditional banking industry. Especially old-fashioned banking models that do not satisfy the expectations of millennial customers. The evolving trends in the banking industry are dictated by new entrants, such as newly established digital banks and fintech companies deploying technologies at a radical speed and attracting customers with their innovative digital products. Therefore, it is inevitable for companies, not only in the banking industry, to adopt a radical shift from creating and managing financial products, to providing modern, financial management tools demanded by customers and tailoring the offerings to the clients' requirements.

Ten years ago, corporations such as Exxon, GE, Microsoft, Gazprom and Citigroup were included in the five most valuable firms of the S&P 500 Index, only Microsoft was a digital company at that time. In April, 2020 the S&P's top five most valuable firms were all digital corporations; Microsoft, Apple, Google, Amazon and Facebook. All five companies have collectively added $4.4 trillion in market cap gains since 2013 and are now the 5 largest stocks in the S&P 500. Moreover, Covid –19 pandemic situation strengthened in having a digital alternative almost for each area whether an industry sector, non-profitable enterprises or governmental departments or any other type of institutions, financial or non-financial ones. The area of finance in businesses, or financial payments by businesses, households, by consumers is evolving and therefore we focus on the transformation process in this area.

Looking forward to the future the obvious question is raised and discussed: What kind of money and payments will be needed to satisfy the needs of a steadily evolving digital economy? Classical banknotes — the Bank's most accessible form of money —is being used less frequently to make payments. At the same time, fintech companies have commenced to alter the market place introducing new forms of money and innovative revolutionary methods of payments.

2. Objectives and methodology

The research subject of the scientific study is the digital transformation in the area of the financing. The main goal of the submitted study is the transformation process of the finance in a global view. Transformation processes are built on the strategy for digital business since it represents the success threshold in contemporary digital environment. The classic banking system faces the threat or opportunity of an open banking system and banks are forced to be prepared to offer next generation services benefiting from third party channels. The partial objectives cover the journey of the banking industry development up to date when digital banking along with fintech as a financial institution compete sophistically to gain the clients to their side. The investigation of the recent growth fintech companies is analyzed, and based on the results, challenges of the digital transformation process are highlighted. Secondary data were used to analyze the development trend in the fintech companies and their growing significance. This transformation possibly will shift the studied phenomenon of digital transformation into the environment of cashless society challenges and proposal of their solutions. Classic research methods are used, critical analysis and synthesis, comparison and deduction and knowledge systemisation. The situation and conditions globally are analyzed leading the governments to make decisions on Central Bank Digitalized Currency – CBDC. The research sample of selected countries is assessed and pointed out whether selected investigated countries have achieved a certain degree towards becoming a cashless society. At last, potential security, trust and fraud issues will be examined resulting in emphasizing advantages and disadvantages virtual world.

3. Digital transformation

The need for business entities' digital transformation is a consequence of the progress in digital technologies, increasing digital competition and resulting digital customer behavior. Verhoef et al. [1] identify three stages of digital transformation: a) digitization -the action to convert analogue information into digital information [1], b) digitalization – the process of deployment of IT or digital technologies for efficient utilization in the business in order to alter existing business processes [2], and c) digital transformation (see systemization of it in **Table 1**).

The result of digitization is analogue information that is encoded into a digital format (0,1). Research also refers to digitization as a change of analogue to digital tasks [2]. Digitalization describes how IT or digital technologies can be used to alter existing business processes [3] and to adopt them for efficient business operations. New online or mobile communication channels, nowadays, enable all customers to connect easily and deal with enterprises immediately without leaving the company's office place. Companies save costs by digitalization, in addition, they operate augmented processes which satisfy customer's demands. Digital transformation is a radical implemented change throughout the company leading to the development of a new business model [4, 5]. Technological progress creates conditions for a company to compete in the digital environment e.g. by creating digital business models that even enhance the company' competitive advantage. In this context the competitive advantage is defined as a value creation process and its ability to be delivered to customers, followed by converting payments received to profits [6]. Digital transformation introduces a new business model by implementing a new business logic in order to create and capture the value [5, 7]. In a digitalized economy, businesses interact with users through many different types of online, or web-based interfaces, often called platforms.

For digital transformation, each of its phases requires digital resources. They are essential for transforming a classical company into a digital one. The influence on organizational structure is enormous, because the changes in the organizational structure must support introduction and adoption of digital changes. But digital technology itself does not guarantee the success unless digital growth strategies are implemented. The successful implementation and results are measured by metrics that also have been altered to adjustments needed in incorporating digital aspects [1].

3.1 Digital transformation strategy for banking industry

Updated business strategy into a digital environment, market position and human capital capabilities are the threshold for the financial institution's success. The emphasis on reshaping of the distribution models, improvement of the value propositions and development of an entirely digitized process for the client will lead

Digital transformation		
Digitization	**Digitalization**	**Digital transformation**
Analogue ⟹ digital task	Alteration of existing business process	New business model development
Digital resources required in each phase:		
Digital assets – storage of data, information and communication infrastructure	Digital agility Digital networking capabilities	Big data analytics capability
Goals that should be achieved:		
Cost savings Efficient use of existing resources	Cost savings & revenue increase Efficient production (via reengineering)	New cost-revenue model, reconfiguration of assets to develop new business models

Table 1.
Three phases of digital transformation elaborated by the author [1].

to augmenting growth and customer satisfaction, forming a steady foundation on which the financial institutions can build and carry on with their innovated activities. A digital transformation strategy should be built on four pillars. The priorities of the banking industry, not only for the banking institutions, but also for similar financial business entities are anchored into four pillars structure [8]. **Table 2** demonstrates briefly their individual characteristics, as follows:

1. The first pillar stresses the goal to digitize the operation process entirely. Digitization of the banking activities from the beginning to the end – all steps are digitized, such as prospecting, advice, sales, onboarding, transactions, and administration.

Benefits: customers' satisfaction, banking employees may be freed for performing more valuable tasks (e.g. sale of different products to the same customer called cross selling, building relationship with clients, or costs saving owing to streamlining a business process).

2. The second pillar encourages to benefit from valuable information being collected, quantitative and qualitative, what is enabled by digital technology. Information itself obtained in time is a tool for success. The manager efficiently converts the information for his company's new revenue opportunities due to Big data analytics - real time analytics, pursuing the spirit of "right insights delivery, to the right person, in real-time" . These analytics tools are used, as follows:

    a. Data analytics – for better clients' understanding, identifying opportunities,

    b. Advanced analytics - for better prediction of loan defaults or improving pricing.

    c. Granular cluster analysis - for comparing an individual consumer product mix to the average for that consumer type (benefit from this information in cross-selling and deepening relationships.)

    d. Data mining -for identifying better prospects and targeting new clients, better pricing (customizing pricing to client's preferences - a tool of increasing revenues and client's satisfaction as well.)

    e. Behavioral analytics -for identifying consumers who show signals of dissatisfaction and plan to change to another bank (a need to create an individual action plans to persuade and keep the client loyal).

3. Third pillar evaluates what possible models may be applied by business entities. There are three digital models proposed: a) as Business as Usual Plus, b) Digital as New Line of Business and c) Digital native. They represent a shift (from a to c) from a partially digital coverage model to the digital native model (newly created digital company, e.g. digital bank). Management should select and support the model with an increasing impact on their customers' experience. Top management should judge the situation and make a decision on investing into technology, new forecasts of potential revenues or possible costs savings should be prepared, so as schedules of activities from retraining older employees, hiring new employees. In addition, implementation of scheduled activities for adopting a needed change must be run. How this can be achieved? Monitoring what qualification must employees have and evaluate if they have capabilities to go through new courses or training, what skills need to be trained obligatorily, decision must be made whether older employees should be requalified or new staff should be employed.

1st Pillar	2nd Pillar	3rd Pillar	4th Pillar
Priorities to focus on under each pillar			
Re-innovation of the client's process	Leveraging of the power of data	Redefinition of the operating model	Building of a digital driven organization
Highlighting activities to be accomplished			
Adoptions:	Tools for success:	Digital models:	Digital business
New operating processes adoptions: • rapid digital onboarding • automated digital lending decisions	• Data analytics • Advanced analytics • Granular cluster analysis • Data mining • Behavioral Analytics	Evaluations and selection of the model best suitable for the company • Business as Usual • A new business Line • Digital native	Finalization of digital business entity Setting the priorities of the digital business

Table 2.
Digital transformation pillars.

Many financial institutions run all three models in different markets, regions and business lines. Hybrid experience links human interaction with digital and self-service functionality into a resulting financial solution offered by the banking industry, it is called a bionic network. It is expected to achieve a 15% increase in revenue, at the same time achieving up to 35% reduction in branch costs and 15% increase in customer satisfaction [8].

4. The fourth pillar supports all activities leading to the final step for the organization which is building a digital driven organization.

A digital driven company sets its priority with a clearly articulated strategy, financial resources available/or to be made available, human capital with specific knowledge, capabilities or digital/analytics skills, agile approach to working duties and an organizational culture with a risk affinity. The best example of a digitally driven organization is fintech companies.

The effective and business supporting legislation for the digital companies in effect is crucial for the smooth operation of any business in the digital environment.

4. Actors of the banking industry in the EU

Most National Banks of the members of the European Union, as e.g. the Slovak National Bank is in the Single Supervisory Mechanism (SSM)[1], which is the first pillar of the Banking Union in the EU. Under the SSM, the European Central Bank (ECB) is the central conservative supervisor of all financial institutions in the euro monetary area and non-euro EU countries that decide to join the SSM. The ECB directly supervises the largest banks, while the national banks act as national supervisors monitoring the other commercial banks in the country. The ECB and the national supervisors work closely together to check that banks comply with the EU banking rules and act immediately when problems arise.

The European Supervisory Authority (European Banking Authority) ('EBA'), established by Regulation (EU) No 1093/2010 f the European Parliament and of the Council (5), EBA's responsibilities comprise in developing and contributing to the consistent

[1] Council Regulation (EU) No 1024/2013 establishes the SSM as a system to supervise banks in the euro area and other participating EU countries.

application of the single rulebook applicable to all Member States and in enhancing convergence of supervisory practices throughout the European Union as a whole[2] [9, 10].

The central bank is an independent national authority in charge of monetary policy, bank regulation and providing financial services. Central banks issue regulations for their members i.e. commercial banks and supervise financial market participants. For instance, regulations are related to the reserves due to acid asset losses to strengthen the stability of the financial system, deposit protection etc. [11]. The National bank apart from other activities, also supervises financial institutions providing payments of a limited or unlimited scale, financial institutions of electronic money (of a smaller volume scale) Financial institutions whose average monthly payments performed (within last 12 months) have not gone over 3 million Euros, those ones operate without a banking license and these are financial institutions of limited financial payment services. Otherwise, over 3 mil Euros, a banking license is required in the EU so as in Slovakia and Czech Republic.

To get to the point of the contemporary situation in banking many relevant achievements have been marked throughout history, as significant landmarks that remind the commencing journey of a "quasi" banker from Babylonia functioning as a safe depositary up to present bankers almost invisible in the world of digital banking.

4.1 Traditional versus digital banking

The history of banking dates back to 2000 BC, when the wealthy people needed to deposit their money safely. The brief history highlighting and summarizing the milestones that significantly influenced development process of the banking industry is illustrated in the series of **Tables 3–5** starting with the function of depositaries until we gradually reach the level of digital banking of the 21st century.

4.1.1 Banking industry: beginnings up to 19th century

2000 BC	Origin of an authorized depositary, predecessors of the banking in Babylon empire, valuables deposited with a trustworthy person, depositary -paid service Greek churches – due to deposit protection, safe deposits, vaults - special rooms in the churches at the beginning free service, only gifts donated to the priests, later paid service, analogy with a contemporary, strong room in the banks.
700 BC	Origin of currency, first coins, in 1600 BC, the precious metals used for payment, that many years later led to coins rise, but bank notes used first time in China 700 AD.
400 BC	Origin of the bankers, evolved from depositaries
1200 AD	The first bank in 1157 in Venetian bank in Italy
1400 AD	The boom of the banks - Florence, Milan, Venezia, Siena (here still exists the oldest functioning bank of the world)
1600 AD	17th century is characterized by the modern banking rise, due to the state regulation needed, central banks arose. Origin of the Central bank-1668 AD Sveriges Riksbank
1872 AD	The first cashless electronic transfer of money using telegraphic network by Western Union

Table 3.
History of banking beginnings - up to 19th century.

[2] Regulation (EU) No 1022/2013 aligns the existing legislation on the establishment of the EBA to the modified framework for banking supervision.

1950 AD	Mainframe computer - the first hall computers for processing information and numerous transactions
1958 AD	First credit card – Bank of America (later Visa) (with magnetic strip, verified by a cardholder's signature)
1967 AD	ATM machine, the first cash machine in London, Barclays Bank, with first time used PIN for verification
1968 AD	Clearing system, in Great Britain, first time automated clearing system BACS (Banker's automated clearing services) needed due to the use of cheques and promissory notes since 18th century
1980 AD	The first telephone banking, by the bank Girobank in Great Britain
1984 AD	The first online shopping in Tesco, using the videotext through television, in Great Britain
1984 AD	The first debit card
1994 AD	The first chip and PIN – technology used in debit and credit cards in order to process the payment or to withdraw cash from ATM, a cardholder must authorize the transaction by entering personal identification. EMV -technological standard for smart payment cards, introduced in Europe, a payment method (Europay, Mastercard and Visa created this standard)

Table 4.
History of banking – 20th century.

4.1.2 Banking: 20th century

The development in the sector of financial technologies is not entirely new, but it definitely effected the financial institutions and commercial banks. It is worth focusing on the era beginning in 1950s and 1960s when the financial industry began its transition from an analogue to a digital industry [12]. The important milestones such as launching of online banking, latest IT developments in internal system of banks and spreading of World Wide Web and the Internet usage led to revolutionary innovations, the most relevant are summarized in the **Table 5**.

4.1.3 Banking: 21st century

Technology progress opened opportunities towards new ways of managing finance, or providing payments among businesses. Bloomberg, a media that delivers business and market news and data and analysis, invented a software called Bloomberg Terminal aimed at professionals for a use in the financial services sector by being able to summon real-time market data. The company is considered as one of the first Fintech companies [12].

4.1.4 Online banking versus digital banking

The global banking arena is going through huge alterations. Digital technology is bringing the progress that has an incredible impact on the way how money is managed. Digital-only alternatives compete with traditional banking. Digital banking is the digitization (or a shift into an online space) of all the traditional banking activities and programs services that were historically only available to customers when physically inside of a bank's branch (**Table 6**).

This includes activities: a) money deposits, withdrawals, and transfers; b) checking/saving account management; c) applying for financial products; d) loan management; e) bill pay and f) account services.

Traditional banks are showing initiative in transforming their operations into digital banking services to attract a millennial generation customer with modern, digital offerings. BNP Paribas (France), JP Morgan Chase (USA), Santander (Spain), HSBC, Barclays (UK), Bank of America (USA), UniCredit (Italy),

	History of digital banking
1993	Temenos AG is founded, a banking software systems provider to retail, corporate, universal, private, Islamic, microfinance, community banks.
1994	Online banking -first time introduced by Stanford Federal Credit Union via their website Microsoft offers integrated online banking via its application Microsoft Money personal finance, 100,000 households in the USA started to use it.
1997	Tangerine' start - becoming the first digital-only bank in Canada.
1998	First Internet Bank starts, becoming the first digital-only bank in the U.S.
2000	First client-side account aggregation invented by eWise in Europe in 2000. eEWise is considered as the origin of FinTech companies, a pioneer of Financial Data Aggregation and Money Management APls, a market leader of Personal Money Management solutions that are based on the patent: personal Data Vault technology. In the USA similar services were introduced by the Yoodle (an innovative software development company providing CMS, customs mobile application and web application services in the USA.
2002	Avoka was founded to help banks and financial institutions in their digital transformations.
2007	The first contactless card introduced in Europe, in 2011 the bank Barclays launched the contactless card for public.
2007	The launch of the iPhone begins shifting digital banking from desktop computers to smartphones. Kony, Inc. is founded to help banks transform their banking operations with a cloud-based mobility, omnichannel and internet-of-things systems and services software platform.
2011	The first payment by the phone launched by Google via application Google Wallet, today known as Google Pay Send.
2016	Millennials succeed in shifting digital banking preferences, signaling to banks that they must move all services online.
2018	Temenos acquires Avoka, the leading provider of digital customer onboarding solutions for financial institutions.
2019	Temenos launches Temenos Infinity, a breakthrough digital front office product with the most advanced cloud-native, cloud-agnostic, API first technology and design led thinking. Temenos acquires Kony, the leading provider of mobile banking apps that support conversational interfaces, artificial intelligence, augmented reality and wearable technologies. According to Temenos' 2019 State of Digital Banking Report, 65% of digitally active large banks reach the 'Digital Promised Land'.

Table 5.
History of banking – 21st century.

Online banking is made with fiat money	**Digital banking** is made with virtual money
Internet banking/virtual banking/e-banking primarily focuses on	Focuses on
• Remote deposits, • Money transfers, • Bill pay • Basic online management of accounts	Digitizing the "core" aspects of banking: every program and activity undertaken by financial institutions and their customers

Table 6.
Differences between online and digital banking.

RBS Group (Scotland), DBS Bank (best digital bank in the world - Singapore), Juniper (BBVA Bank-Spain) are among the top 10 digital banks that succeeded the transformation process [13].

4.1.5 Fintech companies

Digitalization is indeed a breakthrough, also in the world of finance affecting the functioning of all financial services and the way banks provide their services. Most of the changes were a natural result of internal needs of the banks in order to provide higher quality services to customers. The banks themselves took an initiative of innovating their services at the end of the 20th century and beginning of the 21st century. Global economic results were growing, companies invested into modernisation, as many opportunities arose for new players to compete for a market share due to increasing customers' demand. Bankers started placing their goals before the goals of satisfying their clients 'needs, not always playing fair that also led to entrance of new competitors. This boom was ceased by the financial crisis, many banks bankrupted, it many cases banks revealed malpractices of the management, corruption and the companies lost the trust towards their banking institutions. Money being as scarce resource, in some way forced companies to hide cash flows or looking for alternatives offering payments much cheaper and even more efficiently. These also were reasons leading to fintech companies rise.

Fintech as "technologically enabled innovation in financial services that could result in new business models, applications, processes or products with an associated material effect on financial markets and institutions and the provision of financial services" [14]. Some fintech companies began as start-up companies, some of them are already well-established in the global market, representing a sophisticated competitor in the market place. Online shopping developed because of the possibility to make/receive payments, via internet enabled by companies such as PayPal [15]. The need for the capital might be solved by raising the capital through a crowd funding or peer-to-peer lending. **Figure 1** shows the fintech adoption of 6 selected countries according to E&Y survey since 2015.

E&Y survey shows very successful results for FinTech industry that has evolved much faster than the official prediction was. FinTech challengers at present have transformed into professionally managed companies with operating worldwide with a variety of products offered globally. Emerging market countries are world leaders, both China and India achieved the adoption rate of 87%, followed closely by Russia and South Africa, both with 82% adoption. Results for developed countries are best for the Netherlands, the UK and Ireland [16].

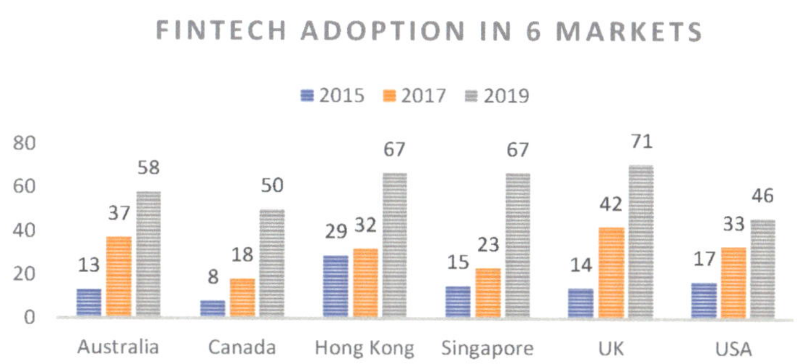

Figure 1.
FinTech increase within 5 years in selected countries.

Challengers and incumbents now compete and they also face a new competitive threat from outside the financial industry. Non-financial services enterprises e.g. retailers, technology platforms, and automakers are evolving their own technology-enabled financial services offerings. These businesses make use of old, existing relationships with customers to offer products enlarged by complementary service offer e.g. insurance and lending, taken by old customers before from the financial providers.

68% of consumers would consider a financial product offered by a non-financial services company. They have trust to retailers (45%), telecommunication firms (44%) as service providers. They prefer using money and making payment using FinTech services e.g. digital-only banking and multi-merchant eWallets [16].

Across the five markets China reaches the highest FinTech adoption rate at 61%. The adoption rate globally is 25%.

SMEs select FinTech globally for offering: a) a range of services/product functionality and features - 66%; b) availability 24 hours a day, 7 days a week - 55%; c) ease in setting up, configuring and using the service 53%, d) more attractive rates/fees - 39%; e) compatibility with daily operations and infrastructure - 38% and f) trust in the providers' team and their reputation - 31% [16] (**Table 7**).

The next paragraph illustrates examples of selected digital banks [17]:

a. Neat (Honk Kong, 2015)- it offers corporate Master cards with competitive exchange rates, budget management software and recording of transactions for expensing purposes. The Neat business account is principally aimed at startups and SMEs, as an alternative to establishment of national business banking options.

b. Doconomy – (Stockholm, Sweden, 2018) - Eco mobile banking service. Doconomy is aimed at users' understanding the environmental impact of their purchasing decisions. Its first solution DO - the world's first credit card enabling users to track their carbon impact and compensate by investing in sustainable, positive impact projects.

c. Nubank, leading fintech in Latin America (Sao Paolo, 2014) launched first fee-free product credit card.

d. Number 26 -N26 – a German digital bank (2013) – one of the cutting edge-digital banks, it offers its clients a current online account, with an intuitive application, money management solutions and fee-free foreign currency withdrawals.

e. Up - Banking (Melbourne, Australia, 2017), a product of collaboration between banks Ferocia and Bendigo Bank. It offers a standard card and current account service; it provides a financial insight – analysis of spending for its users.

f. Tangerine Bank – a subsidiary of Scotia Bank (Canada, 2012) offers more specialized products (backed by a larger traditional bank) -a money back credit

SME globally used FinTech services in 2019 (in last 6 months)				
China	**USA**	**UK**	**South Africa**	**Mexico**
61%	23%	18%	16%	11%

Table 7.
SME FinTech adoption rate.

card, low-fee investing, business accounts, GICs, mortgages, tax-free savings accounts etc.

g. Three UK banks: Starlink Bank (2014), a provider of business banking services, digital checking account; Revolut – challenger banking (2018), online service enables its users to convert money into 24 currencies, up to 5000 GBP a month, money management tools and engages in cryptocurrency trading and Monzo – UK challenger bank with free international payments, money management advice [17].

4.2 Business Payments and Legislation for the EU Banking Industry

The past decade is marked by accepted regulations introduced for banking payment services. E-money licenses (regulated under the second Electronic Money Directive 2009 — 2EMD) are granted to eMoney issuers for the issuance of eMoney.

The Payment Services Directive (PSD) approved in 2007 and effective for use in 2009, permitted payment institutions (PIs) to enter payment services markets. PIs are non-bank business entities that execute payment services of a lower risk. PSD was proposed to guarantee the equal conditions for payment services throughout the Europe, fast service, protecting the customer and a variety of services.

The PSD2 followed the first Payment Services Directive. PSD2 enables two new financial service providers to enter the market:

- Payment initiation service provider (PISP): is able to develop a software bridge between a payee (e.g., a merchant) and payer (i.e., consumer) in order to verify availability of the funds needed for a transaction at payer's account and to initiate a payment, money is transferred from the payer's account to the payee's one.

- Account information service provider (AISP): is able to aggregate online information on one or more payment accounts for a user, accessed via online interfaces of the account servicing payment service providers (i.e., banks).

Introduced changes have had a significant impact on banks and other payment service providers. A new third-party entity enters as a payment provider between the bank and a customer. Banks have to allow the third parties to integrate with their online banking platforms and banks have to provide Third Party Payment Service Providers access to bank's customer account's information, with the consent of the customer. The problem may be trust that is built with time and providing reliable and high-quality service. Banks used to represent a trustworthy business entity [16].

The objective of the EU is to ensure the common payment area, where the fees and terms of payments are equal for citizens and business entities across the EU. Electronic payments, or cash collections, debit/credit card payments, smart phones and online payments. Directives created a base for SEPA payments (Single Euro Payments Area) - fast payments denominated in EURO within EU member states.

5. Digital currency – Fiat currency versus virtual currency

Nowadays, the use of electronic money is growing in popularity, electronic money is a broad term for any money, currency or asset lacking physical substance – it may include representations of a sovereign currency or claims on a real-world commodities [18]. Digital and virtual currencies can either be centralized or decentralized. A centralized currency is any currency that is issued and maintained by a central group or organization, while decentralized currencies are not. For instance, Bitcoin is fully decentralized and its most unique feature is no central authority guaranteeing it or having control over it, as central banks are for conventional currencies [19, 20]. Many investors considered Bitcoin as a speculative bubble rather than a proper currency system [20, 21]. Nowadays, the value of a currency reflects the best judgment about the monetary policy and the "health" of its economy [22].

Virtual currency is distinguished from fiat currency (real money or national currency), i.e. the coin and paper money of a country that is designated as its legal tender. However, it is distinct also from e-money (digital representation of fiat currency).

Digital currency is digital representation of either virtual currency (non-fiat) or e-money (fiat) and it is often interchangeably used with the term "virtual currency". Cryptocurrency refers to a math-based, decentralized convertible virtual currency that is protected by cryptography [23].

Central bank digital currency (CBDC, also called digital fiat currency, digital base money) is the digital form of fiat money (a currency established as money by government regulation and monetary authority or law).

The Bank of England was the first institution to initiate a global discussion on the prospects for the introduction of a CBDC. The central bank of Sweden, Riksbank, is, however, the closest to consider its implementation and started testing technical solutions for its e-krona in 2020 (**Table 8**).

The European Central Bank (ECB) assumes so far conservative and wait-and-see attitude towards CBDC.

The main risk is linked with the fear of introducing a CBDC would precipitate potential bank runs and thus make banks' funding position weaker.

5.1 Central Bank Digital Currency (CBDC)

Bank of England's highlights primarily two relevant models for organizing a CBDC system, so does the Central Bank of Norway [25, 26]:

- **an account-based model**, both value storage and transaction processing are centralized. Money is held in accounts and moves from one account to another within the system;

Digital currency is a digital representation either of			
	Virtual currency (VC)		
Fiat currency (money) Real money/national currency, e-money	**Central Bank Digital currency** (CBDC)		**Non-fiat currency** (money)
Centralized			**Decentralized**
versus **Fiat money - Paper bank notes, coins " - Legal tender"** Country's officially used currency	**E-gold**	**CB issued cryptocurrency** Sovereign "SOV" "Petro" (CBCC)	**Cryptocurrency** **Math-based convertible VC - Bitcoin**

Table 8.
Digital currency [24].

- **a value-based model**, value storage and processing are decentralized. Money is stored locally in a payment instrument, typically a card or smartphone application. Transfers take place directly between parties, without the intermediation of a central third party.

Hybrid variants that combine elements of both primary models are also possible. An example is a model where the money is stored locally, but transactions need to be verified by a third party with a register of all transactions and holdings.

A third model, which can also be considered a hybrid variant, is based on distributed ledger technology (DLT).

Criteria that must be met by a CBDC: three basic functions of money: a) a means of payment that can be used to transfer value between parties, for example in connection with the purchase of a good or service, b) a practical storage of value, and c) a unit of accounting facilitating a value comparison of different goods and services [22].

CBDC can enable a wider access to central bank money, and this would open new opportunities for payments and the way central banks maintain monetary and financial stability. The newly created financial ecosystem could include the following participants: payment providers, mainly payment service providers and electronic money institutions and other non-bank financial institutions.

Although the term CBDC includes the words 'digital currency', CBDC would be something fundamentally different from 'cryptocurrencies' (or 'crypto-assets'), such as Bitcoin. Many crypto-assets are privately issued and not backed by any central party. They are not considered a currency or money because they do not meet all three criteria, mentioned above. They are too volatile to be a reliable storage of value, they are not widely accepted as a means of exchange, and they are not used as a unit of account It is stressed that despite the surge in interest in cryptocurrencies, they are no substitute for cash or payment cards, since cryptocurrencies such as Bitcoin are failing as a form of money and have shown clear signs of being a financial bubble, but their technology could improve the financial system in future [27].

5.1.1 Wholesale and retail CBDC projects

Two main types of CBDC, wholesale and retail sale CBDC are at focus. **Wholesale CBDC** has been the major area of focus, with several central banks around the world launching initiatives as part of an effort to modernize their payments systems.

Wholesale CBDCs are restricted-access digital tokens for wholesale settlements such as interbank payments or securities settlement and are meant to be used by commercial banks, clearing institutions or any other entity that traditionally have had access to central bank reserves. Experiments in this field generally focus on replacing current technologies to realize efficiency gains [28].

Retailsale CBDCs - in Sweden, for example, Riksbank began testing its e-krona digital currency meant for retail use in February 2020. If the e-krona comes into circulation, it would be used to simulate everyday banking activities such as payments, as well as deposits and withdrawals from a digital wallet [29, 30].

In China, the country's central bank has been working on a retail CBDC that would act as an alternative to cash and coins for retail use. In March 2020, the People's Bank of China (PBoC) started trialing the state-run digital currency in several cities including Shenzhen, Suzhou, and Chengdu, as well as a new area south of Beijing, Xiong'an, and areas that will host some of the events for the 2022 Beijing Winter Olympics [31].

A survey among 66 central banks by the BIS found that a large number of central banks around the world are actively developing retail CBDCs. More than 80% of them are currently working on a CBDC project, whether wholesale or retail [31].

5.2 CBDC efforts worldwide

5.2.1 China

China has already been among the global leaders in the transition from a cash to a cashless economy powered by blockchain technology. China's new system is built on digital wallets, QR codes, and utilizing own big tech firms, such as Alipay operating through Alibaba (China's version of Amazon) and WeChat Pay operating via Tencent (China's version of Face-book) [32]. China's system largely disintermediates banks from payment transactions robbing banks of an important and long-standing source of revenue. It creates an alternative payment ecosystem with different incentives between merchants, consumers, and payment system providers.

The PBoC confirmed China's CBDC continuation in pursuing its original plan. As the coronavirus epidemic has caused to speed up global digitization, people are all concerned about the PBoC's issuance and circulation of digital currency, the specific progress is expected with worries [31]. Nowadays, more than 95% of daily micropayments are realized through mobile payments or internet payments.

The Chinese authorities have made an effort to reduce the use of paper money in the economy in a desperate attempt to control the spread of Coronavirus. Authorities still do not have an answer about the speed of the corona spreading among people. In order to control the spread of the deadly coronavirus, the Chinese Central Bank recently announced removal of paper money out of circulation. The People's Bank revealed the plan of disinfecting notes from the economy. The central bank further gave instructions to return disinfected notes back to circulation after holding them minimum one-two weeks depending on a riskiness of region locality. The Bank recommended used notes originating from Hospitals, Wet markets and public transportation to be incinerated [31].

There are numerous established cashless digital payment solutions already established in China. Platforms such as Alipay and WeChat allow users to shop all over the country from the comfort of their smartphones or computers [32]. The bottom line remains paper money as a medium that can spread multitude of human diseases in the most blistering possible way making it a dangerous medium of exchange between humans.

5.2.2 Sweden – the Riksbank's e-krona pilot

The recent sharp decrease in the use of cash in Sweden has made it more difficult to use cash in certain parts of Swedish society. The Riksbank sees potential problems with the marginalization of cash and has therefore initiated a pilot project to develop a proposal for a technical solution for a central bank digital currency, an e-krona that can work as a complement to cash, based on Distributed Ledger Technology (DLT).

Raisons d'être for e-krona - there is no digital state money available to the general public, however, and digital money and payment methods that are available are provided by private market players. The digital money is, therefore, a claim on a private player in contrast to cash which is a claim on the state. An e-krona would offer the general public continuation of accessing the central bank money but in digital form., as it was possible with classic cash.

To be able to, at this stage, test how an e-krona might look and function, the Riksbank is running a pilot project with Accenture to construct a technical platform for the e-krona. E-kronor shall be available 24/7/365 and payments shall be instant. The pilot project will also examine the possibility of building a technology in which the e-krona can be used offline. Accenture's assignment in the e-krona pilot project will run until February 2021.

DLT is a technology that allows to keep databases operated by independent parties synchronized. The network ensures that only valid transactions are recorded. Each participant in the DLT network runs one or more nodes. In the e-krona network, the nodes store e-kronor and receive, validate and forward e-krona transactions.

The test environment will be structured in two tiers. In the first tier, the Riksbank will issue e-kronor to participants in an e-krona network, such as banks. In the second tier, participants will distribute e-kronor to end-users. Similar to today's cash, only the Riksbank will be able to issue and redeem e-kronor.

Participants in the e-krona network distribute e-kronor to end-users and end users can then use various payment methods for e-krona. The consumer or merchant controls their e-kronor with a digital wallet installed as an application, for example, in mobile phone or in the merchant's cash register (terminal). In addition to a mobile application, the pilot will also develop a digital wallet for use in smartwatches and cards. In the future, digital wallets could be created for additional device types and integrated with a payment service provider's mobile application [29, 30].

To be able to use e-kronor for payments, the digital wallet must first be activated at a participant connected to the e-krona network. After activation, the user can, for example, receive e-kronor as payment from another user, pay a retailer with e-kronor, make transfers from their bank account to the digital wallet (and vice versa), and check their e-krona balance.

The e-krona network is private and only the Riksbank can approve and add new participants to the network. All transactions in the e-krona network occur separately from existing payment networks [29, 30].

5.2.3 Bank of Japan and CBDC

The Bank of Japan reported the examination of the concept and role of digital currencies if placed in the general monetary system. The report "Digital Innovation, Data Revolution and CBDC," explains classification of CBDCs into possible two categories: one used by the common public instead of fiat money; and large-value settlements, that are based on the Bank of Japan deposits and adopt modern technologies like blockchain [33].

5.2.4 Norwegian Central Bank developing plans to move to cashless society

The Central Bank of Norway, Norges Bank, also added the study on Central Bank Digital Currencies (CBDCs) dealing with the necessity for forming Norway's cryptocurrency and evaluates this proposition as the one that should have a positive impact on the ability of banks and other financial institutions in offering loans.

The increasing urgency of tackling this matter is a discovery that the contingency of issuance of CBDCs has become more significant because of technological advances and cash usage reduction. Momentarily, Norges Bank has only completed the initial stage of analyzing the need to form a digital currency. There is a plan of continuation if a particular matter requires it [26].

5.2.5 USA - digital dollar

A digital dollar issued by the Fed would enhance scope, access, diversification and resilience in dollar payments and support retail, wholesale and international payment use-cases:

- **Retail payments** on-line cannot be conducted in central bank money. Banknotes remain important in particular to make small payments, although on average physical cash is in decline as a percentage of broader monetary aggregates. A digital dollar would offer a new choice for digital transactions, offer instantaneous peer-to-peer payments, and provide diversification of payment rails, in particular, to grant greater autonomy, especially in times of heightened financial distress. A digital dollar could be distributed to the end-user through commercial banks and trusted payment intermediaries and offer additional mechanisms to ensure and facilitate financial inclusion.

- **Wholesale payments** rely on national payment systems and are usually conducted via inter-bank clearance using central bank money to settle securities and other large-value payments. The important role of central bank money to conduct large value payment transactions implies that access to central bank money has important distributive effects. A digital dollar would offer more diversified access to large-value payments and support the emergence of digital financial market infrastructures [34].

- International payments cannot be conducted digitally in U.S. dollars. A digital dollar would allow establishing more direct monetary relations, reduce risks, address persistent deficiencies of the existing correspondent banking model, enhance competition in international payments and advance financial market integration. The use of a digital dollar in cross-border and offshore transactions would allow making digital payments in central bank money for remittances and large-value payments, including the possibility to conduct offshore securities settlement [34].

A Central Bank Digital Currency (CBDC) would be an electronic form of central bank money that could be used by households and businesses to make payments and store value.

5.3 "De-cashing" - moving to cashless society?

European banks are keen to minimize the rotation of cash and more often propose to shift to digital banking usage. Alike, Norges Bank confirmed continuation of cash issuance as long as there is a demand for it. In the case of cash usage declining, a CBDC can be an alternative to deposit money. The primary purpose of a CBDC is to ensure confidence in money and the monetary system. E-money and crypto-assets are hardly viable alternatives in the near and medium-term.

In addition, the Bank of France also perform out multiple trials to check the integration of a CBDC for cross-bank transaction settlements and encourages all the interested and qualified candidates from the EU to submit their applications [35]. Having followed France's lead, the Bank of Korea has launched a pilot project to test a digital won that will last for 20 months. The system will first be used for micro-payments, and if the tests are successful, it might be fully deployed in late 2021. They are responsible to act and rely on the results of testing before making a decision for the end-users.

A consortium of powerful interests that include Visa and Mastercard, the International Monetary Fund, billionaire Bill Gates and the US Treasury have commenced the process of lobbying for cash to be abolished worldwide and replaced with digital-only currencies. This is still not entirely supported, because people care a lot about their right to use cash. Because of this resistance of the population the consortium may only use indirect measures, like regulations for banks that make cash more inconvenient and expensive for them, a cost, which they pass on to customers. Is it ethical? Many may raise this question, but power what consortium

DOI: http://dx.doi.org/10.5772/intechopen.93987

of the well-off companies have is abused by them for their own benefits. There has even been a study elaborated by the IMF that recommends such indirect measures to get around the resistance of the cash-oriented population [36, 37]. There are arguments where digital payments are safer, maybe much more difficult to be abused by corrupted companies or politicians, therefore the decision should be made with a caution, because people cannot be forced to use digital cash if they do not have a trust towards it. It may have serious psychological consequences on this vulnerable part of population.

Switzerland as the leader in numerous economic sectors, as a driver of innovation, it possesses characteristics that make it a suitable candidate for further development of Blockchain. The Swiss Confederation should aim to become the central global contact for Blockchain opinion leaders, start-ups and related firms at the cutting edge of Blockchain innovations [38].

Czech Republic also sees attractiveness of blockchain which would enable "central bank digital currency bypass the financial sector and issue money to end-users directly through the balance sheet of the central bank. Similarly to cash, digital money would constitute a liability of the central bank. Instead of being the bank of banks, the central bank would become the "bank of the people" or "for the people". Each household or business entity might hold an account at the central bank directly, not using the services of the intermediary [39].

5.3.1 Better Than Cash Alliance BTCA

Based at the United Nations, the Better Than Cash Alliance is a partnership of governments, companies and international organizations that accelerate the transition from cash to digital payments to advance the Sustainable Development Goals. The Alliance has 75 members (national governments from Africa, Asia-Pacific and Latin America, global brands across the agriculture, garment and fast-moving consumer good sectors, UN agencies and humanitarian NGOs) which are committed to digitizing payments to boost efficiency, transparency, women's economic participation and financial inclusion, helping build economies that are digital and inclusive [40].

Main reasons to support digital money are as follows:

- Cost savings through increased efficiency and speed
- Transparency and security by increasing accountability and tracking, reducing corruption and theft as a result
- Financial inclusion by advancing access to a range of financial services, including savings accounts and insurance products
- Women's economic empowerment by giving women more control over their financial lives and improving economic opportunities
- Inclusive growth through building the institutions that form the bedrock of an economy and the cumulative effect of cost savings, increased transparency, financial inclusion, and greater women's economic empowerment [40].

5.3.2 EU situation

Digitisation is transforming the European financial system and the provision of financial services to Europe's businesses and citizens. "In monitoring the evolution and uses of technology, the ECB respects technological neutrality. We do not serve technology – technology serves us. We will only introduce a digital currency if we become firmly convinced that it is both necessary and proportionate to fulfil our tasks in ensuring the stability of our currency. If and when the time comes, we want to be ready – and we will be ready" [41].

The financial ecosystem is continuously evolving, with technologies such as Blockchain, Artificial Intelligence and the Internet of Things moving from the experimental phase, to pilot testing and the deployment stage. Indeed, digitisation of the financial sector can only be expected to accelerate because of the Coronavirus pandemic. At the same time, as people access to their bank accounts and other financial services remotely, and as financial sector employees work remotely, the digital operational resilience of the financial sector has become more important than ever. Digital finance can contribute to tackling the Coronavirus crisis and its consequences for citizens, businesses, and the economy at large in some ways. For several years, the European Union have been embracing digitisation and innovation in the financial sector [42, 43].

5.3.3 CBDC fighting Covid-19 plague

One way of ceasing Coronavirus to be spreading is to reduce the use of cash (paper money) in the economy. The COVID-19 pandemic might push the development of CBDC. The current situation challenges the momentum of a try and implementation of these initiatives. As coronavirus is raging in the entire world and countries are in a strict lockdown, the society looks for a digital alternative to traditional cash payments.

As coinidol.com, a world blockchain news outlet has reported that many countries including China and Hungary are looking to minimize cash use. It might even lead to an overall decrease in cash circulation. In spite of debates on Central Bank Digital Currencies (CBDC) have been ongoing for a long time, we are witnessing the attempts and efforts of practical implementation also under these coronavirus pandemic times.

The coronavirus crisis is forcing the EU to redraw its digital strategy and important legislation is now likely to be delayed, according to several people involved in the process. Working remotely is also causing considerable strain on the EU's IT system [44]. To make sure the compliance requirements are met, banks will need the digital support of Fintech firms more than ever.

6. Digital transformation challenges

Each industry, but especially financial and banking industry are exposed to enormous progress in the technology, digitisation, social media and mobility that may be used to benefit the people and companies. As there are steps of governments introducing and preparing to move ahead from cash to cashless economy, the success of the digital transformation can be influenced by several factors, for instance:

a. The level of internet in the countries, its speed and price availability for companies, institutions and population.

b. Cybercrime, risk of piracy versus security issues

The digital media industry has not been able to fully monetize possible losses due to the cybercrime and piracy. Weak IP regulations and ineffective enforcement has discouraged players to produce original content and IP.

As the digital channel in financial services continues to evolve, cyber security has become a business risk, rather than simply a technical risk. Security breaches can damage reputations and destroy trust, thereby jeopardizing the investments made in digital solutions. Hacking and losses cause by it discourage supporting investment into absolute work digitalisation.

c. Trust towards highly digital products, fear of losing identity, fear of being monitored by SOMEBODY, loss of control.

d. Online payments and their understanding: One of the primary forces impeding the growth of subscription and pay-per-view revenue models are the hassles that the consumer faces while making payments on digital platforms, even when they are willing to pay. This is on account of low credit card penetration, fear of using net banking and credit cards online due to security threats and the lack of experience of making transaction online.

e. Speed of introducing the knowledge and training of required skills into each level of education.

f. Social impact on people, isolation leading to individualism.

g. Potential collapse of the system, losses made by this

7. Conclusion

Digital currencies and the emergence of 'Big Tech' are simply the most visible examples of a fundamental transformation. It is a change that is bringing innovation and making many European cities hubs of a demonstrating new FinTech culture. Success of a digital business comprises in a elaborating and implementing digital strategy thoroughly.

The EU has been at the forefront of enabling innovative Fintech solutions, in particular in the payments sector. EU legislation in this area is a key to promoting a transparent, innovative and competitive payments market in the EU. The Electronic Money Directive (EMD) and the first Payment Services Directive (PSD) introduced a licensing regime that allows the issuance of electronic money and the provision of payment services by non-bank financial institutions. This enables the rise of several FinTechs operating in the payments sphere; a trend that has accelerated via new business models based on data sharing.

The EU's 2018 Fintech Action Plan has also supported these developments, and its implementation has recently been concluded with a look to the future by the Expert Group on Regulatory Obstacles to Financial Innovation [45].

In contrast to crypto-assets, a central bank digital currency would be centralized, and so a blockchain or other distributed ledger would not be required (or useful).

More research is required in confirming or refutating possible pros and cons arguments to eliminate subjective opinions (**Table 9**).

New technology in particular has both encouraged and enabled utilizing it in the real life, especially in the financial sector and in turn the market with customers in it, been fuelled by a huge deluge of new providers and products, all eager to enter the payments space.

Cash is still a leader for many countries, therefore to achieve 100% cashless society is not feasible for near future, but the country, government, companies and population must be prepared to face this challenge.

Pros	Cons
Technological efficiency	Requirement of employee requalification in each industry
Financial safety	
Financial inclusion	Lack of qualified labour force
Safety of payments systems	High-quality of IT control required
Protection of money as a public utility	Abuse of IT positioning
Preventing illicit activity (Tax Collection, Combating crime)	Lack of finance/finance redirected into the area which brings benefits to small group of mankind
Banking competition	Innovation race
Monetary policy transmission	Loss of financial control
Issuance of the money under control	Reliance on IT expertise performing audits
	Collapse of the system
Preservation of seigniorage income	Increase in energy consumption

Table 9.
Room for future research.

Author details

Darina Saxunova[1,2]* and Corlise Liesl Le Roux[1]

1 American University in the Emirates, Dubai, UAE

2 Faculty of Management, Comenius University in Bratislava, Slovakia

*Address all correspondence to: darina.saxunova@aue.ae

References

[1] Verhoef P.C., et al.: Digital transformation: A multidisciplinary reflection and research agenda. Journal of Business Research. https://doi.org/10.1016/j.jbusres.2019.09.022

[2] Sebastian, I. M., Ross, J. W., Beath, C., Mocker, M., Moloney, K. G., & Fonstad, N. O.: How big old companies navigate digital transformation. MIS Q. Executive. 2017; 16(3):197-213.

[3] Li, F., Nucciarelli, A., Roden, S., & Graham, G.: How smart cities transform operations models: A new research agenda for operations management in the digital economy. Production Planning & Control. 2016; 27(6):514-528.

[4] Kane, G.C., Palmer, D., Philips, A. N., Kiron, D., & Buckley, N.: Strategy, not technology, drives digital transformation. MIT Sloan Management Review an Deloitte University Press. 2015; 14:1-25.

[5] Pagani, M., & Pardo C.: The impact of digital technology on relationships in a business network. Industrial Marketing Management. 2017; 67:185-192.

[6] Teece, D. J.: Business models, business strategy and innovation. Long Range Planning. 2010; 43(2-3):172-194.

[7] Zott, C., & Amit, R.: The fit between product market strategy and business model: Implications for firm performance. Strategic Management Journal. 2008; 29(1):1-26.

[8] Boston Consulting Group. The Four Pillars of Digital Transformation in Banking [online] 2019. Available from: https://thefinancialbrand.com/71733/four-pillars-of-digital-transformation-banking-strategy/

[9] European Commission https://ec.europa.eu/info/business-economy-euro/banking-and-finance/banking-union/single-supervisory-mechanism_en

[10] Lex https://eur-lex.europa.eu/legal-content/EN/TXT/?uri=CELEX% 3A32013R1022

[11] Amadeo, K.: Central Banks' Function and Role. The Balance, 2018. [online] Available at: https: //www.thebalance.com/what-is-a-central-bank-definition function-and-role-3305827

[12] Teigland, R, Siri, S., Larsson, A., Moreno, A.P., Bogusz, C. I. The Rise and Development of FinTech: Accounts of Disruption from Sweden and Beyond. London, Routledge, 2018, p. 4.

[13] Marcus Lawrence. Top digital banks [online] 2018. [cit. 2018-01-10]. Available from: https: www.fintechmagazine.com/top10/top-10-digital banks-0

[14] Monitoring of FinTech, Financial Stability Board, [online]. 2020. Available from: http://www.fsb.org/whatwe-do/policy-development/additional-policy-areas/monitoring-of-FinTech/.

[15] The official websites of the company PayPal. [online] 2018. Available from: https://www.paypal.com/uk/webapps/mpp/about..

[16] The official websites "EUR-Lex", the details regarding national transposition of the PSD2. [Online] 2018. Available at: https://eur-lex.europa.eu/legal-content/EN/NIM/?uri=CELEX:32015L2366.

[17] Ernst & Young: EY FinTech Adoption Index 2019. 2019, [cit. 201804-20]. Available from: http://www.ey.com/blockchain+Dig.%20Economy/ey-global-fintech-adoption-index-2019.pdf

[18] Ferebauerová, R., Pekárek, O. et al. 2019. Digitální ekonomika a společnost. 1. vyd. České Budějovice: VSERS, 113 s.

[19] Bouri, E., Molnár, P., Azzi, G., Roubaud, D., & Hagfors, L. I. 2017. On the hedge and safe haven properties of Bitcoin: Is it really more than a diversifier? Finance Research Letters, 20, 192-198. doi:10.1016/j.frl.2016.09.025

[20] Selmi, R., Mensi, W., Hammoudeh, S., & Bouoiyour, J. 2018. Is Bitcoin a hedge, a safe haven or a diversifier for oil price movements? A comparison with gold. Energy Economics, 74, 787-801. doi:10.1016/j.eneco.2018.07.007

[21] Kristoufek, L. 2013. Bitcoin meets Google Trends and Wikipedia: quantifying the relationship between phenomena of the Internet era, Sci. Report. 3 . 3415.

[22] Bariviera, A. F., Basgall, M. J., Hasperué, W., & Naiouf, M. 2017. Some stylized facts of the Bitcoin market. Physica A: Statistical Mechanics and Its Applications, 484, 82-90. doi:10.1016/j.physa.2017.04.159

[23] Financial Action Task Force. Virtual Currencies, Key Definitions and Potential KYC/CFT Risks, FATF Report. [online]. 2014. Available from: http://www.fatf-gafi.org/media/fatf/documents/reports/Virtual-currency-key-definitions-and-potential-aml-cft-risks.pdf

[24] Saxunova D., Slivka P. From cryptoanarchy to cryptogovernance environment is Europe successful in managing transition? Digitalization & smart green (r)evolution conference: In: Proceedings of the international scientific conference. 1.st ed.. Bratislava.2018.: EKONÓM. ISBN 978-80-225-4588-4.

[25] Bank of England. Central Bank Digital Currency: opportunities, challenges and design. A Discussion Paper. [online]. 2020. Available from: https: //www.bankofengland.co.uk/-/media/boe/files/paper/2020/central-bank-digital-currency-opportunities-challenges-and-design.pdf?la=en&hash=DFAD18646A77C00772AF1C5B18E63E71F68E4593

[26] Norges bank Papers. Central bank digital currencies. [online].2018. Available from: https://static.norges-bank.no/contentassets/166efadb3d73419c8c50f9471be26402/nbpapers-1-2018-centralbankdigitalcurrencies.pdf?v=05/18/2018121950&ft=.pdf

[27] Carney M. Cryptocurrencies failing as money but technology has promise. [online].2020. Available from: https://www.reuters.com/article/us-britain-boe-carney/cryptocurrencies-failing-as-money-but-technology-has-promise-carney-idUSKCN1GE18N

[28] Fintechnews Switzerland. Interest in Central Bank Digital Currency Surging. [online].2020. Available from: https://fintechnews.ch/blockchain_bitcoin/interest-in-central-bank-digital-currency-surging/35840/

[29] Sveriges Riksbank . Technical solution for the e-krona pilot. [online].2020. Available from:https://www.riksbank.se/en-gb/payments--cash/e-krona/technical -solution-for-the-e-krona-pilot/

[30] Sveriges Riksbank. The Riksbank's e-krona pilot.[online] 2020. Available from: https://www.riksbank.se/globalassets/media/rapporter/e-krona/2019/the-riksbanks-e-krona-pilot.pdf

[31] China Briefing. What is the China Standards 2035? Plan and How It Will Impact Emerging Industries. [online].2020. Available from: https://www.china-briefing.com/news/what-is-china-standards-2035-plan-how-will-it-impact-emerging-technologies-what-is-link-made-in-china-2025-goals/

[32] Auer, R., & Böhme R. The technology of retail central bank digital Currency, BIS Quarterly Review. [online]

Available from: https://www.bis.org/publ/qtrpdf/r_qt2003j.pdf (2020).

[33] Yanagawa N., Yamaoka H. Digital Innovation, Data Revolution and Central Bank Digital Currency, Bank of Japan. 2020. [online] Available from: https://www.boj.or.jp/en/research/wps_rev/wps_2019/data/wp19e02.pdf

[34] Fineksus. 2020. How is coronavirus affecting the financial payments industry and compliance [online]. Available from: https://fineksus.com/how-is-coronavirus-affecting-the-financial-payments-industry-and-compliance/

[35] Digital Dollar Project. Digital Dollars: Electronic Cash vs Digital Currency [online]. 2020. Available from: https://www.digitaldollarproject.org/electronic-cash-vs-digital-currency

[36] Banque de France . Central Bank Digital Currency. [online] 2020. Available from: https://publications.banque-france.fr/sites/default/files/media/2020/02/04/central-bank-digital-currency_cbdc_2020_02_03.pdf

[37] Agur I., Ari A., & Dell'Ariccia G., International Monetary Fund . Designing Central Bank Digital Currencies, IMF Working Papers. [online].2019. Available from: https://www.imf.org/en/Publications/WP/Issues/2019/11/18/Designing-Central-Bank-Digital-Currencies-48739

[38] Better Than Cash Alliance . Government Toolkit. [online] 2020. Available from: https://btca-prod.s3.amazonaws.com/toolkits/2/downloads/btca-]govern-ment-toolkit-FINAL.pdf?1433186805

[39] Hampl. 2017. Central banks, digital currencies and monetary policy in times of elastic money. Central Bankers' speeches. BIS. Speech by the Vice Governor of the Czech National Bank, at the Official Monetary and Financial Institutions Forum (OMFIF) Roundtable, London, 11 July 2017.

[40] Mersch Y., European Union. [online] Available from: 2020. https://www.bankingsupervision.europa.eu/press/speeches/date/2020/html/ssm.sp200511~9f9eec5592.en.html

[41] Deloitte. Innovation – Blockchain – (R)evolution-Swiss Perspective - White paper. [online]. 2017. Available from https://www2.deloitte.com/content/dam/Deloitte/ch/Documents/innovation/ch-en-innovation-blockchain-revolution.pdf

[42] Ciaian, P., Rajcaniova, M. & Kancs, D. 2016. The economics of Bitcoin price formation, Appl.Econ. 48 (19) 1799-1815.

[43] Klein A. 2019. Is China's new payment system the future? [online] The Brookings institution. Available from: https://www.brookings.edu/research/is-chinas-new-payment-system-the-future/

[44] Financial Times. Virus forces EU digital rethink. [online].2020. Available from: https://www.ft.com/content/0c29e958-fdf0-409c-b622-6d6466ded094

[45] European Commission. FinTech Action plan: For a more competitive and innovative European financial sector. 2018. [online] Available from: https://eur-lex.europa.eu/legal-content/EN/TXT/PDF/?uri=CELEX:52018DC0109&from=EN

Chapter 7

The Trouble with Minding Markets: Emotional Finance in Context

D'Maris Coffman

Abstract

The term 'Emotional Finance' normally denotes a methodological approach advocated by Richard Taffler and David Tuckett, which they intended as a challenge both to Behavioral Finance and to mainstream finance and economics. In the wake of the Great Financial Crisis, Emotional Finance received a warm reception from regulators, the financial press, and the CFA Institute. Nearly a decade on, their ideas have largely failed to achieve traction in the academic literature, and continue to struggle to find empirical validation. Their approach is essentially an application of Kleinian psychoanalysis to financial markets, albeit without the terminological rigor that psychoanalytic practitioners might expect. Because their approach is inherently interdisciplinary, it has rarely been subject to scrutiny, as few psychoanalytic commentators feel qualified to comment on financial markets, and fewer finance academics feel comfortable commenting on the psychoanalytic theory. This chapter characterizes the main theoretical claims of Emotional Finance, and subjects each of them to scrutiny, finding them largely untenable. Although financial bubbles are commonplace and emotional responses to markets unremarkable, the subsidiary arguments advanced by advocates of Emotional Finance to support their primary claims are found wanting. The interpretative strategy of Emotional Finance is fundamentally flawed. Although it is fruitful to analyze the role of emotions in financial markets, more precise, rigorous and realistic approaches to these problems are needed.

Keywords: emotional finance, Melanie Klein, David Tuckett, applied psychoanalysis, behavioural finance

1. Introduction

'Emotional Finance', as inaugurated by Richard Taffler and David Tuckett, received a warm reception in the early 2010s from regulators, the financial press, and investment management industry's main professional body, the CFA Institute. Yet outside their immediate social and professional circles, the wider academic community largely ignored both Emotional Finance's challenge to Behavioural Finance and its theoretical and methodological approach, which is, at its core, an application of Kleinian psychoanalysis to interpreting the individual psychology of traders and to describing the group psychology of financial markets. A decade after the financial crisis, industry professionals rarely talk about 'Emotional Finance' at all, except insofar as they see 'emotional biases' as a sub-species of behavioural biases, which hardly amounts to a successful challenge to Behavioural Finance [1]. Because Taffler and Tuckett's approach is inherently interdisciplinary, few practicing psychoanalysts have felt equipped to comment upon their characterisation of financial markets, and yet fewer finance academics have the training or inclination to reckon with Taffler and Tuckett's idiosyncratic handling of psychoanalytic theory.

Emotional Finance, as an intellectual project, rests on four related claims: first, that financial assets are categorically different from other kinds of commodities; second, that financial innovation peculiarly lends itself to being experienced as a 'phantastic object'; third, that regulators can and should design institutional mechanisms that acknowledge the psychodynamics of the dealing room; and fourth, that the recent financial crisis ought to be handled in a manner similar to the post-Apartheid South African regime's Truth and Reconciliation Commission. While agreeing that financial bubbles are banal and that emotional responses to the vicissitudes of the market are nothing remarkable, this chapter argues that financial assets are not categorically distinct; that the term 'phantastic object' is superfluous and its application is a variant of the 'sharpshooter' fallacy; that narrative causation is not formally equivalent to causality; that the relationship between group psychology and individual psychodynamics is under-theorised; and that financial instability is not the same as financial bubbles. Finally, there are other bigger threats to financial stability than those identified by the techniques employed by advocates of Emotional Finance, especially given the periods of relative calm in financial markets between the Great Financial Crisis (2007-2008) and its sequelae in the Eurozone Debt Crisis (2009-2012) and the recent crisis caused by the global coronavirus pandemic in Q2 2020.

2. The nature of financial assets

By far the most problematic claim of Emotional Finance is that financial assets are somehow a special category. In *Minding the Markets*, Tuckett claims there are three characteristics of financial assets that make them unusually amenable to obtaining the status of a 'phantastic object': their volatility, their abstract quality, and the difficulty in determining whether or not a manager's success was attributable to skill or luck ([2], p. xvii). Of these, the volatility argument is the most straightforward and also most peculiar. While it is certainly true that individual listed securities, futures contracts, or financial derivatives contracts may be highly volatile, financial markets themselves are notable for their lack of volatility. This is straightforward to demonstrate empirically because the volatility of the S&P 500 (as measured by the implied volatility of index options for the following 30 days) is itself a tradable index called the VIX or CBOE Volatility Index. Its performance since its inception in 1985 can be seen below in **Figure 1**.

For most of the last thirty-five years, the VIX has hovered around 15 to 25, with a high of 150 during the October 1987 'flash crash'. In the fourth quarter of 2008, after the Lehman collapse, it peaked at around 80. What does this mean? The VIX is a measure of volatility over a 30-day period, annualised, such that a VIX of 20 means that the market is expected to move up or down by 5.8% (or $20/\sqrt{12}$) over the next 30 days. Even a VIX of 80 in means that the market is expected to move 23.12% up or down over the next 30 days, which most recently occurred in Q2 2020 with the outbreak of the COVID-19 pandemic. The daily volatility, by contrast, is calculated by dividing the number by $\sqrt{256}$, or the number of trading days in an average year, which for a VIX of 20, means that the market is expected to move up or down by 1.25% daily.

How does this compare to other commodities, say crude oil, or even to gold, that supposedly safe haven? **Figure 2** answers this question. In the case of crude oil, the CBOE also publishes an Oil Volatility Index, which is markedly higher than the S&P

500, which compares favourably to a volatility index for gold over the thirty-year period from 1990-2020.

Some might complain that this is because oil and gold are exchange-traded and thus subject to added volatility, but, in fact, there is good evidence that exchange-based futures trading lowers volatility rather than amplifies it. We know this because of a natural experiment afforded by the Onion Futures Act of 1958, which banned futures trading in onions [3]. The price volatility of onions is considerably

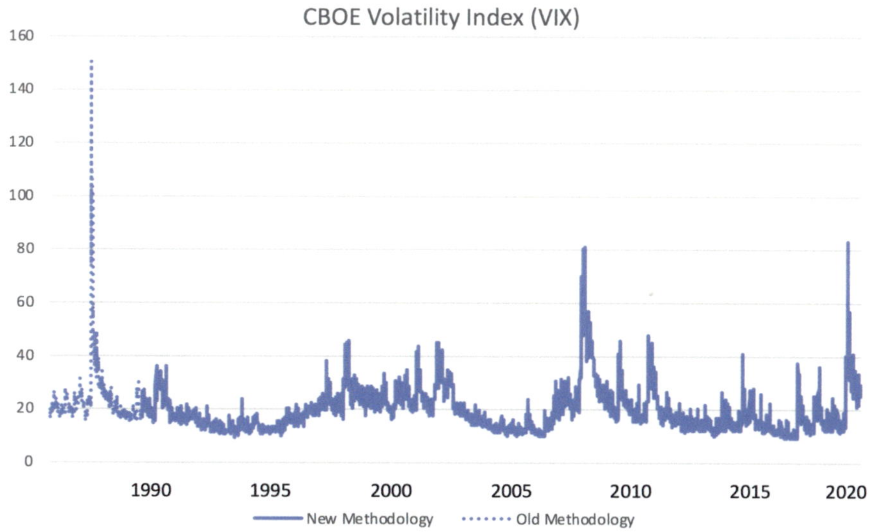

Figure 1.
CBOE Volatility Index (VIX) from December 1985 to October 2020 (daily closings). http://www.cboe.com/products/vix-index-volatility/vix-options-and-futures/vix-index/vix-historical-data (CBOE - Chicago Board Options Exchange).

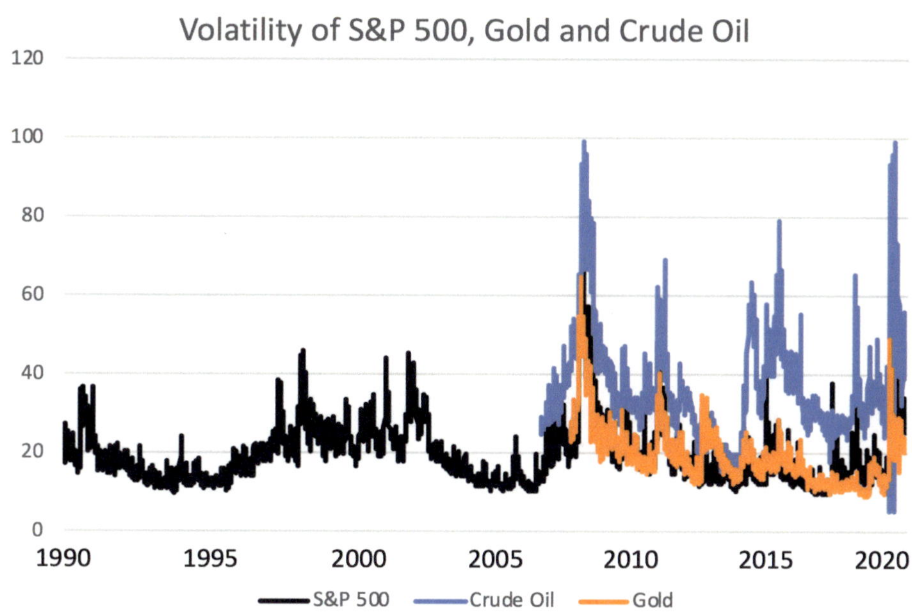

Figure 2.
Comparison of Oil, Stocks, and Gold Volatility Indices 1990-2020. http://www.cboe.com/products/vix-index-volatility/volatility-on-etfs/cboe-crude-oil-etf-volatility-index-ovx (CBOE - Chicago Board Options Exchange); http://www.cboe.com/products/vix-index-volatility/volatility-on-etfs/cboe-gold-etf-volatility-index-gvz (CBOE - Chicago Board Options Exchange); http://www.cboe.com/products/vix-index-volatility/vix-options-and-futures/vix-index/vix-historical-data (CBOE - Chicago Board Options Exchange).

greater than that of either the S&P 500 or of crude oil. The charts in **Figure 3** would not surprise economists or finance academics.

As acknowledged above, individual stocks may move more than the market as a whole, but most investment managers hedge this risk by holding a portfolio composed of a variety of different asset classes, let alone constituents among them. Retail investors, rather than professional money managers, may find themselves credit-constrained and forced to sell if a security falls quickly in value, but most fund managers have either automated stop-losses or the discretion with which to cut their losses. Moreover, over longer time horizons, financial assets are not particularly volatile compared to house prices in major markets in last fifteen years as shown in **Figure 4**.

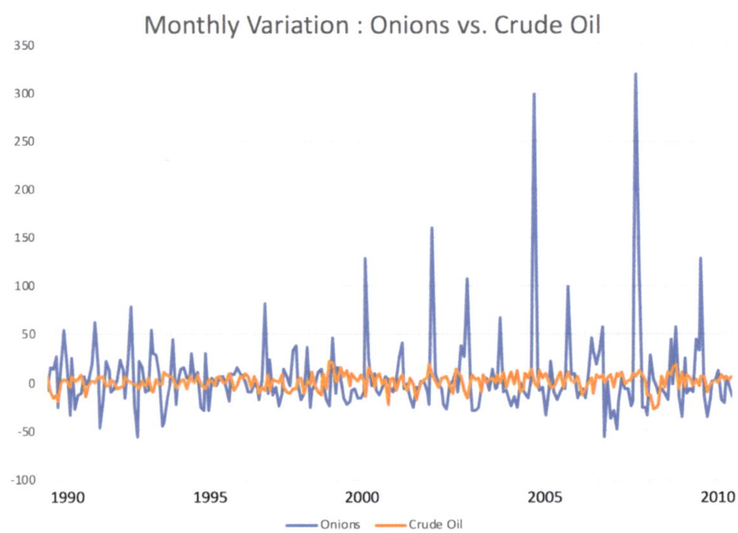

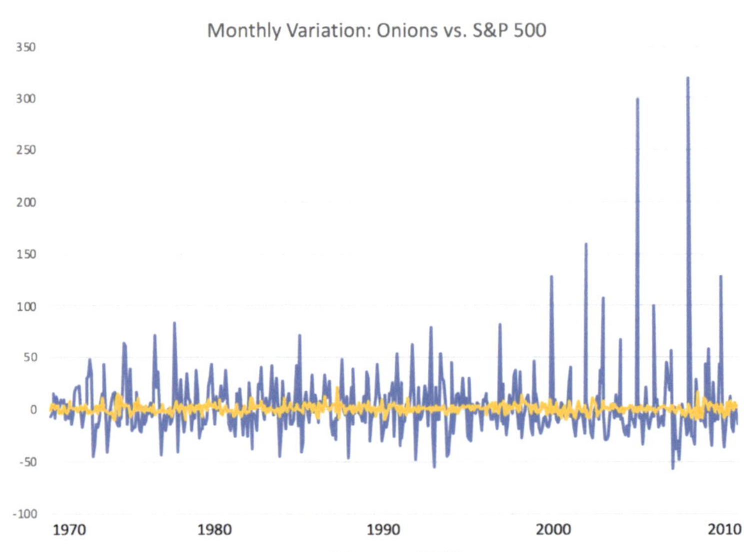

Figure 3.
Onions vs Crude Oil, Onions vs S&P 500. (a and b) https://www.investing.com/indices/us-spx-500-historical-data (Investing.com Historical Data); https://www.indexmundi.com/commodities/?commodity=crude-oil&months=360 (Index Mundi data archive); https://usda.library.cornell.edu/concern/publications/k643b116n?locale=en (USDA Data Library); https://bsic.it/the-onion-paradox-or-why-futures-are-good-for-the-economy/ (Bocconi Student Investors Club Blog).

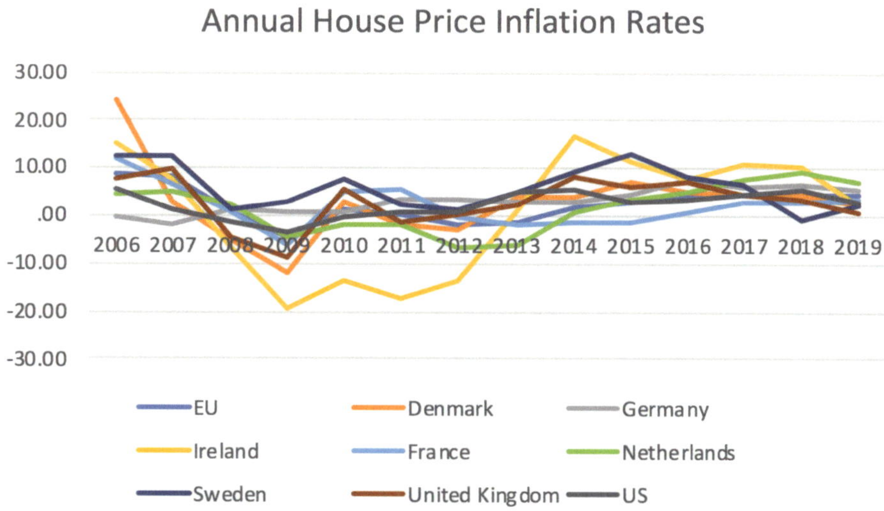

Figure 4.
Annual House Price Inflation Rates, 2006-2020. https ://appsso.eurostat.ec.europa.eu/nui/setupDownloads.do (Eurostat Data Archive); https://apps.bea.gov/iTable/iTable.cfm?reqid=19&step=3&isuri=1&1921=survey&1903=11#reqid=19&step=3&isuri=1&1921=survey&1903=11 (BEA, National Data).

The volatility of the stock market against the risk-free rate is not especially significant even during the Dotcom Crashes. As many commentators noticed at the time of the Lehman collapse, the problem was that most fund managers had spent the majority of their career chasing returns and had little experience of market snaps of any kind. Additionally, market snaps of the kind experienced during the 2008 crash or even the Eurobond crisis of 2011-12 pale in comparison to economic shocks such as that experienced during the coronavirus pandemic in Q1-Q2 2020 as illustrated in **Figure 5**.

This is why financial engineers worked so hard in the period from 2003 to 2006 to create instruments, like mortgage-backed securities and collateralised debt obligations, that gave investors leveraged access to a much more volatile housing market.

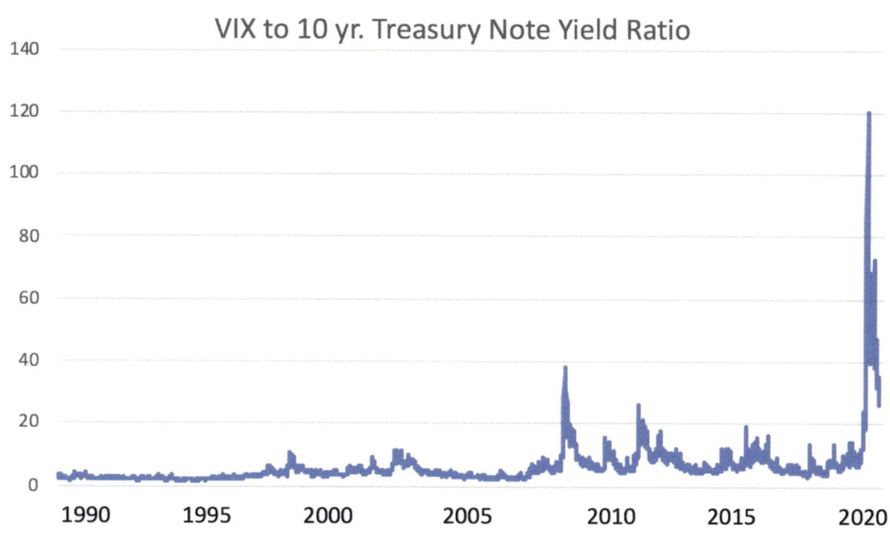

Figure 5.
VIX to 10 yr. Treasury Note Yield Ratio, 1990-2020. https://www.macrotrends.net/2016/10-year-treasury-bond-rate-yield-chart (Macrotrends Data Archive); http://www.cboe.com/products/vix-index-volatility/vix-options-and-futures/vix-index/vix-historical-data (CBOE - Chicago Board Options Exchange).

There is no reason to contest much of Tuckett's characterisation of the problems with the 'efficient-markets hypothesis' except to say that it is was originally developed as a simplifying assumption that made certain classes of models tractable. The slippage that allowed it to become a (flawed) description of reality, let alone an operative ideal and normative regulatory goal, is ideological and not the consequence of the internal logic of the idea. Some markets are efficient and do not forecast prices reliably, as Holbrook Working discovered when he explored North American grain markets in the interwar period or securities in the postwar moment [4, 5].

The second quality of financial assets, identified by Tuckett, which makes them amenable to the psychodynamic processes that he describes is their putative 'abstractness'. This is surely in the eyes of the beholder. As early as Adam Smith [6], economic writers identified two (or three) distinct forms of value: value-in-use and value-in-exchange. Value-in-use can be further distinguished as value-in-consumption or in the income generated by a particular asset, i.e. you could live in a house or rent it out, you could eat the produce of your garden or sell it, etc. Value-in-exchange is what it commands either on an open market or in a barter transaction. For financial assets, there is often little consumable 'value-in-use' except at the margins, insofar as some investors may buy Class A or B shares in Berkshire Hathaway in order to meet Warren Buffett at his annual junket in Omaha and other investors (especially aggressive hedge funds) may purchase shares in order to control a company, oust its leadership, merge it with another, or even liquidate it. Most often, however, financial assets either generate income (which Tuckett suggests is usually calculated through a capital asset pricing model) or are sold on for speculative gains or losses. Modern finance theory holds that efficient markets should arbitrage value-in-use (income) and value-in-exchange, so that the dividend is 'priced into' the share, but in practice many investors are driven by a combination of dividend income and capital gains, and the protection of the latter in the U.S. and UK tax codes has been distorting investment behaviour these last thirty years or so.

Yet, in practice, these instruments are not abstract to those who trade them. Bonds have par values, generate coupon payments, have interest rates and calculable yields based on their prices. Equities may or may not pay dividends, but can be valued on that basis or on the book value of the firm. A variety of options, including the right to buy or sell a security at a particular price, have been well known for over 500 years ([7], p. 2-3). More complex financial derivatives were not abstract so much as they were opaque, in that they were tied to underlying assets that were, themselves, difficult to value. But even if we were to call that 'abstraction', it is by no means obvious that this is the sort of abstraction that lends itself to phantasy. It is equally plausible that relatively simple, graspable items in everyday life are the stuff of phantasies. The very complexity of some of the more recent species of financial assets (especially collateralised debt obligations that were tied to securitised mortgages) made them difficult to value, but the problem was not that investment managers fantasised about them, but rather that rating agencies were put under pressure to score them more highly than they deserved.

Elsewhere Tuckett contrasts financial assets with a television set, where 'a "rational" consumer can consult a range of information about the price and quality and on that basis make a decision' ([2], p. 21). He goes on to argue that the buyer might notice he got a bad deal, might observe the prices of televisions fluctuates as models sell out quickly or not at all, or as new models appear, and he might have buyer's remorse, and even sell it on the second-hand market. Yet Tuckett maintains that 'with financial assets the situation is very different [from television sets] as they have no intrinsic value but one determined by ambiguous information and varying expectations about an uncertain future that plays out in time' ([2], p. 21). This is simply untrue. Bonds represent claims, either preferential or subordinated, on the business revenue or tax revenue of the firm or sovereign that issued them, equities represent residual claims against the book value of a firm, whereas financial derivatives (swaps, options, etc) represent contractual arrangements that can, and have, been litigated. The fortunes made by vulture funds that purchased collateralised debt obligations composed of subprime mortgages or of junior Greek debt is an indication that these financial assets do have values that are calculable.

What is more difficult to calculate, and is indeed often uncertain, is the depth of the secondary market at a given time, and hence the liquidity risk. Tuckett commits the same error as proponents of the efficient-markets hypothesis do when he ignores what is known in the trade as "the limits of arbitrage", in that he assumes that buyers are not credit constrained and only buy or sell because of their sense of the direction of the market. The reality is very different, in that people and institutions can be forced to sell for a range of reasons (to raise money to meet current obligations) and institutions, like pension funds, can be forced to purchase risky assets because they have to match their assets with their liabilities to generate the returns needed to meet obligations that are years away. Liquidity risk is particularly acute in a financial crisis where people are not buying or selling anything at any price, but anyone who has tried to sell a television set near the end of the month can tell you that the used market also depends on the proximity of the average consumer to a weekly or monthly pay day, depending on the price level. Sensitivity to liquidity risk is difficult to know *ex-ante*, but it is not analytically difficult to grasp.

Moreover, the distinction between risk and uncertainty in Tuckett's account is problematic. Risk is calculable based on an ergodic assumption that the future will be like the past. To a surprising degree, this assumption holds in financial markets, as the 'equity risk premium' (the premium paid to investors for buying equities over government debt securities) has not changed much in 150 years, and, as the finance literature has decisively shown, has made owners of shares better off than those who eschew the risks attendant to them [8, 9].

Moreover, as **Figure 6** illustrates, the majority of the 'total return' from stocks comes from dividends not from price appreciation, which belies the idea that shares do not have a 'value-in-use' or income component that is tangible and real.

The returns above are for U.S. equities as an asset class (i.e. they represent 'beta'), and say nothing about particular securities or vintages. Yet it is precisely because retail investors and professional money managers can buy (and sell) index-funds that active managers have to try to 'beat' the market. That is where the pressure comes, to generate 'alpha', which Tuckett correctly notices is ephemeral, and, according to adherents of the efficient-markets hypothesis, at best idiosyncratic and at worst a statistical mirage. The money managers that Tuckett identified have an incentive to depict their performance as a result of their skill, but given the survivorship bias (firms that get unlucky fail and disappear), the charge that even the big winners are probably 'lucky monkeys' is not without some real plausibility.

So, yes, returns are 'uncertain,' but what does this mean? 'Uncertainty' refers to the 'unknown unknowns' of Knight and Keynes, but hardly matters much to the everyday operation of markets, which have remained remarkably continuous and well-funded in all but a handful of cases (some of the more exotic CDOs still do not trade at any price) through the last crisis. The reason that discussions of 'uncertainty' were back in vogue in the 2010s is that markets in 2003-2007 under-priced risk, because the models could not account for uncertainty. Once-in-a-lifetime events (the so-called Black Swans) are important to risk managers, but for Tuckett's argument to work they have to be an everyday feature of markets, which they, by definition, are not. Tuckett is describing the life of an onion trader not a financial asset manager. This is precisely why more recent work on emotions in financial

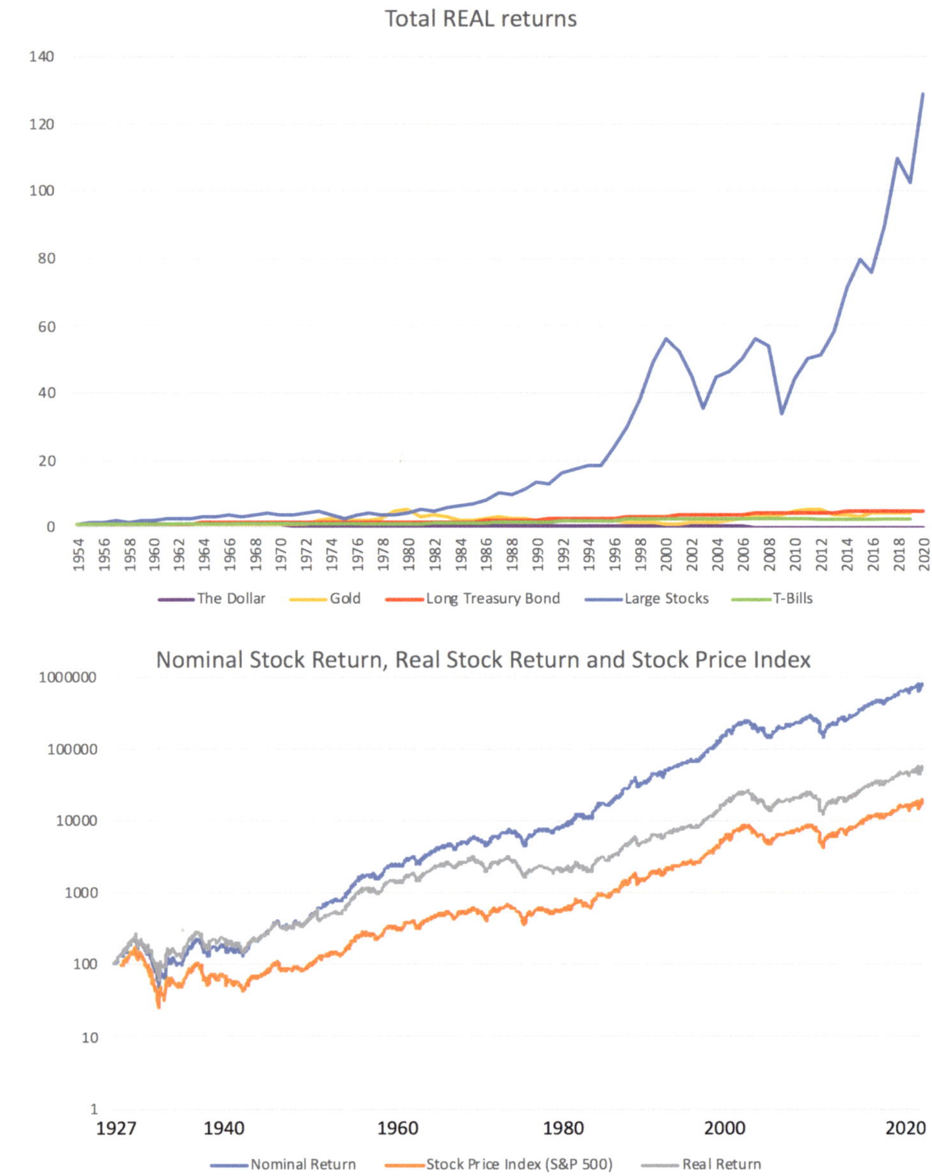

Figure 6.
Nominal and Real Returns from Stocks and the Stock Index, 1927-2020. (a) https://www.statista.com/statistics/1032048/value-us-dollar-since-1640/ (Statista archive); https://www.macrotrends.net/1333/historical-gold-prices-100-year-charthttps://onlygold.com/gold-prices/historical-gold-prices/ (Macrotrends); https://fred.stlouisfed.org/series/DGS20#0https://www.multpl.com/s-p-500-historical-prices/table/by-year (St Louis Federal Reserve Archive); https://seekingalpha.com/article/4311451-stocks-bonds-bills-and-inflation-returns-for-94-years-ending-december-2019 (Seeking Alpha Blog). (b) https://finance.yahoo.com/quote/%5EGSPC/history?period1=-1325635200&period2=1603238400&interval=1mo&filter=history&frequency=1mo&includeAdjustedClose=true; https://www.officialdata.org/us/stocks/s-p-500/1927?amount=100&endYear=2020 (Yahoo Finance); https://www.in2013dollars.com/us/inflation/1927#:~:text=In%20other%20words%2C%20%24100%20in,inflation%20rate%20was%20%2D1.69%25. (CPI Inflation Calculator).

markets has eschewed the problematic articulated by Taffler and Tuckett in favour of understanding how emotions affect participants in markets under ordinary trading conditions [10].

While a middle class, middle-aged Londoner might indeed see a television as ordinary and mundane and a share as 'exotic' and 'abstract', but as seen in the London riots of 2011, ordinary people did risk their livelihoods, reputation (and a possible

DOI: http://dx.doi.org/10.5772/intechopen.95094

criminal record) and even lives to snatch televisions and trainers from shops. Before globalisation, not so long ago, consumers in emerging markets invested television sets with almost magical properties. If television sets are in the eye of the beholder, it is equally plausible that various financial instruments are mundane, familiar and more or less rationally estimable by people who trade them every day. Is financial innovation, in its first incarnation then, any different?

Tuckett thinks so. He cites tulips, subscription shares (in the South Sea Bubble), and a host of other items ([2], p. 18) as inherently generating outsized excitement because they represented 'financial innovation', but these assertions are not proven. In some cases, as with tulips and subscription shares, the characterisation of them as novel financial innovations is just wrong ([7], pp. 2-4), as futures trading in Baltic grain had preceded that in tulips by over half a century, and the Bank of England offered subscription shares to English investors decades before the South Sea Company directors did. In other cases, it is easier to explain the erratic valuations in terms of Akerlof's lemon problem, which can be summarised as those who cannot tell good wine from bad will overpay for the latter and undervalue the former [11]. This is not to deny that bubbles form in financial markets or that they are further fuelled by fantastic narratives about the value of the assets, which are their focal point. But let us not forget that the 'bubble' in the early noughties was not in collateralised debt obligations, but rather in housing market where price rises were fuelled by the advent of subprime mortgages, which are neither especially abstract nor backed by something intangible. The trouble is not with the role of fantasies in bubbles, but rather with the theoretical formulation of these 'phantastic objects.' In short, there is nothing unique about financial assets.

3. What is a phantastic object?

The theoretical edifice of Emotional Finance equally depends on the usefulness of the term, 'phantastic object', as a plausible unit of analysis. Tuckett [2] gives his most recent definition of a phantastic object as 'subjectively very attractive "objects" (people, ideas or things) which we find highly exciting and idealise, imagining (feeling rather than thinking) they can satisfy our deepest desires, the meaning of which we are only partially aware' ([2], p. xi). According to Tuckett, he had 'coined the term' as an attempt to explain a situation where 'a story gets told about an object of apparent desire (such as a dotcom share, a tulip bulb, or a complex financial derivative), which becomes capable of generating excitement in a situation where outcomes are inherently uncertain' ([2], p. xiv). He reports that 'the term conjoins "phantasy" as in unconscious phantasy and "object" as in representation.' What does this mean? Tuckett further explains: 'the phantasy stimulated is about more than just a story of getting rich. Rather it is a story about participation in an imagined object relationship in which the possessor of the desired object plays with the omnipotent phantasy of having permanent and exclusive access to it and all good things' ([2], p. xiv). Although Freud and Klein both long ago recognised that all object relationships are ambivalent, Tuckett sees ambivalence (and with it a degree of abstraction, ambiguity and uncertainty) as necessary ingredients of this heady emotional stew [12, 13]. Yet the insistence on ambivalence, for emphasis, is hardly a cardinal sin.

The more serious problem arises, however, when we pick apart this notion of 'phantasy.' For Tuckett and Taffler, the usual citation is Freud's meditation on creative writing and daydreaming [14]. Here Freud develops a theory, no longer accepted even in literary theory, that a child's fantastical play is very similar to the creative writer, because both the child and the writer are able to distinguish their intensely rich libido-cathected worlds and the characters they create for them from external reality ([14], p. 142-3). Phantasies, both conscious and unconscious, come to replace play, for Freud, as 'the growing child when he stops playing, gives up nothing but the link with real objects; instead of playing, he now phantasises' ([14], p. 144). Adults populate their phantasies with their internal objects both in manifest and disguised forms. In that limited sense, Tuckett's 'phantastic object' is simply any object that has found a place in an adult's unconscious phantasy, or what Freud constructed as the 'psychical reality', which is unique to each individual. Exactly how 'financial assets' become the paradigmatic 'phantastic object' remains to be shown, unless what Tuckett really means is that financial assets evoke some memory of a part-object or maternal breast.

To complicate matters, Freud recognises that children rarely conceal their fantastical play, whereas 'the adult, on the contrary, is ashamed of his phantasies and hides them from other people. He cherishes them as his most intimate possessions, and as a rule he would rather confess his misdeeds than tell anyone his phantasies ([14], p. 144).' If so, it is all the more remarkable that the fund managers whom Tuckett interviewed were willing to tell their 'phantasies' to him, over the course of one meeting of 70 minutes or so, unless, if by analogy to Freud's neurotic patient who hopes for a cure, they confess their phantasies to Tuckett in hopes of absolution for speculative excess ([14], p. 145).

Freud's explanation of what causes adults to hide their phantasies in shame arises from the fact that they are 'either ambitious wishes, which serve to elevate the subject's personality; or they are exotic (sic) [erotic] ones' ([14], p. 146). But he cautions, 'we will not lay stress on the opposition between the two trends; we would rather emphasise the fact that they are often united' and just as often reparative ([14], p. 146-7). Even the most overtly 'ambitious, egotist wishes' have some element of sexual gratification involved, if merely auto-erotic in the most narcissistic of states. Freud finishes by comparing 'phantasies' to 'dreams' and noting their quality of wish fulfilment ([14], p. 148). All of this is very familiar to psychoanalysts, but Tuckett's neologism has lost the crucial sense, found in Freud, of erotic wish fulfilment, presumably because draining it of the erotic makes the concept more palatable to Tuckett's audience. The Strachey translation's tendency to render 'fantasy' as 'phantasy' (which is now the conventional usage in Britain) further reinforces the impression that it has little to do with sex, however alien the spelling may seem to American readers.

If we allow that conscious and unconscious narratives which adults weave about their internal objects are invested with libido and contain sexual gratification and conquest as elements of their function as wish fulfilment, then there is nothing unusual, let alone alarming, about a particular investment or set of investments acting as the vehicle, in such a fantasy, to unlimited wealth and with those resources the means to sexual conquest. Buyers of lottery tickets do this every day. To the extent that a particular object occupies a stereotyped place in such narratives, such that it becomes 'very attractive' and 'idealised' to an individual, let alone a group, then we have something closer to a 'fetish' or 'an inanimate object worshipped … for its magical powers or as being inhabited by a spirit' ([15], p. 57). Fetish objects also provoke the 'divided states' that Tuckett describes ([2], p. xi), possess 'magical powers' and lead to 'potency the [fetishist may] otherwise lack' ([15], p. 57). Whereas many sexual fetishes function by synecdoche (feet, hair, clothes, footwear, etc), others do so by metonymy, offering a substitute object ([16], p. 132). There are two further features that sharpen the similarities between 'fetish object' and 'phantastic object', namely '(a) the fetish has multiple meanings derived by condensation, displacement and symbolisation from other objects, and (b) the fetishist behaves as though [the fetish object] actually were these other objects and is no more disturbed by incongruity or absurdity than a dreamer is while dreaming' ([15], p. 57).

Ironically, Tuckett's example of Aladdin's lamp is usually explained as a fetish object rather than a phantastic one. The use of 'pseudo-psychoanalytic' language ('phantastic object' in place of 'fetish object') may be more acceptable to the audience, but it has the consequence of dislocating the concept within a wider psychoanalytic discourse.

Although Tuckett does not acknowledge this in his own discussion, the Emotional Finance presentation of 'phantastic objects' also depends on these meanings derived from 'condensation, displacement and symbolisation' ([15], p. 57). Before exploring that in detail, it is first worth considering the alternative source of 'phantastic object' as offered by Tuckett, namely in the definition of 'phantasy' offered by Laplanche and Pontalis in their rival to the Rycroft volume ([17], pp. 317-321), which invokes the principle that 'the use of the term "phantasy" cannot fail to evoke the distinction between imagination and reality (perception). If this distinction is made into a major psycho-analytic axis of reference, we are brought to define phantasy as a purely illusory production which cannot be sustained when confronted with a correct apprehension of reality' ([17], p. 315). As they note, 'certain of Freud's writings appear to back up this type of approach. Thus in "Formulations on the Two Principles of Mental Functioning" (1911b), Freud sets the internal world, tending towards satisfaction by means of illusion, against an outside world which gradually imposes the reality principle upon the subject through the mediation of the perceptual system' ([17], p. 315).

For Taffler and Tuckett, the 'reality' of financial markets ultimately strips the 'phantastic objects' of their value if not their meaning, as the inevitable crash and de-idealisation leads to anger and revulsion [18]. As Laplanche and Pontalis also notice, modern psychoanalytic usage extends 'phantasy' to a range of conscious, preconscious and unconscious fantasies, thereby muddling the extent to which repression plays a role ([17], p. 315). They suggest, instead, distinguishing between day-dreams that serve as compromise-formations, common 'unconscious phantasies' that appear as precursors to neurotic symptoms, and unconscious fantasies that offer the seeds of wish fulfilment in dreams. With Tuckett's formulation, the narratives about 'phantastic objects' appear to be mostly preconscious, in that the fund managers are not necessarily aware of them until prompted by their interlocutor, but then venture them freely. Whether or not this is plausible in a psychoanalytic sense remains debatable, as Tuckett's formulation appears to ignore both the roles of secondary revision and of repression.

As with Freud, Laplanche and Pontalis also link phantasies to desire, which does not even merit an index entry in Tuckett [2]. In Laplanche and Portalis, they emphasise the extent to which wish fulfilment evokes the 'hallucinatory memory of satisfaction' (1973, p. 318), or the maternal breast, which is a kind of primordial 'phantasy-object'. Yet they also acknowledge, 'the relationship between phantasy and desire seems to us to be more complicated than that. Even in their least elaborate forms, phantasies do not appear to be reducible to an intentional aim on the part of the desiring subject ...', and crucially 'it is not an object that the subject imagines and aims at, so to speak, but rather a sequence in which the subject has his own part to play and which the permutations of roles and attributions are possible' ([17], p. 318). Read that way, Tuckett's 'phantastic object' is, in effect, a contradiction in terms, in that it is not the object itself that the subject desires, but rather the outcome of the script, i.e. unbridled wealth, beautiful women (or men), and universal gratification. In other words, we're back to ordinary explanations that turn on greed, lust, and gluttony.

As to the relationship between the internalisation of the so-called 'phantastic object' and the processes Rycroft alludes to of 'condensation, displacement and symbolisation', these are, in effect, what Tuckett evokes when he describes the 'divided states' of idealisation and de-idealisation that he postulates occur in the minds of traders. There may well be a value in thinking about how financial assets relate to Marxian and Freudian notions of 'fetishism,' but Tuckett forecloses this possibility with his neologism.

To summarise, there are two separate etymologies of 'phantastic object' in Tuckett's writings with Taffler on the subject. The strain that depends most heavily on Freud is very hard to distinguish from more conventional uses of 'fetish object' while the version that depends strictly on Laplanche and Pontalis is oxymoronic. Either 'phantastic objects' are essentially fetish objects, denuded of the explicit eroticism, or they are an inherently self-contradictory attempt to bridge the gap between part-objects expressed in paranoid-schizoid states (where what the infant desires is the maternal breast) and vehicles for the realisation of erotic phantasies in less regressed states of mind. The love affair, in short, is not with the financial asset or the car or the suit, but rather still with idea of 'getting the girl' or 'winning the game.'

The latter is simply an instance of superfluity and proliferation of neologisms, which in turn muddles the waters, whereas the former suggests something of the very problematic hermeneutic strategy employed by those who advocate for Emotional Finance.

4. Narrative causation versus causality

Interpretation is not explanation; causation is not causality. In the social sciences, this is almost a cliché, but they are important caveats. Causality rests on the identification of a specific mechanism by which X has an effect on Y. Explanations can be realistic in the sense that they try to account for external reality, or epistemic (anti-realist) in the sense that they strive for the internal consistency of the empirical model. Much of Tuckett's complaint with modern economics is that it strives for the latter, whereas the natural sciences present themselves as interested in the former, except perhaps in cosmology.

In finance, the movement of prices is easy to explain: they rise when there are more buyers than sellers, they fall when there are more sellers than buyers. The willingness to buy or sell is, indeed, partly influenced by individual expectations of future prices, such that for markets to function there has to be heterogeneity of belief. There is nothing at all surprising about that. Predicting the movement of prices is an occult science, whether practiced by 'chartists' who do 'technical analysis' or by punters who pontificate on the market outlook for a particular stock. Interpreting price behaviour (explaining why markets rose or fell) lies somewhere in between, though much of it depends on normative judgments about 'value'. To imagine that you are in an asset-price bubble is to imagine that the current prices of an asset have diverged from some 'rational' judgement of fundamental value.

Tuckett retains that notion of 'rationality', though he attributes it to an uncertain, yet-to-be-experienced 'objective reality' rather than to the price discovery mechanisms of the market. Now he is by no means alone in that, as Behavioural Economics speaks of 'bounded rationality,' but the problem is whether or not any of this can be apprehended ex-ante. Tuckett identifies the 'drowning out' of naysayers as a feature of the euphoria he describes, yet some of these naysayers, like Nouriel Roubini, have successfully predicted ten out of the last three crises, whereas Warren Buffett made an even greater fortune on Berkshire Hathaway's derivatives book, even as he preached about 'weapons of mass destruction'. Some people are hypocrites, others are stereotyped market commentators, and even stopped clocks are right twice a day. It should not be forgotten that the people who made the most money in the Great Financial Crisis where those who shorted subprime mortgages, often against the interests of their own clients. The most successful currency trade in modern times, the Black Wednesday bear raid organised by Soros, was, in fact, a mean-reversion trade designed to force sterling out of the European Exchange Rate Mechanism. It just took two billion pounds to do it. In other words, the trick about shorting anything is timing it. To echo the line often mis-ascribed to Keynes, 'markets can remain irrational longer than you can remain solvent.'

Tuckett [2] variously declaims any attempts at quantification, though his most recent work aims in that direction by attempting to exploit insights from Big Data [19–23]. Instead, what Tuckett's approach is offering is an interpretative strategy, which serves mostly as an elaboration of the latter stages of the Minsky-Kindleberger model of an asset-price bubble [24], which identifies states of 'displacement, new opportunities, boom, euphoria, dismissal, unease, panic, revulsion' ([2], p. 16). What the Minsky-Kindleberger model describes is not a mechanism of causality but a causal chain. Psychoanalysis, with its roots in Aristotelian casuistry (with the assumption of a relationship, albeit a complex one, between infantile conflicts and adult neuroses), is especially well-suited to such an exercise. Moreover, psychoanalytic theories of causation are also multi-valent. Aristotle identified four cases: material, formal, efficient and final. Freudian psychoanalysis, on the other hand, tends to consider symptoms simultaneously in terms of 'origins, genesis, function, meaning and expectation' ([25], pp. 22-36). For example, your euphoria might well have its genesis in the rising price of a stock (or falling if you shorted it), might have its origins in an outpouring of enthusiasm for a new technology in which the particular firm has an advantage, might be a function of the fact that institutional investors have decided they need exposure to that sector, may mean that firms that rely on older technologies will experience hard times, might have been expected given the success of a similar technology in a more advanced country. None of these interpretations of your euphoria have anything to do with causality in any formal sense (that the number of buyers in the market started to outnumber the number of sellers); but rather this strategy reflects a mode of analysis of narrative causation that is liberating because it disrupts established narratives and opens up the possibilities of new ones. This is why Tuckett eventually became interested in 'conviction narratives', because that seemed to present a means of moving from causation to casuality [20, 22]. Unfortunately, this strategy creates a hermeneutic circle.

As post-structuralist literary critics subsequently noticed, these narratives generally are organised around one of four tropes: metaphor, metonymy, synecdoche, and irony, which correspond to the emplotments of romance, tragedy, comedy/ farce and satire [26]. Tuckett's case studies of investment managers do all follow similar trajectories, but figural causation is an artefact of the mimetic function of narrative not a feature of reality [27]. The reason that people have not learned from previous crises is because there is less to learn than some might imagine. To suggest otherwise is to suggest that there is some path dependent group psychological structuring of financial bubbles, such that they all have the same denouement, regardless of the particular asset at their core. To the extent that this is true, it is obvious (and just an elaboration of Minksy-Kindleberger), and to the extent that it is not obvious, it is wrong (in that the focal point of bubbles does matter) for reasons that should become clear in the next two sections.

5. From phantastic objects to *groupfeel*

As Tuckett explains, 'groupfeel' has replaced his earlier usage of 'groupthink' as a way of aggregating the individual emotion states of participants in a market. He is surely correct that groups display elements of 'consensus seeking, group polarisation, out-group stereotyping, and the suppression of dissent' ([2], p. 66-67), but what becomes harder to understand is why he sees financial markets as 'groups' in the sense that a notion of 'groupfeel' would apply. Financial markets are nothing if not competitive arenas, and despite the existence of social spaces in which collusion might occur (c.f. LIBOR-fixing), the notion that the market is subject to these dynamics is implausible. Individual firms may be, which is significant only insofar as some bulge-bracket firms become the dominant dealers in particular financial assets. Tuckett is likewise correct that the structure of the industry means individual managers may be more concerned with short-term performance than with longer-term results, but that has nothing to do with phantastic objects and everything to do with how compensation is structured. This is also one of the few areas in which the market does 'zero-sum,' as those managers who outperform the market benchmark are richly rewarded in fees, whereas those who underperform benchmarks get sacked. That said, zero-sum games are not especially known for displaying the sorts of group psychologies found elsewhere.

Behavioural Finance, instead, offers 'herding' as a heuristic that mangers use to main-chase the perceived 'market leaders'. This is not necessarily an emotional response (as one might prefer to think oneself smarter than other traders), but rather a rational one of achieving safe but possibly sub-optimal returns. Even so, it is a simplification to suggest that risk-on/risk-off maps to divided states (paranoid-schizoid and depressive positions), unless one assumes that the 'market norm' is one of stagnation, which, at least in equities, is discredited by the data presented in **Figure 6**. What Tuckett has, in fact, done is taken a typical risk management heuristic of the directors of trading desks on dealing floors, which is to remove from the floor traders who are losing on a given day and to cap the winnings of those who appear to be 'streaking', and used it as a synecdoche for the market as a whole. That interpretative strategy makes very little sense, however, when you consider that the *reason* that the risk manager is pulling the trader is that the frustration and disappointment causes him to exaggerate risk, whereas the success encourages him to underrate risk vis-à-vis the market as a whole. Crucially, in Tuckett's model, the problem is not the distance between the judgements of individuals and the group, but rather the distance between the phantasies of market participants and his notion of 'reality', which can only be apprehended *ex-post*, but seems in fact to be based upon some notion of equilibrium and rationality that hovers behind the precise notions that he and Taffler try to critique [28], hence the hermeneutic circle.

6. Conclusions: financial instability and asset-price bubbles

The final problem with Emotional Finance is the specification of the problem. Financial bubbles are nothing new. One recent work of economic theory written by a former practitioner called them 'banal' and ubiquitous [29]. Janeway suggests that problem is not with asset-price bubbles, per se, but rather that some of them are productive whereas others destructive. Asset-price bubbles that focus on 'general purpose technologies' or infrastructure (canals, steamships, railways, electrification, information computing technology, etc) tend to be socially beneficial. The rush of speculation generates a tolerance for Schumpterian waste. Once the music stops, individual firms may go bankrupt, but the roads, canals, bridges, and rail lines remain.

Debt-leveraged bubbles, particularly in real estate, can wipe out private wealth and cause contagion to other aspects of the economy, generating great hardship, but those are usually generated by central banks that use household balance sheets to smooth aggregate demand, as happened in the late 1990s and early 2000s. Tuckett's analysis makes no distinction on the basis of the focal point of the bubble.

Bubbles are all equally suspect, in that they are formed around 'phantastic objects' that promise fool's gold. Underlying Tuckett's work is the peculiar fantasy that it is possible to train regulators to identify asset-price bubbles based on their recognition of a kind of prodromal euphoric state as evidenced in the chatter of traders, particularly on the Bloomberg platform. The idea is then to install circuit-breakers, as a kind of market nanny decides 'enough is enough.' The problem with this is that it begs the regulatory equivalent of the Texas sharpshooter fallacy, whereby a gunman sprays the side of a barn with a shotgun and only then steps up to draw the bulls-eye. We can only guess at the number of 'dangerous' bubbles that will be so averted!

One final point remains to be made. Tuckett calls for a 'Truth and Reconciliation' Commission to investigate the financial crisis in the same manner as the Apartheid-era crimes in South Africa. Leaving aside the question of how successful the latter was, the former is hardly worthy of such an intellectual and moral project. The Great Financial Crisis was not the end of the world as we know it, particularly from the vantage point of 2020 when the effects of COVID-19 lockdowns are so much greater. If the Great Financial Crisis was a searing experience for the Millenial generation, it was not because of economic realities, but because of the political responses to the crisis. Austerity policies which produced widening inequality in the developed world are neither 'necessary evils' nor the product of the 'inner logic of capitalism,' but rather are ideological and political projects pursued with the blessings of the median-voter.

The most dangerous thing about Tuckett's proposals for 'minding markets' is that they de-politicise the regulatory process, putting it in the realm of regulating human emotion, rather than in the sphere of political economy. For Tuckett, based in the United Kingdom, the irony of the financial crisis is that the neo-liberal experiment in 'light touch' regulation and low levels of taxation (especially on capital gains) happened under New Labour. The Tories came to power on the back of New Labour's mistakes, and have followed the 'tried and true' strategy of austerity while blaming the 'pain' on their predecessors and on the European Union. The electoral calculus of such a strategy produced Brexit. The glee with which the political elite have pursued these aims and the docility of the electorate in the face them is a much worthier target of study via notions like 'groupfeel' and 'phantasies' that produce master narratives. Rather than minding impersonal markets, we'd do better to mind our own tendency to deny the damage done by those who used the financial crisis to justify policies that they fully intended to pursue anyway. If 9/11 was George Bush's excuse for invading Iraq, the collapse of Lehman Brothers in its vicissitudes offered the Tories a pretext for dismantling the welfare state. In the era of COVID-19, the main challenge for regulators and central banks alike will be resisting pressure from politicians the world over to encourage bull markets deliberately in order to maintain consumer and investment confidence in the face of damage to the real economy and especially the attendant job losses. In addressing such questions, 'Emotional Finance' has little to offer, despite the sense of *Déjà vu* involved.

Acknowledgements

The author would like to acknowledge a number of people with whom she has discussed this subject over the years, including Professor Michelle Baddeley, Dr Stanley H. Shapiro, Dr Frederick Fisher, Dr Margot Waddell, and Dr David Bell, and the members of the London Consortium's 'Psychoanalytic Thought, History and Political Life Forum,' which was where she gave a version of this paper as a seminar in June 2014. Special thanks to the organisers, Dr Shaul Bar-Haim, Dr Benjamin Poore, and Dr Helen Tyson, and particularly to Professor Daniel Pick, Professor

Jacqueline Rose, Dr Matt ffytche, Dr Manuel Batsch, and Dr Akshi Singh for their comments. A version was also circulated in September 2015 at the New Imago Forum at Jesus College, Oxford where useful suggestions were made. The author would also like to thank her research assistant, Mr Eskil Välilä, for redrawing the graphs with updated data, which required considerable research, and for rendering them to suit the formatting guidelines for this publication.

Conflict of interest

The author declares no conflict of interest.

Data sources for figures and graphs

Figure 1: http://www.cboe.com/products/vix-index-volatility/vix-options-and-futures/vix-index/vix-historical-data (CBOE - Chicago Board Options Exchange).

Figure 2: http://www.cboe.com/products/vix-index-volatility/volatility-on-etfs/cboe-crude-oil-etf-volatility-index-ovx (CBOE - Chicago Board Options Exchange); http://www.cboe.com/products/vix-index-volatility/volatility-on-etfs/cboe-gold-etf-volatility-index-gvz (CBOE - Chicago Board Options Exchange); http://www.cboe.com/products/vix-index-volatility/vix-options-and-futures/vix-index/vix-historical-data (CBOE - Chicago Board Options Exchange).

Figure 3 (**a** and **b**): https://www.investing.com/indices/us-spx-500-historical-data (Investing.com Historical Data); https://www.indexmundi.com/commodities/?commodity=crude-oil&months=360 (Index Mundi data archive); https://usda.library.cornell.edu/concern/publications/k643b116n?locale=en (USDA Data Library); https://bsic.it/the-onion-paradox-or-why-futures-are-good-for-the-economy/ (Bocconi Student Investors Club Blog).

Figure 4: https ://appsso.eurostat.ec.europa.eu/nui/setupDownloads.do (Eurostat Data Archive); https://apps.bea.gov/iTable/iTable.cfm?reqid=19&step=3&isuri=1&1921=survey&1903=11#reqid=19&step=3&isuri=1&1921=survey&1903=11 (BEA, National Data).

Figure 5: https://www.macrotrends.net/2016/10-year-treasury-bond-rate-yield-chart (Macrotrends Data Archive); http://www.cboe.com/products/vix-index-volatility/vix-options-and-futures/vix-index/vix-historical-data (CBOE - Chicago Board Options Exchange).

Figure 6a: https://www.statista.com/statistics/1032048/value-us-dollar-since-1640/ (Statista archive); https://www.macrotrends.net/1333/historical-gold-prices-100-year-chart; https://onlygold.com/gold-prices/historical-gold-prices/ (Macrotrends); https://fred.stlouisfed.org/series/DGS20#0https://www.multpl.com/s-p-500-historical-prices/table/by-year (St Louis Federal Reserve Archive); https://seekingalpha.com/article/4311451-stocks-bonds-bills-and-inflation-returns-for-94-years-ending-december-2019 (Seeking Alpha Blog).

Figure 6b: https://finance.yahoo.com/quote/%5EGSPC/history?period1=-1325635200&period2=1603238400&interval=1mo&filter=history&frequency=1mo&includeAdjustedClose=true; https://www.officialdata.org/us/stocks/s-p-500/1927?amount=100&endYear=2020 (Yahoo Finance); https://www.in2013dollars.com/us/inflation/1927#:~:text=In%20other%20words%2C%20%24100%20in,inflation%20rate%20was%20%2D1.69%25 (CPI Inflation Calculator).

Author details

D'Maris Coffman[1,2,3]

1 Bartlett School of Construction and Project Management, University College London, London, United Kingdom

2 Department of Economics, Management and Quantitative Methods (DEMM), University of Milan, Milan, Italy

3 London Institute of Psychoanalysis, London, United Kingdom

*Address all correspondence to: d.coffman@ucl.ac.uk

References

[1] Baker, H.K., Filbeck, G. and Ricciardi, V., (2019). The Psychology of Financial Professionals and Their Clients. *Investments & Wealth Monitor*, pp.15-20.

[2] Tuckett, D. (2011). *Minding the Markets: An Emotional Finance View of Financial Instability.* Palgrave Macmillan.

[3] 'The Onion Paradox or Why Futures are good for the Economy: BSIC', Bocconi. (8 December 2013) See http://www.bsic.it/the-onion-paradox-or-why-futures-are-good-for-the-economy/

[4] Working, H. (1960). 'Note on the correlation of first differences of averages in a random chain'. Econometrica 916-918.

[5] Working, H. (1942). 'Quotations on commodity futures as price forecasts'. Econometrica 39-52.

[6] Smith, A., 2010. *The Wealth of Nations: An inquiry into the nature and causes of the Wealth of Nations*. Harriman House Limited.

[7] Coffman, D. and Neal, L. eds. (2014). *A History of Financial Crises.* 4 vols. Routledge.

[8] Dimson, E., Marsh, P. and Staunton, M., (2009). *Triumph of the optimists: 101 years of global investment returns*. Princeton University Press.

[9] Siegel, J.J., (2002). *Stocks for the Long Run: The Definite Guide to Financial Market Returns and Long-term Investment Strategies*. McGraw-Hill.

[10] Duxbury, D., Gärling, T., Gamble, A. and Klass, V., (2020). How emotions influence behavior in financial markets: a conceptual analysis and emotion-based account of buy-sell preferences. The European Journal of Finance, pp.1-22.

[11] Akerlof, George A. (1970). 'The Market for "Lemons": Quality Uncertainty and the Market Mechanism,' in The Quarterly Journal of Economics. 84:3, pp. 388-500.

[12] Freud, S. (1909) 'Bemerkungen Über einen Fall von Zwangsneurose', G.S., 8, 269; G.W., 7, 381. (52, 161, 169, 170, 322) [Trans.: 'Notes upon a Case of Obsessional Neurosis', C.P., 3, 293; Standard Ed., 10, 155.]

[13] Klein, M. (1932). *The Psycho-Analysis of Children. The International Psycho-Analytical Library*, 22:1-379. London: The Hogarth Press.

[14] Freud S (1908). Creative writers and day-dreaming. SE 9, 141-53. London: Hogarth.

[15] Rycroft, C. (1997). *A Critical Dictionary of Psychoanalysis*. Penguin [1968].

[16] Bowie, M. (1991), *Lacan.* Harvard University Press.

[17] Laplanche J, Pontalis JB (1973). *The language of psychoanalysis*. Nicholson-Smith D, translator. New York, NY, London: Norton and Hogarth.

[18] Tuckett, D., Taffler, R. (2008). 'Phantastic Objects and the Financial Market's Sense of Reality: A Psychoanalytic Contribution to the Understanding of Stock Market Instability'. Int. J. Psycho-Anal., 89:389-412.

[19] Baddeley, M., (2020). Hoarding in the age of COVID-19. Journal of Behavioral Economics for Policy, *4*(S), pp.69-75.

[20] Chong, K., & Tuckett, D. (2015). 'Constructing conviction through

action and narrative: how money managers manage uncertainty and the consequence for financial market functioning.' Socio-Economic Review, 13 (2), 309-330. doi:10.1093/ser/mwu020

[21] Nyman, R., Kapadia, S., Tuckett, D. A., Gregory, D., Ormerod, P., & Smith, R. (2018). 'News and narratives in financial systems: exploiting big data for systemic risk assessment'. Bank of England Staff Paper.

[22] Shiller, R.J., 2020. *Narrative economics: How stories go viral and drive major economic events*. Princeton University Press.

[23] Tuckett, D., Smith, R.E. and R. Nyman. 2014. 'Tracking phantastic objects: A computer algorithmic investigation of narrative evolution in unstructured data sources.' Social Networks. 38: 121-133.

[24] Kindleberger, C. (1978). Manias, Panics and Crashes: A History of Financial Crises. Macmillan.

[25] Sherwood, M. (1969). *The Logic of Explanation in Psychoanalysis*. Academic Press.

[26] White, H. (1978). *Tropics of Discourse: Essays in Cultural Criticism*. JHU Press.

[27] White, H. (2000). *Figural Realism: Studies in the Mimesis Effect*. JHU Press.

[28] Aren, S. and Hamamcı, H.N., (2020). Emotional finance: determinants of phantasy. Kybernetes.

[29] Janeway, W.H. (2018) *Doing Capitalism in the Innovation Economy: Markets, Speculation and the State*. Cambridge University Press. 2nd edition.

Chapter 8

From Money-Centered to People- and Planet-Centered Ledger Economics: Leveraging the Hidden Wealth of Underutilized Productive Capacity

Thomas Fisher and Joel Hodroff

Abstract

This chapter introduces a for-profit way to repair persistent problems in free enterprise economics and commerce. Today, continuous advances in technology and human capabilities fail to produce a commensurate, across-the-board rise in the standard of living and quality of life for households and communities. Instead, win-lose competition over money and proliferation of competitive duplication put downward pressure on profits, wages and the purchasing power of families. Despite an ever-growing economic pie, everyone does not enjoy a secure income. This is a money issue, not a productivity issue. Eventually, so-called equilibrium is achieved when businesses downsize, merge and/or fail. But businesses fail while there are still unmet needs for their products and services revealing a missed business opportunity. An innovative alternative is to monetize and market currently underutilized productive capacity using a new form of business scrip termed Ledger Dollars (L$) L$ increase purchasing power within a cooperative network of business and community stakeholders. L$ are analogous to loyalty rewards—backed by unsold products and services—but reward more than consumer spending and enhance cooperation and eco-sustainability. Ledger Dollars constitute a new financial asset class designed to improve traditional fiat-centered economics and advance the now popular Triple-Bottom-Line of People, Planet and Profits.

Keywords: triple-bottom-line economics, people-and-planet centered commerce, monetizing excess productive capacity

1. Introduction

The global economy knows *how to build* nearly anything, but it does not know *what to build* to solve our pressing social, economic, and environmental challenges. This is evident in the persistence of problems like inequality and unsustainability. Our modern economy has not solved these problems because nearly everything we know about economics and commerce was inherited from an era of scarcity, which drives win-lose competition over money, a grow-or-die business imperative, economic disparities, and damage to the natural environment [1].

This win-lose competition over money creates a dilemma. Businesses seek more customers, while people seek more of the very goods and services that businesses want to sell, with money often the only missing ingredient for commerce to occur, even though we invented money to promote needed commerce. At the same time, many people have useful skills for community economic development, with no way to put those people to work because of a lack of money to make that happen. This "lack of money" dilemma hits economically disadvantaged communities especially hard, and increases the challenges of closing economic disparities.

While this dilemma is accepted as normal by economists—as well as by business, community and government leaders—it makes no sense. These problems may seem solvable by issuing more money, but the more we issue money, the more competitive startups and businesses grow, generating more downward pressure on each enterprise's market share, prices, and profits. It also impacts employee wages, which affect family purchasing power [2].

Modern economies have more wealth producing ability—measured in underutilized capacity – than the money to distribute it. Many of our economic problems—from affordable housing and healthcare to world hunger and clean water to education, training and employment—can be solved not by issuing more money, but by questioning the assumption that win-lose competition over money is the most efficient way to provide the greatest economic good for the greatest number. Turning currently underutilized business capacity into profitable production and sales—at the marginal cost of production—is the win-win foundation for a needed update to free-enterprise economic thinking.

Unbridled competition over money is a double-edged sword. Free-enterprise competition is a powerful engine of economic growth. It increases customer traffic to a given destination, while improving consumer choice, quality and service, all while holding down prices. Competition is also our model for economic growth, creating jobs and expanding the tax base by rewarding entrepreneurs for hard work, risk and innovation. However, extreme competition over money puts downward pressure not only on a company's ability to perform, but also on employee wages, which stall or decrease when unbridled competition increases. That creates a large and growing gap between what a normal economy can produce and what employees, families and communities can afford to buy with their artificially restrained wages.

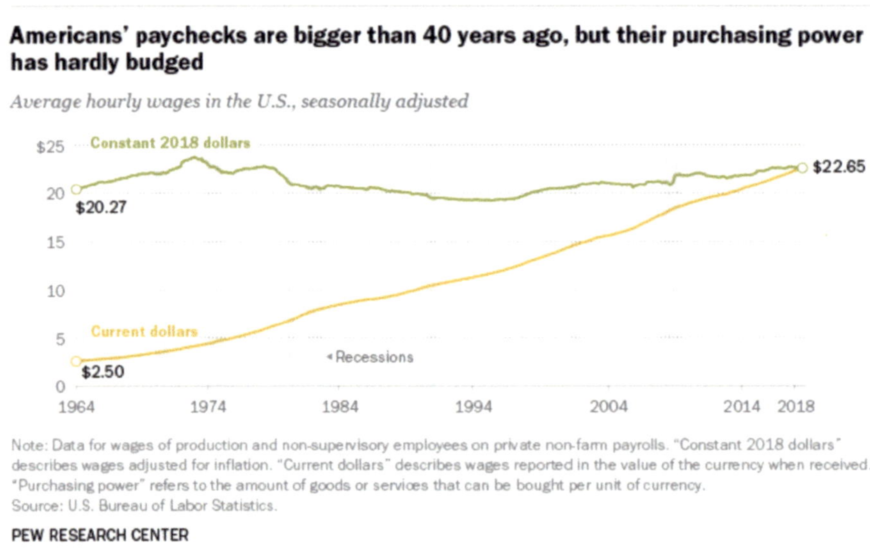

The cycle of innovation, growth, maturity and decline applies to most products and industries, and is well understood. The hidden anomaly is that our wealth-producing capabilities constantly improve with advances in technology, infrastructure and human skill, knowledge and creativity. Yet the standard of living and quality of life go up and down with the money-driven boom and bust cycles of the business cycle. Economists insist that falling prices benefit everyone in the end, and that new jobs created by ongoing innovation replace old jobs that are lost. Yet, downward pressure on market share from local-to-global proliferation of competitive duplication causes the growth of excess or underutilized business capacity, creating wasted wealth [3].

2. Confusing money with wealth

This wasted wealth stems from a flaw in how we think about and use money. We have made money the object of competition and the goal of the economic game. The simple yet mysterious fact is that economics, commerce and the popular culture all confuse money (our tool of wealth creation) with wealth (the goods and services). Of course, money is a critical tool in the equation, but it should not itself be the objective of economics. This confusion of money and wealth begins to explain our seemingly intractable social, economic and environmental challenges, even as all the other factors of production are only improving rapidly [4].

Confusing money and wealth is akin to confusing a map with the terrain the map represents. Economics will take a great leap forward when we distinguish money from wealth and introduce a next generation of money to mobilize real and available economic wealth wherever the dollar fails to do so. This is an enormous business opportunity, because there is so much untapped wealth in the world, side-by-side with so much unmet need. This serves no one: not businesses, individuals, communities, or society. This is not just an issue for the poor. Many individuals and families are just a paycheck or a layoff away from dire economic circumstances.

This is a societal problem, not a personal failing; it reflects a repairable shortcoming in our free enterprise system. And no one is to blame for this: not the rich, the poor, the banks, foreign competition, the government, the political left or right, or human nature. We all suffer from outmoded ways of thinking and outdated economic tools and practices. Blaming one group or another - all of them equally caught in a system they did not invent - gets in the way of a solution.

3. Awash In productive capacity

If we look across the economy, it is overflowing with excess productive capacity. College desks are empty more than they are full; restaurant tables are empty more than they are full. There are extensive off hours at fitness clubs, movie theaters, oil change shops, beauty salons and elsewhere. We are living in a world of wasted capacity and yet we are already overbuilt to meet the needs of everyone on the planet. For example, food is an abundant renewable resource, yet people go hungry across the world. Meanwhile, global agrobusiness is one of the most powerful industries on the planet and they want more customers. Business wants more customers and people need more goods and services, and yet, while humans invented money to match buyers with sellers and work to do with people who need jobs, all that's missing is money [5].

The automotive industry offers another example of excess capacity. While numerous people are driving old and perhaps dangerous vehicles, and others can afford no vehicle at all, thousands of auto dealerships are awash in high quality new and used cars. Only money or purchasing power is missing to match eager sellers with eager buyers. The same is true of education. While there is much agreement on the need for a more educated workforce, we do not know how to make college education affordable for all. Many people, young and old, desire a college education that they simply cannot afford (and affordability is a money issue not a wealth production and distribution issue). Colleges and universities have enormous numbers of unfilled desks and compete for student tuition dollars. For the most part, they each have enough infrastructure, instructors and staff to serve many more students, and could easily increase teachers and staff if a source of funding was available for everyone who wants to go to school. Scholarships are a means of discounting tuition, yet many youth leave college saddled in debt—again a money issue!

4. What we have not learned from economic downturns

The hidden lessons of the 2008–9 US housing market crash and subsequent global economic downturn are revealed in the movie The Big Short [6]. The movie ends with three revealing statistics: in the US alone, $5 trillion in wealth disappeared; 8 million people lost their jobs; 6 million families lost their homes. We also know that many millions of people lost some or all of their life savings and large numbers of businesses failed. Why are these well-known figures critical for repairing the US and global economies? Because the simple fact is that *no real wealth disappeared*: no buildings, no technology or global economic infrastructure, no labor skill, management knowhow or human creativity disappeared, no products disappeared off retail shelves, and not a single ounce of materials or a joule of energy disappeared. So what *disappeared* causing the devastating economic consequences on people and communities?

Technically, only valuations fell. Valuations are the price in dollars that one might expect to receive when selling stock, a company, a home, or other real and valuable material assets. In other words, during an economic downturn, numbers in computers, called money or stock, shrink. Nothing in the material world that constitutes wealth nor any of the factors of production, described above, disappear or diminished. In fact, the factors of production continue to improve during economic downturns, which ultimately help to set the stage for eventual recoveries. In truth, once again, only money goes missing to put people back to work and turn idle productive capacity into new consumable wealth for society.

This is, in part, what makes life in the modern world so stressful. Advances in technology cause us to chase money at an ever-increasing rate, rather than allowing us to enjoy time in nature, family and community time, personal growth and development time, religious and spiritual time, and so forth. It is outside our sense of possibility that technology could do the lion's portion of the work, leaving people to enjoy ever-shorter working hours by sharing what is left. Instead, people are today chasing after a living at the ever-increasing, 24–7-365 pace of technology. And we are paying the price with our health, and the health of our families, workplaces and communities. Technology could eliminate most repetitive, boring, and dangerous work, allowing people to enjoy life more. Why instead are ever-growing numbers of people feeling anxious about their economic futures and depressed about their situations? Put bluntly, the dynamics of the economy have hard-wired us to chase money for survival (and, of course, for many to get ahead).

5. Rethinking supply and demand

As a solution to the dilemma of businesses with desirable goods and services existing side-by-side with eager customers lacking purchasing power, we propose creating a next generation of money—backed by the underutilized wealth of society—to stretch purchasing power in fiat currencies beyond what is available today. Fiat currencies have a critical role to play as a means of exchange, but a single currency does not efficiently distribute both what is abundant and what is scarce. A new accounting protocol can stretch current financial resources to distribute evermore available wealth. Pairing the dollar with a second currency, as a measure of wealth, addresses this dilemma, expanding production and distribution for what is already or could easily be in sufficient supply, e.g., food, shelter, healthcare, education, and so forth. In such a system, the ratio between dollars and the second currency in the price of an item would denote its relative scarcity or sufficiency.

Consider how the sharing economy accomplished rapid economic growth when mobile apps and social media had a fraction of the economic impact that they have today. A decade ago, it exploded onto the scene creating millions of jobs and billions of dollars of new wealth. On the one hand, the sharing economy demonstrated how to capture, monetize and distribute the excess productive capacity of solopreneurs—an empty room in someone's home or an idle car and driver. On the other hand, filtered through win-lose competition over money, someone had to take the hit for all this economic growth. Hotels, motels and their employees took the hit from the rise of Airbnb, while cab drivers, limo drivers and their companies took the hit from the rise of Uber and Lyft. This showed how the outdated economics of scarcity, based in win-lose competition over money, can stifle efforts to monetize excess capacity.

We need, instead, to move toward "Continuous Economic Improvement", where every advance in the factors of production—technology; infrastructure; human skill, knowledge and creativity; our ever-growing access to nature's abundant and free renewable resources—raises the standard of living and quality of life for everyone, shortens working hours across-the-board and, ultimately, eliminates traditional economic growth and creates a Circular Economy.

When we monetize excess capacity, as in the sharing economy, not with dollars, since the lack of dollars has created the problem to begin with, but with another measure of wealth, a second currency, we can address the paradox of our having excess wealth and insufficient cash. It also enables us to close disparities, whether it's for women or communities of color or youth, which is hard to do in a cash economy because of a lack of dollars. In a dual currency system, if somebody pays you in the second currency, you can pay for things on a part cash/part second-currency basis, stretching your purchasing power and get more of what you need.

The traditional approach to closing disparities include: local, state and national government programs; philanthropy and volunteerism; corporate social responsibility and social entrepreneurship; cooperative enterprises; women and minority owned businesses; public education campaigns; wellness campaigns; green products and services; microlending; collective impact initiatives and so forth. Just as millions of businesses compete over market share with their products and services, millions of government agencies, schools and community programs compete for tax allocations, and millions of non-profit and community organizations compete for philanthropic funding and volunteer time. In the end, this proliferation of competitive duplication within and across sectors creates immense inefficiency. Greater efficiency is at the heart of economic progress and environmental sustainability.

Continuous Economic Improvement would operate not by holding down production to the level of available purchasing power, but by raising the purchasing power for individuals, families and communities by capturing he ever-increasing productive capacity in the world. In order not to disrupt what was already working well in the economy, Continuous Economic Improvement would not raise employer labor costs, increase taxes or increase debt. It has three cornerstone premises:

- Business innovation and the profit motive is more effective than politics to solve social, economic and environmental challenges. When joined with institutional power and resources and community wisdom and mobilization (empowered by social media and other modern information technologies), it would be an unstoppable force for the common good.

- Modern technology, global economic infrastructure, renewable resources and eco-sustainable business practices can now produce more than enough food, housing, education, healthcare, travel and entertainment options for everyone on the planet to enjoy a high quality of life and a healthy balanced lifestyle.

- Money, commerce and citizen empowerment could be immediately brought into the 21st Century with another step in the history of money innovation. We would go from barter to coins to paper currency to electronic commerce to ledgers as part and parcel of economic history.

6. Ledger economics

An economics based on ledgers recognizes that transactions that once involved exchanging tokens – cash and coins – are now increasingly done through credit and debit cards, which amounts to digital bits moving from one ledger to another. This represents a transformation in the history of money. Unlike cash and coin tokens, ledgers do not crash or inflate in value, do not experience scarcity or hoarding, and do not lend themselves to speculation or theft. Moreover, ledgers allow us to measure not just the exchange of cash, but other currencies as well, accounting not only for money, but also for other forms of capital that we have not tallied before [7].

The role of ledgers as a measure of untapped wealth has broad implications for many of the chronic challenges we face. Impoverished communities, for example, may lack money, but they often have extraordinary amounts of social and cultural capital, which, if accounted for, can enable these communities to address their own problems and meet their own needs without depending upon government programs or non-profit charity. Ledgers also enable us to have economic activity that does not destroy the natural environment in the process by accounting for work that has environmental benefits as equally as that which does not. Likewise, ledgers provide a way for businesses that have excess capacity and owners who have under-utilized goods and services to put those assets to work meeting the unmet needs of customers and consumers.

Ledgers measure wealth, while U.S. dollars – and the national currencies in other nations –remain primarily units of exchange. But there are also other features that distinguish these two types of currencies. A ledger currency – let us call them Ledger Dollars (L$) – could stretch U.S. dollars through dual currency transactions. For example, a $20.00 restaurant meal might cost $12.00 and L$ 8.00, much like the economics of senior discounts or '2 for 1' dining. Or a $20 fitness club pass might cost $4.00 and L$ 16.00, based on the much lower marginal cost of production at a club than at a restaurant.

Bank-issued dollars – or other national currencies – are government money, backed by debt and taxes. Ledger Dollars are more like loyalty rewards (frequent flyer miles, Hilton Honors, Starbuck Points, etc.) which are business-issued currencies backed by real business products and services. But unlike loyalty rewards, L$ are not rewarded for consumer spending and do not promote the competitive advantage of one business over another. National currencies are scarce by their very nature and therefore they command interest and dividends in the market. They are also party to the ups and downs of speculation and part-and-parcel of inflationary and recessionary problems as well. In contrast, Ledger Dollars are purely symbols—mere entries in a ledger—used to match production of goods and services with business, employee, customer, family and community wants and needs. There can never be a shortage of symbols—inches, gallons, pounds or numbers— to get needed work done in communities. And through the efficient match of customer purchasing power to available products and services, we can finally solve the pesky problems of inflation and recession.

U.S. dollars or other national currencies are a blunt instrument to address economic inequity, as traditional money chases the highest rate of return and as interest and dividends bring evermore money to those who already have money. Ledger Dollars, instead, encourage a more level economic playing field through smarter production and distribution of real wealth. Finally, U.S. dollars encourage consumerism to promote traditional economic growth, which has negative social and environmental consequences. In contrast, Ledger Dollars promote a higher quality of life by engaging everyone in greater economic efficiency and voluntary sharing of currently idle resources, advancing better living, with less consumption [8].

Traditional Economics and Commerce versus Dual Currency Commerce and Ledger Economics

Category	**Fiat-based Economic and Commerce**	**Dual Currency Commerce and Ledger Economics**
Philosophy	Competition over scarce resources—in the face of unlimited wants and needs—creates the greatest good for the greatest number.	People and planet-centered economics and social entrepreneurship. Breaks no laws of free enterprise economics; fiat/dollars distribute what is scarce; Ledger Dollars distribute what is sufficient/abundant. Business-led, market-based, profit driven, yet immediate not trickle down.
Economic Driver(s)	Maximize shareholder value through increased profits (not a bad thing, just an incomplete approach)	Triple bottom line: people, profits, planet; seeks an equitable win for all stakeholders, while protecting the environment
Currency Innovation	Not a field of economics; latest design innovation was paper tokens to digital tokens riding banking and Automated Clearinghouse (ACH) ledgers	Transitions economics and commerce from solely using a fiat token currency to a dual currency combination of a fiat currency and a ledger currency
Economic domain(s)	Revolves around what is measured in fiat currency	3 domains: fiat economy; non-fiat monetized economy; unrecognized and nonmonetized excess productive capacity economy
Price setting	Supply and Demand sets prices in fiat currencies only leaving extensive underutilized productive capacity side-by-side with extensive unmet needs	• *Total Supply* recognizes the sum of available wealth in all three domains (see above) • *Total Demand* recognizes all unmet needs across the planet • *Supply* of goods and services in the modern era outstrips humanity's ability to consume in many categories of production • What remains scarce is subject to either fiat only pricing or a higher ratio of fiat to Ledger Dollars in the price

Traditional Economics and Commerce versus Dual Currency Commerce and Ledger Economics

Category	Fiat-based Economic and Commerce	Dual Currency Commerce and Ledger Economics
Competition vs. Cooperation	Competition over money leaves wealth on the table and drives win-lose results	Dual Currency Commerce balances competition and cooperation to lift everyone up together
Impacts of labor-saving technology, outsourcing, mergers and acquisitions	Many people lose their jobs, while other people are left working longer and harder.	Advances in technology and sharing work globally raises everyone's standard of living and quality of life, while shortening working hours, and reducing damage to the natural environment
Quality of life considerations	Drives longer working hours and business versus labor workplace dynamics; degrades the natural environment; social issues (crime, workplace stress, addiction) are considered "personal problems"	Continuous economic improvement drives: ever-higher quality of life; ever-shorter working hours; ever-less damage to the natural environment by thoughtful and cooperative distribution of work, material sufficiency, and leisure; social problems (crime, workplace stress, addictions) are addressed as social issues
Diversity, Equity and Inclusion	Disparities remain and expand because fiat money seeks the highest rate of return and results in money flight from communities	Disparities become relatively easy to close at the marginal cost of production through the monetization of excess productive capacity
Governance	Government banking regulations and one-size-fits-all civil legislation	Governance by protocol (akin to the Internet, Visa/MC, and the 12 Step program of Alcoholics Anonymous). Algorithms govern currency distribution based upon available resources. Mass customization allows all network stakeholders to determine rules and regulations within customized communities
Relationship to growth	Based on consumerism and the inherited "grow-or-die" business imperative	Seeks to build a Circular Economy with a values-based economic engine; recognizes extensive underutilized productive capacity and replaces growth imperative with efficiency; does not need consumerism, so focuses on quality-of-life considerations
Healthcare	Focus is on institutional care and treatment, not prevention; highly profitable activities include: treating cancer and diabetes; diagnostics and pharmaceuticals; cardiovascular medicine (a heart attack is a major economic event, while quitting smoking lowers the GDP)	Focus is on individual, family and community health and wellness through addressing the Social Determinants of Health and Health Disparities. Wellness investments are low-cost, including healthy diet, moderate exercise, economic stability and wellness education, etc.

7. Money innovation

Ledger economics represent a paradigm shift in how we think about money and look at wealth. Consider that nothing in the physical universe changed when human perception shifted from the earth at the center of the universe to the sun at the center of the solar system. Yet, that shift in perception opened the door to enormous advances in science and society. Using the solar system as a metaphor, money has long stood at the center of society's economic universe. This has led us to subordinate all that we do to the availability of money, including much that communities value: families, education and healthcare, God and spirituality, hobbies, healthy balanced lives, culture, the natural environment and more.

Ledger Dollars put those values, rather than cash, at the center of the economic universe. Money should revolve around values and not the other way around, especially since money is just a means to our ends, something that we designed and that we can redesign if it no longer helps us achieve what we most value. The redesign of money may sound odd, but we have done this before, innovating new tokens of exchange when necessary.

Historically, money innovation has been technology-driven, following the accelerating pace of economic evolution. In the 1800s, the United States transitioned from gold and silver coins to paper currency, as the dominant form of money. During that time, virtually every state and every bank issued their own paper money. The system was unworkable, and thousands of banks failed. In response, the equivalent of an industry standard was set for paper currency. It consisted of a single national currency and a Federal Reserve System. Then, a hundred years later the phenomenon was repeated.

In the early years of the credit-card-industry banks, department stores, gas stations and others each issued and processed their own credit cards. The young industry had operating losses of tens of millions of dollars. An industry standard was set that provided workability and profitability for the banks. It was the VISA platform (followed quickly by MasterCard) [9]. We can learn a great deal from the standard that was set, because it included a new financial instrument (the electronic debit and credit), a new payment platform and a cooperative network of banks and retail merchants. Virtually everything proposed here can be created rapidly through a cooperative network made up of banks (and the payment systems industry), retail merchants and cardholders, which was the original vision of VISA's Founder. Money innovation has also enabled the democratization of wealth:

- The agricultural era brought the transition from bartering to gold coins over a 3,000 to 5,000 year period, with coins made possible by the technologies of smelting and metal casting

- The industrial era, over a period of 300 to 500 years, saw the transition to paper currency and checks, all made possible by printing and paper making

- Today's high-tech global era, fueled by the transition to electronic banking, credit cards, e-commerce, and now mobile apps, has matured over a mere 30 to 50 years, all made possible by computers, plastics, and the Internet.

That increasing pace, from millennia to centuries to decades, has demonstrated not only the growing rapidity of money innovation, but also its feasibility as a way to address unmet needs. And if that pace continues, we think that it could be just a matter of 3 to 5 years to see the emergence of a monetary system that revolves around and supports what communities most value: a second currency, enabled by mobile apps, social media and blockchain and able to absorb excess assets, compensate voluntary work, and increase the quality of life of everyone.

We cannot solve society's greatest challenges with a tool – money – that is insufficient for the tasks we want it to do. But this is not impractical or overly idealistic at all when you realize that society operates at only a fraction of its social, economic and environmental potential. We have all the tools that we need to make a rapid and sustainable economic transformation happen and a universally high quality of life available to everyone.

Over 70 years ago, with no computers or global economic infrastructure - and with only on-the-job training for the so-called unskilled members of society - the U.S. went from the depths of the depression to full employment and global war production in a mere 18 months. The three key ingredients of this extraordinary economic feat were a common cause, a funding source, and a cooperative mobilization in contrast to everyday competition over money. A common vision, modern technology, a new wealth accounting protocol, and cooperative mobilization could enable a 21st century ledger-economic system that works at the pace of mobile apps and social media.

Ledger Dollars integrate the best features of many popular currencies

Money Type	Most useful features	Least useful Features
Fiat/national currencies	• Proven and tested, highly productive, mainstream system (Coin of the Realm) • Used across the private, public, nonprofit, cooperative and social impact sectors • Engine of innovation including social entrepreneurship • Rewards risk, innovation and hard work • Already functions from local-to-global	• Money-centered not Triple Bottom Line-based • Elevates competition over cooperation and fails to distribute what is abundant • Does not address gaping economic disparities • Money flows to the highest rate of return causing community impoverishment • History of economic crashes; inflation and recession • Unsolved problems lead to political fighting rather than united solutions • Money competition is hard-wired for growth rather than sustainability
Barter	• Widescale use in both B2B and C2C exchange • Mobilizes excess business capacity • Popular workaround for lack of fiat currency	• No effective and widely used model of B2C exchange • Too much bartering disrupts a company's cash flow • Most businesses use in-kind contributions as the way to support community economic development
Loyalty Rewards	• Global currency backed by business excess capacity • Demonstrates fully functioning dual currency pricing, accounting and transaction settlement technology	• Loyalty rewards are a competitive weapon in the market • Thousands of competing rewards does little to address economic development • Rewarding spending increases disparities and does not support sustainability
Community Currencies and Time Dollars	• People helping people in local economic exchange • Human scale activity • Supports relationships	• Rarely accepted by Merchants • No proof of scalability • Lifestyle choice, not systems-change lever

Ledger Dollars integrate the best features of many popular currencies		
Money Type	**Most useful features**	**Least useful Features**
Cryptocurrencies	• Leverages blockchain technology for secure, cost-effective, and immutable transactions; demonstrates scalability • Generally governed through rules-based protocols; decentralized design may support community autonomy and mass customization • Helping to make Money Innovation a mainstream concept • capital accumulation, which has created new infrastructure that can be applied to upgrading the economy	• Mining as the source of origination does not provide significant social value; some argue environmentally harmful energy use • So far economically ineffective: rarely accepted by merchants; creates few jobs despite the speculative frenzy; does not close disparities, etc. • Unstable value inside speculative markets; serious risk to investors
Anticipated results by combining the best features of multiple currencies and platforms		
Ledger Dollars used within a Dual Currency Ledger Economics Network	• Stretches dollars rather than competes with dollars; mainstream with a profit motive in dollars • Backed by goods and services through dual currency contracts with Merchants • Denominated in every country's fiat currency for ease of pricing • Rewards many types of social good • Delivers new wealth into the economy at the marginal cost of production to close disparities • Technology is at hand in the loyalty rewards industry across the globe; relatively easy to launch and scale • Ledgers do not crash; suffer inflation, recession or money flight from communities; akin to loyalty rewards, Ledger Dollars are an accounting protocol, not a circulating token; they are issued, redeemed, and taken off the books • The system is managed by governance protocol (akin to the Visa/MC Interchange or the Internet); money supply is managed by algorithms; addresses the Triple Bottom Line of People-Profits-Planet	

8. A dual-currency ledger dollar system

The Dual-Currency Ledger-Dollar (DCLD) system has four main stakeholder groups: Individuals, Merchants, Sponsors, and System Operators.

Individuals download the DCLD app and receive a first monthly dividend on their smart phones or other digital device. The app reveals where to earn and where to spend Ledger Dollars. It helps people to find community organizations, schools, employers and government agencies offering L$ to volunteers, students, employees, and government benefit recipients who seek to earn additional Ledger Dollars above their monthly allocation. For participants in the system, it not only has the tangible benefit of increasing their purchasing power at participating merchants, but also intangible advantages like feeling valued for contributing to thriving communities, meeting like-minded people, and helping create a better world that works for everyone.

Sponsors are the community-oriented organizations that aggregate and report the rewardable activities of network participants. A public school, for example, could reward parents or local residents who tutor struggling students. It could also reward those students for putting in the effort to improve their academic performance or engage in service learning in the community. Employers would do the same for participating employees who join company volunteer groups, wellness teams or green teams. Community organizations reward volunteers. Healthcare systems reward patient compliance, donating blood, and better health outcomes. Government agencies distribute L$ to benefits recipients. Indeed, any socially valuable activities can lead to earning extra Ledger Dollars. In this way, Sponsors can improve volunteer recruitment and retention, advance community wellbeing, increase their impact, attract funder attention and support, and reward the engagement of their own employees.

Merchants determine the *ratio* of U.S. dollars to Ledger Dollars to accept and any restrictions on when they will accept the second currency. Merchants benefit by increasing the number of customers, while selling targeted excess capacity at the marginal cost of production plus an incremental cash profit. They pay a modest marketing fee on dual currency sales and receive useful demographic data on community participation, free L$ employee benefit, and excellent community PR.

System Operators include payment processors and merchant services organizations; consultants to the private, public, nonprofit, cooperative, and social impact sectors; algorithm architects who see that the L$ supply makes a good match between monetized excess capacity and unmet family and community needs and others who help to aid the transition from a dollars-only economy to a dual-currency ledger system.

Stakeholder Benefits in a Dual Currency Ledger Economics Network (DCLEN)	
Individuals	• Increased purchasing power and reduction of economic insecurity • Greater job opportunities (better match of work in communities with people who need jobs) • Continuous economic improvement means more personal, family and community time • Akin to the GI Bill (1944), 1–2 gap years of domestic or international service can provide youth with fully funded college educations
Merchants	• Increased customers, sales and profits • Improved employee recruitment and retention from improved benefits and thriving workplace cultures • Excellent community PR
Sponsors	• Ledger Dollars expand funding to achieve goals and help to recruit and retain the best talent • Voluntary Dual Currency Sliding-Scale prices are a unique form of support to close disparities • A share of system transaction fees (akin to affinity donations)
System Operators	• A share in system transaction fees • Innovative spin-off business opportunities • A leadership role in sustainable economic development

9. How it works for individuals

Sonya is a nurse in a community clinic who hears about recovery dollars from a coworker. She downloads the mobile app and receives a first monthly dividend of L$ 100.00. That dividend is determined by an algorithm based upon the volume of merchants in the network and their redemption patterns: The more merchants who join and the more people seek their products and services, the larger the dividend grows to over time.

DOI: http://dx.doi.org/10.5772/intechopen.95562

Using the merchant directory and location map, Sonya finds a local gym where a standard $99.00 membership now costs her $50.00 plus L$ 49.00, which would be akin to the gym offering a 50% discount to attract new members. This stretches Sonya's cash and brings in extra revenue to the gym, given the low marginal cost of accommodating another customer on underused equipment and facilities.

Eager to earn more recovery dollars, Sonia uses the app to locate community sponsors who could use volunteers. When she spends two hours a week volunteering with a sponsor in the network, Sonya earns L$ 20.00/hour, which adds an additional L$ 160.00 per month to her account. Sonya also finds that a local food co-op allows customers to pay 10% of their total shopping bills in recovery dollars, which not only increases their purchasing power, but also builds a more cooperative economy by incentivizing customers to volunteer.

On the weekend, Sonya notices that the app continually highlights new merchant offers in her neighborhood and she finds a "L$ Deal" at a hair salon (shampoo and cut for $30.00 and L$30.00 for new customers). She meets some of her volunteer friends at a restaurant where their $80.00 tab is $55.00 and L$25.00 (tax and tip in cash). Sonya also donates L$20.00 to a teen group raising money for a local sports team. Spending L$ help her save cash on every day purchases and support her favorite causes from the savings.

The system can also incorporate a feature to help close social and economic disparities without resorting to tax dollars. A bit like rounding-up for a cause or paying-it-forward at the drive-through, economically well-off participants voluntarily pay further up the US dollar side of Dual Currency transactions, making it possible for economically disadvantaged participants to transact in fewer dollars and more Ledger Dollars. For example: on a $20.00 meal that was priced at $12.00 and L$8.00, a more financially well-off person can voluntarily pay $18.00 cash and L$ 2.00 (or tithe and pay $22.00), which would allow a lower-income person, to pay $6.00 cash and L$ 14.00 for their $20.00 meal. In both cases, merchants gets the dollars that they contracted for, but unlike when everyone pays the same price, some people voluntarily pay with more cash allowing others to pay with more Ledger Dollars. This is a market-based, people-helping-people model that could grow up and reduce the need for so many tax-funded government programs.

10. How it works for employers and communities

One use of currently wasted wealth is intended to increase employee compensation without raising cash labor costs for employers. The process improves employee wages and benefits by utilizing empty restaurant tables, off-hours at fitness clubs, excess retail inventory, and so on. Instead of downsizing companies to match money-based demand in the market, it raises people's purchasing power up to the level of available business capacity.

Many employers know how to use a portion of their excess capacity as a perk or a benefit for their own employees. Employees who work for an airline enjoy free or discounted flights. Those who work at universities generally enjoy free or discounted classes. Fitness club employees enjoy free or discounted memberships, while restaurant employees enjoy free or discounted food. This is true across the private sector, as well as in the public sector (public universities) and the nonprofit sector (YM/YWCAs). It is noteworthy that if businesses operated at full-capacity, with 100 percent cash customers, this common form of employee benefits would not exist, confirming the existence of underutilized business capacity.

Ledger economics makes the excess capacity of employers available to all employees as a perk or benefit for working within a network of cooperating businesses, government agencies and nonprofit organizations. Imagine the pooling of all this excess capacity into a "virtual community warehouse" for sustainable economic development, accessed not only by employees, but also by all those earning rewards within the community.

The warehouse would be virtual because none of the products need to be purchased in advance or stored somewhere special, as with traditional bricks-and-mortar retail. Instead, they remain where they are normally produced and sold—at the airlines, the university, the fitness club or the restaurant. This system simply captures currently underutilized business capacity to offer people new purchasing power, to attract more customers, and to give communities new economic resources.

The free-enterprise system manages excessive competition, easily and without government regulation, by setting needed standards across any given industry. Capitalist countries have yet to apply this principle to proliferation of competitive duplication within the economy, whether at the local, state or national levels. Why set industry standards? Consider how impractical it would be if there were 15 different types of electrical outlets to accommodate 15 different styles of electrical plugs on consumer products. To avoid this mess, an industry standard is set to which all manufacturers of both electrical outlets and consumer products adhere. The same is true of Internet Protocol on the World Wide Web, which did not require government regulation, but instead grew out of collaborative development and agreed upon design principles.

The virtual warehouse would work in the same way. The participating merchants would establish a standard that everyone would agree to follow as part of the mobile app, with instructions to participating customers and sponsors on how to access the excess capacity and how to document the community hours that volunteers have donated in exchange for additional recovery dollars. When everyone has something to gain from a system, the participants involved in it have a strong incentive to agree on an industry standard so that all can benefit.

11. Ledger dollars and the IRS

Will people have to pay income taxes on the Ledger Dollars they receive as a dividend or earn through their community work? While it is not possible to know the answer ahead of a formal ruling, there are useful precedents. Since the merchant is simply taking less cash and not keeping and spending a circulating currency, then Ledger Dollars are clearly not a barter dollar. Barter dollars are considered commercial in nature and taxable (with taxes due in US dollars). This system operates, instead, like a universal employee discount network, and discounts are not taxable income.

Ledger Dollars are similar to the discounts that employees enjoy from their own employers' excess capacity: discount flights for airline employees, discount classes for university employees, discount meals for restaurant employees, etc. And by awarding Ledger Dollars to volunteers and others, participating employees and non-employees benefit from discounts at businesses everywhere in the network. A third precedent is a community currency know as Time Dollars [10]. Time Dollars are a people-helping-people, noncommercial, community economic development currency, and they are not taxable as income. There was a ruling many years ago by the Minnesota Department of Revenue that state welfare recipients who earned Community Service Dollars (a predecessor currency) through volunteerism would not have their welfare benefits reduced, which is one more positive precedent.

While cryptocurrencies are taxable if there are capital gains from the sale of an investment in crypto, Ledger Dollars, taken off the books as soon as they are redeemed, is not an investable or speculative instrument, which is yet another reason why Ledger Dollars might not be taxed as income. Ultimately the issue is not whether this second currency will be taxable, but rather how much can this system upgrade the economy and help to create a universally high quality of life. A mature system could fund many of the community economic development needs that taxes are used for today, with the idea that an ever-more efficient economy will result in less need for government services paid for through taxation.

The factors of wealth production are all at hand and continuously improving: technology, global infrastructure; human knowledge and creativity, innovative business models, access to the earth's free and abundant renewable resources. Yet large numbers of people in the US and around the world still face a low and/or deteriorating quality of life. This can be seen in poverty and widespread economic insecurity, poor public health and safety, workplace stress, social and economic disparities, crime, addictions, youth at risk, pollution, and so forth... all of it based on an outdated paradigm of economic scarcity. We can immediately begin to move beyond all of these age-old problems by recognizing the enormous amount of untapped wealth that exists in the world and leveraging it to everyone's advantage. Once we see that we are drowning in wealth, while searching for money (our own invention), we can begin to create more sensible and sustainable economies the world over.

If, in fact, our inherited framework for economics—scarce resources and unlimited wants and needs—is outdated, then so, perhaps, are other theoretical and practical inheritances from that earlier era where that framework came from. Today's cultural obsession with blaming the rich, the poor, the right, the left, the military, foreign competition and the like prevents thoughtful and intelligent discourse toward new solutions. A common vision of Continuous Economic Improvement for all can transcend the current left-versus-right polarization and the tendency to blame anyone, when in fact this inherited system is overdue for a 21st Century update.

Ledger economics can help us call a truce between the political left and right and the stalemate that prevents innovative solutions from emerging. For Conservatives and Libertarians, ledger economics is completely voluntary and self-funded, as well as business-led, market-based, and profit-driven. For Liberals and Socialists, it offers immediate rather than trickle down benefits and environmentally sustainable rather than growth-based commerce, while closing rather than increasing disparities. By combining this new financial resource with a mobilization of business-community stakeholders, we can end the blame and create a dual-currency, ledger-based, equitable-and-sustainable economy, based on continuous economic improvement [11].

Economics and Politics beyond Left–Right-Compromise

For Conservatives and Libertarians	**For Liberals, socialists and greens**
100% voluntary: No forced participation by government or other authorities; breaks no rules of free enterprise economics	**Immediate not trickle down:** the available underutilized business community resources
100% self-funding: no need for higher taxes or deeper debt to raise everyone up with the engine of dual currency efficiency	**Equitable:** closing disparities through the mobilization of massive underutilized productive capacity is rapid and inexpensive rather than attempting to close disparities with ever elusive fiat resources

Economics and Politics beyond Left–Right-Compromise	
For Conservatives and Libertarians	**For Liberals, socialists and greens**
Business-led, market-based and profit-driven: Dual Currency Commerce is purely a social entrepreneurial business innovation entering the market making use of new technologies to create greater efficiencies	**Ecologically sustainable:** there is no need for traditional growth when the world is already overbuilt to meet all need across the planet. For example, short-term, food is an abundant renewable resource and global agribusiness wants more customers. This is purely a matter of money and will; not at all about skills, infrastructure, lack of demand, etc. Long-term, we can make communities everywhere self-sustaining and interdependent through shared technologies and sustainability best practices.
For everyone **Mass Customization:** There is no need to fight and suffer over who gets their way regarding controversial issues. The Internet demonstrates that in the high-tech era, a shared platform can also allow everyone to pursue their own interests. In the same way that porn-blocker can be applied to a phone, a computer, or a television, communities of common values can voluntarily choose to participate in customized economies that are "for or against" abortions, drugs; marriage equality; guns; vegan lifestyles; prostitution, and so forth. Why? Because akin to the Internet, if you are willing to follow the protocol to get on, you can do what you want whether it is: e-commerce; pornography; charitable fundraising; art; sports; pro or against environmentalism, free speech, etc.	

Author details

Thomas Fisher[1*] and Joel Hodroff[2]

1 University of Minnesota, Minneapolis, USA

2 Rapid Recovery Alliance, Minneapolis, USA

*Address all correspondence to: tfisher@umn.edu

DOI: http://dx.doi.org/10.5772/intechopen.95562

References

[1] Lietaer, Bernard (2001) The Future of Money: Creating New Wealth, Work and a Wiser World, London, Random House Press.

[2] Drew Desiler, (August 7, 2018) For most U.S. workers, real wages have barely budged in decades, Pew Research Center

[3] Wann, David (2007) "Simple Prosperity: Finding Real Wealth in a Sustainable Lifestyle" New York, St. Martin's Griffin.

[4] Toffler, Alvin and Toffler, Heidi (2006) "Revolutionary Wealth" New York, Knopf.

[5] Hodroff, Joel (1993) "The Currency Exchange: Community Economic Development through Business Entrepreneurship" Self-Published: http://www.dualcurrency.com/files/The_Currency_Exchange_0-19.pdf; http://www.dualcurrency.com/files/The_Currency_Exchange_20-44.pdf

[6] Lewis, Michael (2010). *The Big Short: Inside the Doomsday Machine.* New York, W.W. Norton.

[7] Hodroff, Joel (2003) "Sustainable Prosperity: Capturing Underutilized Business Capacity to Revitalize our Economy and Transform our Quality of Life" Self-published: http://www.dualcurrency.com/commercepages/whitepapercomplete.html

[8] Hodroff, Joel (1991) "How 'Collective Self-Help Groups' and Computer Networks are Organizational Models for the Democratic Transformation of Society" Self-published: http://www.dualcurrency.com/files/Self-Help_Groups_and_Computer_Networks.doc

[9] Hock, Dee (1999) "Birth of the Chaordic Age" San Francisco, Berrett-Koehler Publishers

[10] Cahn, Edgar and Rowe, Jonathan (1998) Time Dollars: The New Currency that Enables Americans to Turn their Hidden Resource-Time-into Personal Security & Community Renewal Chicago, Family Resource Coalition of America

[11] Henderson, Hazel (1996) "Building a Win-Win World: Life Beyond Global Economic Warfare" San Francisco, Berrett-Koehler Publishers, Inc.

Chapter 9

Tunisian Fintech: An Ecosystem under Construction - Can COVID 19 be the Fuel to Ignite the Construction of Tunisian Fintech?

Salma Zone

Abstract

Fintech leads the most powerful technology and finance in the industry. Appearing recently in the newspapers, this term describes the disruptive challenge in the financial sectors. Fintech has primarily emerged in the world, and then Europe followed the lead before it starts in Tunisia. Although Fintech attracts the customers through the innovation and the technology, it worries users because of the absence of the intermediaries. Fintechs create metamorphosis in the financial field of digital disruption and really shake up the reserved world of banking services, savings, means of payment, and financing. The main idea of this chapter is to describe the Fintech ecosystem in Tunisia. It is about situating the concepts around Fintech by studying the reasons for its emergence and its business segments. Then, the analysis provides the elements of the Tunisian ecosystem of Fintech, the issues, and the challenges. This chapter aims to capture the essence of this phenomenon by discussing the challenges for both Fintech startups and traditional financial.

Keywords: Fintech, startups Fintech, Fintech ecosystem, Tunisia

1. Introduction

Fintech refers to innovation in financial services through technology. This financial technology combines financial products or services with technology to compete with, or cooperate with, financial institutions [1–3].

This term dates back to the 1980s and derives from the confusion between finance and technology. It becomes popular following the 2008 crisis. Innovations give birth to business models, processes and new products, and applications. These will drive the financial markets, financial institutions, and financial services allocation solutions (Financial Stability Board).

The innovations in finance have a phenomenal boom thanks to finance professionals who reconsider the progress of the financial system. These innovations combine with innovation, technology, flexibility, simplicity, and efficiency. Less expensive and more efficient for users, Fintechs are shaking up finance leaders. The term Fintech remains largely unknown in Tunisia.

The Fintech Industry: Fintech global investment in the first half of 2018 is $ 31 billion. These investments are equal to those of the integrity of the year 2017 [4].

In France, Finance startups insured 200 million Euros in the first half of 2018 [5]. These spectacular revolutions are ensured by Blockchain technology (a division which is evolving rapidly but which has not reached the stage of maturity) and startups which disturb the act of payment.

The technology finance industries are already having a significant impact on the finance industry. Investing in technology finance is a priority [1, 6]. It should be noted that global investments in Fintech technology companies are quite significant, although they are declining following current events [7]. Traditional financial institutions are now investing in external tech startups as collaborative tech companies.

Note that China and the United States are the main countries in startups and Fintechs. According to the 2019 ranking of KPMG and H2 venture [8], the top 10 Fintechs are: Ant Financial (China), Grab (Singapore), JD Digits (China), GoJek (Indonesia), Paytm (India), Du Xaoman Financial (China), Compass (United States), Ola (India), Opendoor (United States), and OakNorth (United Kingdom). These Fintechs are raising more than $ 70 billion (up 35% from last year) and more than $ 18 billion in the past 12 months.

Who can be Fintechs?: Fintechs are generally startups. A startup is a young company that anticipates powerful growth and uses innovation to create its activity. These Fintechs can be large groups that have long been subject to financial services and that invest in innovation. Companies that have gone beyond the startup youth and have had great success can also be Fintechs (Fintech scale-ups). Fintech startups differentiate themselves from traditional financial companies with personalized niche services, data-based solutions, an innovative culture, and an agile organization. Fintechs:

- Coexist with traditional financial institutions but differentiate themselves by innovative, efficient, and economical technologies. Traditional financial institutions are looking either to modernize their systems to work with Fintechs or adopt technologies and replace their systems.

- Collaborate with financial institutions through purchasing, investing in financial services and products. The financial institutions are in this case the clients, donors or partners of these Fintechs.

- Compete with traditional financial institutions by directly offering consumers financial products and services at the lowest cost.

2. Literature review: understanding Fintech

To recognize this disruptive innovation, an introduction to the emergence of Fintech and the identification of study segments and areas of Fintechs will be illustrated.

2.1 The emergence of Fintech

Fintech grows through phases of evolution ranging from the electronic medium, the Internet revolution in the 1990s, the use of smartphones in the mid-2000s, and the crisis of 2008 [3].

In 1915, the acceleration of financial data and linkages changed the financial technology infrastructure. Through electronic means, the deposit institutions in the Federal Reserve in the United States (Federal Wire Network) transferred the funds.

From the 1960s, ATMs became more profitable than the creation of bank branches. The adoption of technologies for finance has been developed to illustrate this new financial inclusion. In the early 1990s, the financial market was affected by the reduction of physical contact with banks due to the Internet revolution. This revolution has led to the development of electronic finance (E-finance). Several business models are developed as a result of the synergy between trust and technology such as online banking, online brokerage services, mobile payment, and mobile banking [9, 10]. This financial revolution has disrupted banking and insurance through indirect access to accounts, business negotiation and the gathering of information about online financial products and services, and downsizing of banks. This period is marked by the progress of e-finance.

In the mid-2000, mobile finance flourished thanks to the proliferation of smart phones. Finance is experiencing a revolution through mobile payment and mobile banking. Customers can access their account and make transactions via their mobile device. Mobile technologies are introduced in financial institutions.

In 2008, the global financial crisis combined several economic models to find solutions. Internet technologies, social networking services, social media, artificial intelligence, big data analysis, e-finance, and mobile technologies are used for the financial solution. Technology is no longer seen as a threat to the industry but rather as a sustainable competitive and differential advantage. Following the crisis, the search for opportunities promotes the use of technology in finance.

The Internet and mobile devices have therefore transformed the financial ecosystem by using technology in all the components of the financial activity value chain: transaction costs are reduced, execution times are faster, management information is more up to date, internal communication is more fluid, interaction with existing and potential customers is more practical, and access to professional knowledge in financial management is more convenient.

Thus, Fintech has developed following globalization in the twentieth century which accentuated the transmission of data. Second, the introduction of ATMs negated the need to establish bank branches. Then, e-finance encouraged customers to stay at home to provide their financial services. Finally, mobile finance has made it even easier to access these services.

Today, high-tech developed economies are already talking about Fintech 3.0 with no longer ATMs or electronic finance or mobile finance. The current era encompasses Blockchain, WealthTech and RegTech. The diversity of Fintech startups is spectacular [4].

These Fintechs multiply and are born from threats. Indeed, the evolution of the banking sector is caused by the appearance of GAFA (Google, Apple, Facebook, and Amazon) having today the greatest financial power that constitute a threat for the traditional financial institutions. They constitute the lobbying on the monetary departments and ensure the execution of banking services. Likewise, the proliferation of telephone operators, who have a large customer portfolio and great technological innovation through big data, artificial intelligence, and others, allow startups to become financial operators without banking authorization. Fintech becomes a domain and gives birth to an industry in its own right.

2.2 Fintechs by segment

Fintechs are in strong evolution every year and are increasingly in competition with traditional banks [9]. Indeed, Fintech encroaches on certain sectors reserved for banking such as payment (Paytechs), daily banking services (neobank), credit (crowdfunding or crowdlending). Some are complementary to the banking sector by monitoring regulatory constraints (regtechs) [11, 12]. The different Fintechs are illustrating in **Table 1**:

Segment	Definition
Neobanks	They are 100% digital dematerialized banks without branches and which offer innovative and low-cost banking services (accounts, payment cards, online pools, payment applications, wealth management or automated investment tools, etc.)
Paytech	It is a solution that optimizes all types of payment
Crowdfinding or crowdlending	It is a crowdfunding platform that connects project leaders, business creators, SMEs or individual or professional investors. This platform calls on a large number of people to finance a project either in donations with or without rewards (crowdfunding) or in the form of loans (crowdlending) or else capital financing (crowdequity)
Insuretech	It is an innovation in the insurance field and plays as a comparator to collaborative insurance and 100% digital health insurance
Regtech	It is an innovation that offers technological solutions that meet the regulatory and compliance constraints of mainly banking players

Table 1.
The segments of Fintechs.

3. Fintech ecosystem

Technological innovation can be valued by two components: the first relates to the roles of ecosystem participants; the second emphasizes the analysis of the support mechanisms of this ecosystem.

3.1 Participants in the Fintech ecosystem

The expansion of the Fintech industry is linked to a stable ecosystem where its players assume their roles. The union between these actors ensures good governance and the value creation. Diemers et al. [13] present three essential participants in this ecosystem which are presented in **Table 2**.

Key participants	Roles
Government	It is called upon to implement a regulatory framework which facilitates the entrepreneurial ecosystem
Institutions	They bring expertise to the ecosystem and tie up relationships with Fintech startups.
Entrepreneurs	They provide technological solutions

Table 2.
The participants in the Fintech ecosystem.

By setting up the procedures and regulations for a Fintech ecosystem, the government is encouraging entrepreneurs who bring technology. The innovative but sometimes disruptive contributions of entrepreneurs are accepted by the institutions. This gives entrepreneurs access to finance and market expertise. These institutions will build relationships with Fintech startups by seeking to strengthen their competitive positions.

3.2 The pillars of conducting a Fintech ecosystem

To contribute to innovation, stimulate the economy, facilitate collaboration in the financial system, and allow consumers to benefit from the financial industry, the Fintech ecosystem must call for efficient management based on the allocation of regulations, the organization between the different participants, and the innovation of technologies (see **Figure 1**).

- **The allocation of regulations** at the level of the Fintech environment ensured by the government can reframe the Fintech ecosystem and define the procedures, rules, and mechanisms to understand and follow. These regulations can soften trade and tax regulations to facilitate the management of Fintechs and facilitate their integration into the economy. The weight of the government and its allocation of regulations can vary depending on the extent of Fintech in the country [13]. The interest of Fintechs depends on their profits with long-term promises of law [14].

- **The organization between the synergies of the different participants** is a performance pillar, the establishment of the Fintech ecosystem. Everyone must find their profit and create value by defending their interests. Startups promote technology in collaboration with technology developers by lowering operating costs and making profits. These startups must collaborate with traditional financial institutions with skills and effective potential in the financial sector. Traditional financial institutions, with competitive advantages in terms of scale costs, focus on unbundled products and services and collaborate with Fintech startups to benefit from their technologies. Mobile network operators provide low-cost infrastructure and benefit from the use of large numbers of consumers. Customers can manage their accounts according to their needs by counting on several financial institutions. The government

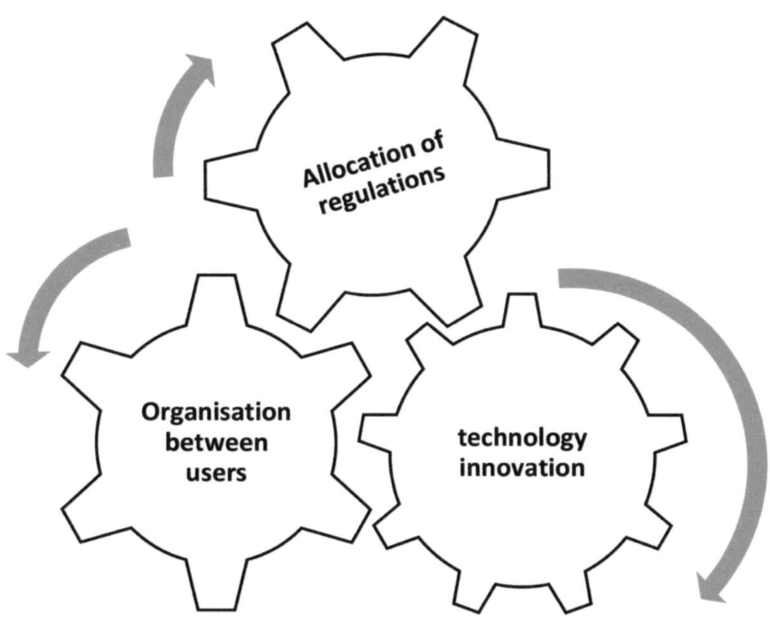

Figure 1.
The pillars of conducting Fintech ecosystem.

succeeds in stimulating technology and innovation by encouraging global technological growth.

- **Innovation in the field of finance** to help startups in launching innovative services to guarantee sustainability and meet user needs. The innovation of financial expertise will help structure the Fintech ecosystem. At this level, regulations must support technology in order to guarantee a technological financial industry.

4. Fintech in Tunisia

According to GFI 2020 [15], Tunisia ranks 196 globally and 6th in the Middle East and North Africa (MENA) region with a score of 3668 points.

The Middle East and North Africa (MENA) has the highest rate of unbanked people in the world. In Tunisia, 64% of adults are financially excluded or underserved, in part because of the difficulty of reaching a physical bank location. Regardless of these results, the GFI 2020 considers that the evolution of Fintechs in Africa and the Middle East will be rapid and a real game changer and essentially in Africa.

In Tunisia, the call is certainly to acquire the necessary skills to better understand innovative financial technologies and seize the opportunities offered by Fintechs. According to the TCB (Tunisian Central Bank) governor, Fintechs master these technologies perfectly, understand user experience effectively, and apply agile organization. Fintechs have successfully changed the banking and financial ecosystem and usage preferences. The various stakeholders in the banking and financial sector (banks, financial institutions, regulators, payment infrastructures, etc.) must adapt to this new situation.

The Fintech industry is already prevailing in Tunisia; it has developed thanks to startups that have emerged and revolutionized technology with innovative solutions to banking products and services.

4.1 Tunisian Fintech segments

The Tunisian entrepreneurial ecosystem offers several indices encouraging technological finance in Tunisia like the venture capital index, technology absorption networking process innovation. In 2018 [16], thanks to the collaboration between the public and the private sector, innovation took off in Tunisia and entrepreneurship registered a very great dynamic.

According to the Global entrepreneurship and Development Institute (GEID) which measures the dynamics of the entrepreneurship ecosystem, Tunisia is ranked in November 2019 the 1st in Africa, 6th in the MENA region, and 40th in the world.

The ecosystem has bet on skills and experience by supporting entrepreneurs at their young ages through coworking spaces, investors, accelerators, incubators and non-governmental organizations without forgetting Tunisian startup. Also the startup act comes to facilitate technology. This legal framework is developed by the government using a participative and collaborative approach between all stakeholders in the entrepreneurial ecosystem. It is dedicated to startups by encouraging entrepreneurs to dare to undertake and launch their startups by supporting their developments and by encouraging investors to invest in these startups.

The startups Fintechs are 38 [17]. Fintechs that have benefited from a startup label being part of the startup act are listed in **Table 3**.

DOI: http://dx.doi.org/10.5772/intechopen.93427

Startups	Presentation of startups	Segment	Promotion
PAYPOS Tunisie	Development of innovative electronic payment solutions and in the digitalization of compatible banking and financial services	FinTech	March 2019
Expensya	Expensya offers automation of expense reports – worldwide	Fintech	March 2019
Kaoun	Kaoun implements identification and automation products to make financial services faster and more accessible to everyone	Fintech	April 2019
Dqlick	Dqlick is an insurtech specializing in digitalization and digital transformation in the field of personal insurance	Insurance Tech	April 2019
MEDCRETECH	MedCretech offers a Blockchain application to trace and streamline the life cycle of real estate. Website: www.medcretech.com	Blockchain & Cryptocurrency	April 2019
PEAK	PEAK technologies specializes in the development of management and control solutions for transactional operations based on Blockchain technologies. Website: www.peak-cs.com	Fintech	April 2019
PAYMEE	Development of mobile payment solutions and online payment gateways. Website: www.paymee.tn	Fintech	April 2019
	Swiver is an ERP in SAS mode intended for VSEs and SMEs to digitize their financial management process	Fintech	May 2019
Neapolis Development	Develop offshore and Edit digitalization and robotization solutions for the insurance and banking sector	Insurance Tech	May 2019
deep'era.ai	DEEPERA is a Fintech. Its objective is to democratize finance by offering "Investment advisory for everyone!" through AI models	Fintech	June 2019
INSIGHT PLUS	Insight + designed and developed the first manual currency exchange cloud application (BBE) in Tunisia dedicated to exchange offices.	FinTech	June 2019

Startups	Presentation of startups	Segment	Promotion
Sobflous	Sobflous is an electronic wallet (web and mobile) that offers users phone recharge, money transfer, and merchant payment and invoice payment services. Website: www.sobflous.tn	Fintech	June 2019
TRANSIN	SmartIN is an AssurTech which offers innovative solutions for enriching and improving services in the insurance sector	Insurance Tech	July 2019
CATRiM	Catrim develops innovative solutions for the trading rooms of investment banks. Website: www.catrimtech.com	Fintech	July 2019
universa	Universa is a new generation of blockchain as a cooperative register of state changes, carried out by licensed and trusted nodes, and is capable of handling thousands or tens of thousands of transactions per second (±20,000TPS)	Blockchain & cryptocurrency	July 2019
getpay	GETPAY is a payment platform backed by merchant marketplaces. Website: www.astontechnologies.tn	Fintech	Setember 2019
	Lightency is developing a platform for the exchange of electricity between individuals and brings together all the stakeholders in the sector on the same platform in order to reduce costs	Cryptocurrency & Blockchain	October2019
TLedger	Tledger offers financial and non-financial institutions access to a network allowing real-time financial transactions through APIs and mobile wallets. Website: www.tledger.tech	Cryptocurrency & Blockchain	October 2019
k2lis	K2LIS is a digital microfinance platform accompanied by its electronic web and mobile wallet for microfinance institutions and their beneficiaries.	Fintech	Dècember 2019
	PayGrant is a platform for targeting clearing through mobile payment"	Blockchain & Cryptocurrency	January 2020

Startups	Presentation of startups	Segment	Promotion
	SQOIN is specialized in blockchain, having developed solutions to facilitate e-commerce through an exchange of tokens on the blockchain. Website: http://sqoin.us/coin/Bacem Bergaoui	Blockchain & cryptocurrency	January 2020
	UTIK provides personalized services to build digital trust through risk identification and preaching, cryptography and an infrastructure for decentralized applications. Website: http://www.utik.co	Blockchain & cryptocurrency	January 2020
Coinsence.org	Coinsence offers a central collaboration platform allowing organizations and communities to issue their own community currency to activate resources, facilitate exchange, and finance collaborative projects. Website: http://Coinsence.com	Blockchain & cryptocurrency	February 2020

Table 3.
Fintech startups in Tunisia.

4.2 Support and management mechanisms for the Tunisian Fintech ecosystem

The TCB has taken initiatives and is positioning itself as a regulator and a facilitator with the Tunisian innovation ecosystem and Fintechs. The objective is to assist the operation of Fintechs despite the rigidity of the regulatory framework. In fact, Tunisia is engaging in a participatory approach in order to co-conserve the new financial services. This global approach is based on the vision of the TCB which aspires to be "a modern, proactive and efficient Central Bank at the forefront of economic and financial transformations" [18] (see **Figure 2**).

TCB has set up a Fintech committee, a regulatory sandbox, a TCB Lab, a TCB Web, and regional and international cooperation.

1. Establishment of a *Technological Hub* which is essentially based on optics of inclusiveness and a participative approach thanks to the creation of a Fintech committee. This committee acts as a regulator between the TCB and the Fintech ecosystem. It cooperates with stakeholders on innovative initiatives.

2. Launch of a *Regulatory Sandbox* on January 21, 2020: in order to certify financial inclusion and innovation and transform the banking model by going toward the restructuring and digitalization of banks and the banking and financial ecosystem. This test environment will allow Fintechs to test innovative solutions on a small scale and with real voluntary customers under the aegis of the BCT. The BCT as regulator will be able to understand the innovations and adjust the regulatory framework if necessary. Fintechs will also adhere to the regulations in force.

3. Creation of a *TCB-Lab* in order to digitize certain internal processes, watch over financial and technological innovation, transform the banking and financial profession, spread an image of openness and modernism, and build relationships with the environment.

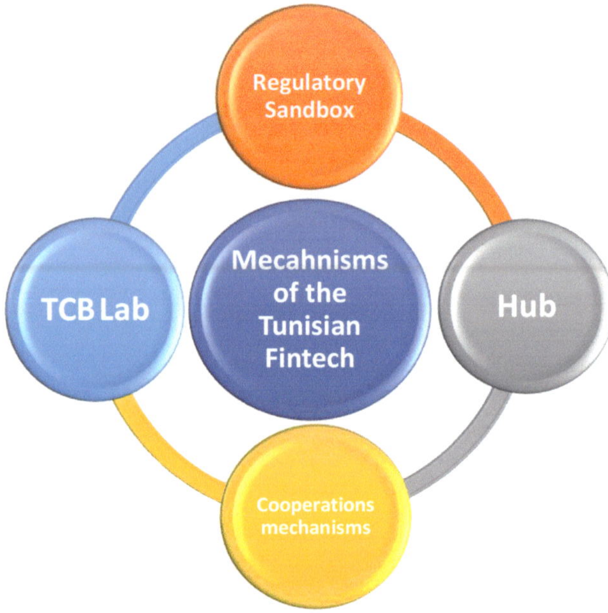

Figure 2.
The mechanisms of the Tunisian Fintech ecosystem.

4. Establishment of coordination and cooperation mechanisms to guarantee *regional and international exchanges*. This was highlighted by the merits of regional and international coordination and cooperation "Bali Fintech Agenda" developed by the World Bank and the IMF (International Monetary Fund). Thus, the TCB participated with the "Maghreb Fintech Committee" and the Board of Governors of Central Banks of the Arab Maghreb and the "Regional Fintech Working Group".

4.3 Roles of the TCB in the Fintech from the sandbox ecosystem

Tunisia's policy tends to promote the Fintech ecosystem. In fact, aware of the need to follow technological and financial developments, the TCB is committed to fostering financial involvement, supporting financial stability, protecting Fintech users, and prospering the emergence of Tunisian Fintech on a regional scale, national, and international.

4.3.1 Roles of the TCB as a facilitator

Through the Sandbox, the TCB:

- Fosters Fintechs with innovative solutions that provide access to households and businesses who find it difficult to defend their interests by financial institutions.

- Monitors and tests the innovative completions offered by these Fintechs.

- Guarantees the security of the financial system by assessing the risks associated with these Fintechs.

- Protects Fintech users from risks through innovative solutions and complaint mechanisms.

4.3.1.1 What's the TCB regulatory sandbox?

According to Dorra Marrakchi, Regulatory Sandbox Project Manager Governor's Office, TCB needs to release new challenges and open new horizons in a full scale environment for the benefit of national innovated actors and companies [19]. TCB uses Sandbox consisting in a helpful test environment with high value and powerful tools. This Sandbox has global data's referential and technical and legal expertise in order to hold up innovate potential projects.

Through the sandbox, TCB, as a regulator, improves the development of the position of startups on the market and also helps financial institutions to benefit from the supports and skills made available to them.

Sandbox needs innovate actors of the financial market, startups, and approved institution of the ecosystem with innovate solutions. As a result, the Sandbox is intended for all legal persons with or without an approval, in particular startups, without limiting either the list of activities or that of the products concerned by the Sandbox.

TCB considers regulatory Sandbox as a win-win opportunity. Registered companies will be able to communicate on the skills and experiences of TCB and its partner institution whether legal or technical, to acquire the necessary credibility expertise and maturity for a better competitiveness expertise and international market. On the other hand, TCB as a regulator is taking the chance to approach the market innovators understand the new challenges and difficulties they are facing and then to provide the right answers such as making adjustments to the regulatory framework for the supervisory processes, if necessary.

Applications for the regulatory Sandbox will be open starting from today, January 21, operations will be done in cohort mode and each test phase will last on average nine successive months. The application process is simple and transparent and it's available on the "TCB Fintech" website. Of course, admittance will need strict criteria. These will be listed with more details on the website as well as the international operating rules considered by TCB to ensure a safe work place which all related stakeholders.

4.3.1.2 Conditions of access to the Sandbox and eligibility criteria

To access the Sandbox, certain criteria must be met.

- The solution proposed by startups must be highly innovative and guarantees an expansion of the ancient habits of financial institutions. This solution must provide a significant competitive advantage over existing offers on the market. Thus, potential Sandbox candidates must present a product or service or solution that offers radical or incremental innovation, that changes techniques or tools, transforms existing practices or that changes an existing product.

- The end customer will be able to identify the direct or indirect benefits of the product or financial service. These benefits are estimated or demonstrated quantitatively.

- The objective of testing the innovative solution of potential customers must be communicated clearly and formally. Thus, the TCB guarantees the communication of risks and possible indemnities.

- The solution must be technically tested in a laboratory environment and the test results should be made available to the TCB.

- The regulatory tests must be approved from a protection and technical point of view. Each candidate must present appropriate regulatory plans and respond to client protections and must take into account technological watch in order to minimize risks and losses.

- The solution must be demonstrated by the candidate via a realistic business plan and must be deployed nationally and internationally

To register in the Sandbox, the candidate must complete the online form and describe their skills, financial situation, and area of activity. It is necessary to specify the financial service to be tested, to describe the satisfactory eligibility criteria, to introduce the regulatory test plans, and to specify the impact of the Fintech experience. The application process also includes a communication plan which stops the revelation of the risks and the important information on the candidate and the Sandbox.

4.3.1.3 Operation of the Sandbox

The operation of the Sandbox [20] is based on five pillars:

- Cohorts: the duration of the test period is 9 months from the date of notification of admission to the Sandbox. It can be extended for 3 months on the basis of a written request motivated by the requester. The extension request must be sent at least 1 month before the end of the test period.

- Access fees: access to the Sandbox is subject to an access fee estimated at 100 Dinars payable once Fintech is accepted into the cohort.

- Quantitative thresholds: the parameters of the tests are determined according to the number of clients, funds, and other relevant variables. These parameters are decided on a case-by-case basis depending on the nature of Fintech and its risks.

- Reporting: reporting will be done at a frequency that takes into account the nature and complexity of the solution to be tested. A final report is drawn up at the end of the test period.

- Communication: the communication of information about the candidates selected and the solutions under test is the exclusive responsibility of the TCB.

The TBC reserves the right to make the acceptance of applications subject to certain modifications, and possibly not to follow up on applications if none of them appears acceptable to it either from a technical point of view or because of the details proposed or for any other reason.

The Sandbox process can be interrupted at the request of the candidate and at the request of the TCB.

4.3.2 TCB Fintech regulatory framework

According to Kaouther Bouzamitha, Director of common Law studies and legal Monitoring, Today Fintech has main challenge to financial regulation [15]. This is why at the Central Bank of Tunisia, the managers are keenly aware of the urgent need to develop and to modernize financial regulations to make the country among the countries that allow entrepreneurs to engage in innovate and high value activities. This can be summed up in one word: anticipation. The TCB vision is clear: technology is not just a tool, it is a source of inspiration and progress.

TCB, as a regulator, is a welfare regulator, and a protector regulator regulation is also a protection and even a freedom. Then TCB takes a proactive approach which aims to develop financial regulation in collaboration with Fintech to prevent it from being imposed the goal that is not to control in order to punish but rather to support the strategy set up by Fintech.

4.3.3 The TCB guarantees national and international exchanges

The BCT is committed to ensure the emergence of Tunisian Fintech on a national and international scale by acting with the various stakeholders. It is developing regional and international coordination and cooperation mechanisms, as highlighted by the "Bali Fintech Agenda" drawn up by the World Bank and the IMF. Thus, it participates in the work of two committees which meet twice a year and each time it is necessary:

- The Maghreb Fintech Committee under the aegis of the Board of Governors of the Central Banks of the Arab Maghreb, created in November 2018.

- Regional Fintech Working Group under the aegis of the Arab Monetary Fund, created in December 2018.

Everyone watching over innovative technologies in the banking and financial industry and international best practices for interacting with Fintechs; contributes to financial inclusion in the Maghreb region and to the harmonization of the Maghreb regulatory framework to remove any barrier to financial innovation; promises financial innovation in the region by giving external visibility to Maghreb Fintechs, coordinates and exchanges experiences and with other regional and international Fintech Committees, sets up a common strategy for managing the risks inherent in the activity of Fintechs; launches studies and surveys on Fintech opportunities and challenges.

5. Tunisian Fintech facing Covid 19

Startups have no choice: they adapt or die. For some sectors, this meant a complete transfer of services, for others, it could mean a change in priorities or roadmap. Some industries have been much more affected than Fintechs as the tourism, but the flexibility and the redistribution of resources are essential, especially with fundraising which should slow in the coming months to a few years. Covid-19 could encourage some institutions to invest more in the digitalization of their processes, which can be an opportunity for startups to attract new customers.

Two examples of Fintechs which have ensured innovations to overcome the COVID 19 pandemic are illustrated.

Digiconstat which is a Fintech selected by the financial regulator Al Madina Takaful in Oman (Capital Market Authority CMA) among the 10 Fintechs to digitize the finance sector in Oman and help insurance companies reduce their claims management costs and fight against fraud. This Fintech, which raised 600 thousand dinars, concluded an agreement during this pandemic period to guarantee the continuity of the insurance service for automobile victims via digital. During this period, Al Medina Takaful policyholders will be able to report the claim and be able to follow up on their report via their phone in a few minutes.

In partnership with Trntrust, **Kaoun** is developing client identification software that goes through the eKYC process and can have a free DIGIGO electronic signature. When the coronavirus struck, Kaoun launched a Flouci application allowing you to register for government services or file your taxes. This signing of documents is free until May 31 during this lockdown period.

In addition, Kaoun has launched a service that opens bank accounts for sub-bank and non-bank accounts in free partner institutions. This service will allow them to access financial services regardless of social distance. For small businesses that have had to close their physical location, they have benefited from digital technology to provide a bank account or to benefit from remote credit via partner banks and microfinance institutions.

Likewise, in order to secure donations from Tunisians of any amount to ensure a stock of medical supplies and in collaboration with the SEBITAR platform, Kaoun sets out to secure by its technology the backend any transfer to the SEBITAR team. Thanks to Kaoun, the hospitals which submitted their needs for medical supplies and the Tunisians who made the donations by choosing the supplies to which they wish to contribute ensured the transfers in full safety on the SEBITAR platform which takes care of the purchase of these supplies.

6. Conclusion: challenges of Tunisia

Fintech is a recent development. It is very difficult for Tunisian financial institutions. This chapter is one of the first studies to develop Fintech in Tunisia.

After giving a conceptual overview of the emergence, segments, participants, and pillars of Fintech management, the chapter presents how Tunisia is taking root and how it is building its Fintech ecosystem thanks to the roles of government, startups, and financial institutions.

Tunisia thus adopts financial technological acceleration. Since January 2020, and thanks to the support and steering mechanisms, it has come up to date with Fintech and takes care of the birth of a sector at an embryonic age. The TBC plays strategic and legal roles in maintaining the Fintech ecosystem.

However, the TCB declared in October 2018 its collaboration with Ernst and Young and the World Bank to seek an international operator in Fintech which will help it to get started in e-payment through different services such as Paypal (2018). Knowing that Paypal exists in Tunisia but to ensure consumption and or purchase yet not allow online sale (Paypal merchant). After a long study, this request is refused following the Tunisian exchange laws. Tunisia must change its laws to be able to benefit from this service.

Likewise, Tunisia has a low bank account of Tunisians. Far from being a handicap, it is an opportunity for the development of Fintechs that can conquer a market. In fact, Fintech can exploit a deposit of banking services which is not based on the opening of accounts but on secure and fast payment facilities.

The Tunisian market is too heavily regulated which can slow Fintechs down. The choice becomes either being a Tunisian Fintech that focuses entirely on markets outside with friendlier regulations, or spends more time deploying solutions in local environments and using that expertise to expand to other similar environments using the same learning and techniques when relevant. The type of investors and their motivations here differ, the second being more impact investor driven.

Tunisia hopes to become a pioneer by implanting the blockchain in the TCB, digital payment, and cryptocurrencies according to the declarations of the governor of the TCB. Regarding "deceasing," the TCB is collaborating with other financial institutions and will launch initiatives soon. The stakes are high.

Note also that Fintechs can threaten certain jobs in finance. According to Marcos Lopez Prado and the British firm TMS Market, finance jobs will disappear in 2020. The forecasts in the United States will record 1.3 million jobs such as customer service positions, financial managers and compliance officers and loans. In parallel, the big banks, according to Lea Nonniger analyst at Business Insider US, will invest in automation where the labor cost is quite low, that is to say artificial intelligence, machine learning, etc.

It is certainly true that digital will bring innovative solutions to the banking sector and establish a high value sector. Tunisia has made great strides in this area but is currently encountering dilemmas such as:

- Management of disruptive innovations following disruptive technologies which invents new technologies such as big data, artificial intelligence, Iot, robotization, blockchain, etc.

- The measuring between an old and structured world and a new innovative and unstructured world. Was it necessary to keep the market shares and develop them afterwards? Opt for IT and intelligent mutations while preserving the operational adaptation to user needs to new innovative and efficient technological solutions?

Will Tunisia be able to conquer these dilemmas?

The central bank has yet to adopt blockchain in practice, and its interest is still at an exploratory level. Initiatives must be taken to speed up the operating mechanisms. It is true that technology has its advantages and disadvantages, but the premise of technology is definitely there. From faster and cheaper transactions and more reliable systems to decentralized nature, better security, and better immutability, the technology has real benefits.

Should we therefore prepare for a profoundly transformative technology, do not allow technological developments to overtake and protect economic operators and the financial system from the risks that may arise from these technologies (money laundering, tax evasion, fraud, etc.) without block access to the technological revolution and deprive itself of its positive aspects.

To change customer behavior, technology is a small part of the equation. Accessibility and a good user experience are essential. There are two schools of thought. One that sees this as a top-down approach (the state imposing a series of measures and use cases on citizens to elicit aggressive behavior from customers) and the other is more of a free market approach that aims to increase competition to make services better and therefore more attractive to customers. The two are not mutually exclusive and one cannot replace the other for optimal long-term results.

The government is called upon to take certain initiatives. This is first and foremost the initiative for the financial consolidation of the public sector – administration and businesses – associated with a better targeted and more equitable social policy, with a view to freeing up budgetary space for the benefit of productive investment.

Then, it is necessary to promote the economic initiative by the reform of the legislative and regulatory device and the simplification of the administrative procedures for the benefit of the companies, and the adoption of a governance system based on the risk management in conformity with the standards and good international practices. However, this requires the acceleration of the promulgation of the law on the regularization of exchange offenses and the effective establishment of exchange offices. At the same time, foreign exchange regulations will have to be deeply reconsidered, in consultation with the authorities and professionals, with a view to greater openness to the outside world for the benefit of residents and non-residents, companies or individuals.. It is a question of taking care to identify in a precise way the opportune measures to be implemented as well at the level of the current operations as those of the Capital account, in order to give to stimulate the inflows of currencies by an adequate accompaniment of the exporters of goods and services and support for the internationalization of Tunisian companies.

Finally, the strengthening of international cooperation and the support of which is necessary for the consolidation of the national economy in the medium term and its integration into the world economy. Likewise, strengthening the attractiveness of the Tunisia site to foreign investments is essential, in order to climb them to a higher level, even to faithfully reflect the real potential of the country. In this perspective, and while working to consolidate its action inherent in its missions, and at their head price stability, by a deep restructuring and strengthening of its capacities, the BCT will soon adopt a "multi-year strategic plan," including the objective is to identify the means and resources to be implemented to ensure its qualitative transformation and to reach the tune of modern central banks, to carry out its missions in accordance with its new statutes laid down in the framework of the law 2016–2035.

Author details

Salma Zone
University of Monastir, Tunsia

*Address all correspondence to: salma.zone@fsegma.u-monastir.tn

References

[1] Kim Y, Park Y, Choi J. The adoption of Mobile payment services for "Fintech". International Journal of Applied Engineering Research. 2016;**11**(2):1058-1061

[2] Chiu IH-Y. Fintech and disruptive business models in financial products, intermediation and markets-policy: Implications for financial regulators. Journal of Technology Law & Policy. 2016;*21*:55-112

[3] Lee I, Shin YJ. Fintech: Ecosystem, business models, investment decisions, and challenges. Business Horizons. 2018;*61*(1):35-46. DOI: 10.1016/j.bushor.2017.09.003

[4] KPMG. The Pulse of Fintech 2018 Biannual global analysis of investment in fintech [Internet]. 2018. Available from: https://assets.kpmg/content/dam/kpmg/xx/pdf/2018/07/h1-2018-pulse-of-fintech.pdf

[5] France Fintech. The French Fintech have raised a record od 200 million eurs since January [Internet]. 2018. Available from: https://francefintech.org/en/les-fintech-francaises-ont-leve-un-record-de-200-millions-deuros-depuis-janvier/

[6] PwC. Blurred lines: How FinTech is shaping financial services [Internet]. 2016 Available from: https://www.pwc.de/de/newsletter/finanzdienstleistung/assets/insurance-inside-ausgabe-4-maerz-2016.pdf

[7] KPMG. People perspectives possibilities, KPMG global review [Internet]. 2019. Available from: https://home.kpmg/xx/en/home/campaigns/2019/12/global-annual-review.html

[8] KPMG. Fintech100: Leading Global fintech innovators [Internet]. 2019. Available from: https://home.kpmg/xx/en/home/insights/2019/11/2019-fintech100-leading-global-fintech-innovators-fs.html

[9] Webster IP. Fintech: Are banks responding appropriately? [Internet]. 2015. Available from: http://www.ey.com/Publication/vwLUAssets/EY-fintech-are-banks-respondingappropriately/$FILE/EY-fintech-are-banks-responding-appropriately.pdf

[10] Arner DW, Barberis JN, Buckley RP. The Evolution of Fintech: A New Post-Crisis Paradigm? University of Hong Kong Faculty of Law Research Paper No. 2015/047; UNSW Law Paper No. 2016-62; 2015

[11] Saksonova S, Kuzmina-Merlino I. Fintech as financial innovation – The possibilities and problems of implementation. European Research Studies Journal. 2017;**XX**(3A):961-973

[12] Giorgio BN, Giacomo C, Alberto FP. FinTech and Banks: Friends or Foes?9-30, Handbook: European Economy Banks, Regulation, and the Real Sector [Internet]. 2017. Available from: http://european-economy.eu/wp-content/uploads/2018/01/EE_2.2017-2.pdf

[13] Diemers D, Lamaa A, Salamat J, Steffens T. Developing a FinTech ecosystem in the GCC, Let's get ready for take off [Internet]. 2015. Availbale from: http://www.strategyand.pwc.com/media/file/Developing-a-FinTech-ecosystem-in-the-GCC.pdf

[14] Thomas P. The FinTech Opportunity, NBER Working Paper No. 22476, Issued in August 2016. Available from: https://www.nber.org/papers/w22476.pdf. doi: 10.3386/w22476

[15] The Global Fintech Index 2020 Finde able the global Fintech Index

City Rankings Report. Available from: https://findexable.com/wp-content/uploads/2019/12/Findexable_Global-Fintech-Rankings-2020exSFA.pdf

[16] GEI. Global Entrepreneurship Index. 2018. Available from: https://thegedi.org/global-entrepreneurship-and-development-index/

[17] DisrupTunisia. Available from: https://www.disruptunisia.com/annuaire-startup-tunisie

[18] Available from: https://fintech.bct.gov.tn/fr/Mot-du-gouverneur

[19] Available from: https://fintech.bct.gov.tn/fr/sandbox

[20] Goo J, Heo J-Y. The impact of the regulatory Sandbox on the Fintech industry, with a discussion on the relation between regulatory Sandboxes and Open Innovation. Journal of Open Innovation: Technology, Market, and Complexity. 2020;**6**:43. DOI: 10.3390/joitmc602004